What's Love Got to

Do with It? Transnational

Desires and Sex Tourism in

the Dominican Republic

DENISE BRENNAN

DUKE UNIVERSITY PRESS

DURHAM AND LONDON 2004

© **2004 DUKE UNIVERSITY PRESS** | All rights reserved
Printed in the United States of America on acid-free paper ∞
Designed by Rebecca M. Giménez | Typeset in Monotype Dante
by Keystone Typesetting, Inc. | Library of Congress Cataloging-
in-Publication Data appear on the last printed page of this book.
Fourth printing, 2007

WHAT'S LOVE GOT TO DO WITH IT?

A BOOK IN THE SERIES

LATIN AMERICA OTHERWISE:

LANGUAGES, EMPIRES, NATIONS

Series editors: Walter D. Mignolo, Duke

University; Irene Silverblatt, Duke

University; Sonia Saldívar-Hull,

University of California

at Los Angeles

FOR BELKIS AND NANCY

CONTENTS

ABOUT THE SERIES

L atin America Otherwise: Languages, Empires, Nations is a critical series. It aims to explore the emergence and consequences of concepts used to define "Latin America" while at the same time exploring the broad interplay of political, economic, and cultural practices that have shaped Latin American worlds. Latin America, at the crossroads of competing imperial designs and local responses, has been construed as a geocultural and geopolitical entity since the nineteenth century. This series provides a starting point to redefine Latin America as a configuration of political, linguistic, cultural, and economic intersections that demands a continuous reappraisal of the role of the Americas in history, and of the ongoing process of globalization and the relocation of people and cultures that have characterized Latin America's experience. Latin America Otherwise: Languages, Empires, Nations is a forum that confronts established geocultural constructions, that rethinks area studies and disciplinary boundaries, that assesses convictions of the academy and of public policy, and that, correspondingly, demands that the practices through which we produce knowledge and understanding about and from Latin America be subject to rigorous and critical scrutiny.

Sosúa, a town in the Dominican Republic, is a crossroads of personal desires and impersonal forces. European clients in Sosúa meet Dominican and Haitian women for paid sex. With sensitivity and compassion, Denise Brennan introduces us to women determined to do more than survive; they have dreams of improving their lives, helping their families, and leaving the D.R. for the excitement and security of Europe. Few do.

This rich and engaging book brings a subtle ethnographic lens to a complex exchange. Sex work is never just about money and sex; it is about hopes, possibilities, and the realities of transnational capitalism and the local structures of class. Forcing us to conceptualize sex work "otherwise," *What's Love Got to Do with It?* unscrambles the transnational economics of desire and intimacy and shows how sex workers, with few opportunities and fewer resources, strategize to make a way for themselves in a global economy of enduring inequalities.

ACKNOWLEDGMENTS

I am deeply grateful to Dr. Bayardo Gómez and the staff of the Centro de Promoción y Solidaridad Humana (CEPROSH), particularly Hemilce Guerra, Giovanni Ferreira, Miriam de Castro, and Roque Cid. I am also indebted to CEPROSH's peer educators for their willingness to share their time and insights. Belkis Hernández and Nancy Gómez have been caring and generous friends, as well as talented field assistants who threw themselves into this project. Without their generosity and help, this book would not have been possible. Many thanks as well to Sosúa's residents, who have helped me in so many ways over the years. Dear friends Sylvie Papernik and Corey Price, in particular, always looked out for me, and Lisa Brody and her family warmly opened their home to me in Santo Domingo whenever I was in the capital.

So many people have provided comments. I would like to express deep gratitude to Sarah Mahler and to an anonymous reviewer, both of whom spent much time drafting very detailed suggestions; Nina Glick-Schiller, Linda-Anne Rebhun, Ian Condry, Colleen Cotter, Anne Allison, Steve Rubenstein, Yuka Suzuki, Kate Frank, and Penny Saunders have generously provided feedback on different parts of the book. Participants in an anthropology reading group— Walter Armbrust, Jean-Paul Dumont, Mark Ingram, Gwen Mikell, Sylvia Onder, Joanne Rappaport, and Susan Terrio—also have given me valuable comments. Ongoing dialogues with fellow sex worker rights advocates Kathy Moon, Ann Jordan, Melanie Orhant, Penny Saunders, and Elizabeth Bernstein have helped me make sense of the sex trade in Sosúa.

My colleagues at Georgetown University, in the Department of Sociology and Anthropology and in the Women's Studies Program, have provided me with a supportive work environment. Denise Goitia, Beth Hallowell, Kristen Saad, and Sabra Thorner have been dedicated, creative, and inspiring research assistants. I am particularly grateful to Beth, who, always energetic and thorough, helped me with the final stages of the book. Sarah Aponte at the Dominican Studies Institute has, on many occasions, helped me track down Dominican resources, and Ana Aparicio lent a hand with the glossary. Mark Padilla has answered many a query on the sex industry in the Dominican Republic. I am grateful to the following funding sources: the Georgetown Summer Academic Grant, Georgetown Competitive Grant-in-Aid, Georgetown Junior Faculty Fellowship, Fulbright Fellowship Program, Yale Center for International Area Studies Summer Research Grant, and Andrew W. Mellon Pre-Dissertation Field Research Grant. This project began under the tutelage of Patricia Pessar, Marc Edelman, and Hal Scheffler, the most supportive and insightful advisors a graduate student could hope for. I owe a mountain of debt to Patricia, who has inspired me on so many levels and who gave so much to this project over the years. This project finished up under the editorial eye of Valerie Millholland, who, with the help of Miriam Angress and Kate Lothman, has showed tireless dedication to its publication. Thanks.

Finally, dear friend Marybeth McMahon read and commented on the book with great enthusiasm and skill. My parents, Mary and Arthur Brennan, have been endlessly supportive and have provided loving child care. Emily and James have been patient, expecting to see "the book" at every turn, in every bookstore. And I do not know how this book would have been done without the patience, encouragement, and editorial talents of my husband, Doug. In him I have found a true partner.

Last, I have been fortunate to spend my days listening to the stories of such courageous women. I cannot imagine a more rewarding job. I owe them many, many thanks for sharing so much with me.

INTRODUCTION: ELENA AND JÜRGEN

Elena, a twenty-two-year-old Dominican sex worker in Sosúa, the Dominican Republic, was released from jail after being held for two days.[1] She had paid the police 500 pesos (U.S.$42) —the standard bribe sex workers must pay for their release.[2] While she was in jail, her younger sisters, ages fourteen and sixteen, took care of her five-year-old daughter, Mari. In their care, Mari announced to her aunts that she too was going to go out in the *calle* (street) "so the police will arrest me and I can be with Mom."

Elena had been arrested in the middle of the day while out running errands with her friend Andrea, another sex worker. The police plucked her from the streets and brought her, along with nineteen other Dominican women, to a jail thirty miles away in Puerto Plata (the largest city on the north coast). She was not yet dressed for cruising the tourist bars, but the police knew she was in the sex trade since, like most sex workers in Sosúa, Elena had been arrested before. During this roundup, however, the police also had arrested women who were not in the sex trade—six of the nineteen, according to Elena's and Andrea's count—thus rendering real Elena's young daughter's fears of being arrested just for walking in the street. The police did not arrest Andrea, however, as her boyfriend was on the police force. Besides, she had not worked the tourist bars as a sex worker for months: she had met a German client who paid her rent and other expenses and promised to marry her and to bring her to Germany to live with him as his wife. It was a stroke of luck that Elena was with Andrea, who notified Elena's family and paid the bribe Elena needed to get out of jail. Because of Andrea's relationship with this German client, who sent her international money wires, she had enough money on hand to help out her friend.

Building Transnational Ties

Elena went to the beach the afternoon of her release. She came back ecstatic to her one-room wooden house. She had run into a German client of hers, Jürgen, who had just returned to Sosúa to see her. They had been sending faxes to one another since he left after his last vacation, and he had mentioned in one of his faxes that he would be returning. He did not know where she lived but figured he would find her that evening at the Anchor, Sosúa's largest tourist bar, where foreign male sex tourists went to drink and dance and where foreign men went to pick up Dominican and Haitian women working in Sosúa's sex trade.[3] Jürgen brought her all kinds of presents from Germany, including perfume and a matching gold necklace and bracelet. Elena was thrilled, and, as she showed off her gifts, talked about Jürgen as a smitten school girl might: "He is adorable. You know he is older, like my father.[4] He is very sweet. I am going to spend the entire time with him while he is here. We will go to the beach, and he will take me to nightclubs and restaurants." She began preparing for a night out on the town. Her sisters would look after her daughter while Elena stayed with Jürgen in his tourist hotel for the duration of his vacation. She rushed off to the hair salon, where the stylist straightened her shoulder-length black curly hair and shaped it into a sophisticated French twist. She looked elegant. She chose the evening's outfit carefully, with plenty of help from her sisters, daughter, and friend, a young sex worker who also lived with them without paying any rent because she had very little money.

Elena took care of these four girls with her earnings from sex work. They all rotated between sharing the double bed and sleeping on the floor. Spending time with a tourist on his vacation meant Elena would receive more gifts, maybe even some for her family, as well as earn a steady stream of money. These girls helped primp Elena, selecting billowy rayon pants that moved as Elena did, and a black stretch shirt with long sheer sleeves that was cropped to reveal her slim stomach. She was meeting Jürgen at the Anchor, where I saw her that evening and where she stood out in the bar crowded with sex workers vying to catch the attention of visiting male tourists.

Later in the week I ran into Elena and Jürgen at a restaurant on the beach. Jürgen invited my husband and me to join them for a drink. Elena's daughter, Mari, was eating a fish dinner, and Elena's two younger sisters were snacking on sodas and french fries. At one point, Jürgen reached over to wipe Mari's runny nose, and Elena cleaned something from Jürgen's forehead. They touched each other affectionately and looked much like a family on a beach outing. Not far away on the beach were Elena's three older sisters (two of whom used to be sex workers but now were married to Dominican men) and their children playing in the sand. Everyone was in a bathing suit, except for Jürgen, who wore jeans and a long-sleeve denim shirt that he had unbuttoned, revealing his large stomach. He was sweating profusely but refused to swim; even Elena's teasing could not induce him to take a dip. Jürgen spoke in English to my husband and me, and then I translated for Elena, who did not understand English or German. Jürgen could not speak Spanish. He explained to us that he was interested in buying some land and building a house. He wanted to live part of the year in Sosúa and part in Germany. He asked me, "Have you seen Elena's place? It's horrible." After I told Elena what he had said, she hinted, "Well if he wants to buy me a larger house, he can." When the check came, Jürgen insisted on treating us to drinks, and Elena also waved our money away.

A week later, as I was walking along the beach, Jürgen called out to me from the same bar where I had seen him earlier in the week. His vacation was coming to a close, and he was flying back to Germany the next day. He planned to return to Sosúa in a couple of months. Elena was at a bar next door getting ice, and when I saw her and asked how she was, her face dropped; she began crying. I had not known how much this relationship meant to her. Maybe Jürgen represented more than just money, nice meals, and gifts. I had heard sex workers often distinguish between relationships for love (*por amor*) or for green cards (*por residencia*), but Elena's tears broke down that distinction.

Despite Jürgen's most ardent promises, there was no telling what he would do once he left Sosúa. Elena knew all too well that she might not ever see him again. Whether or not clients stay in touch with sex workers is out of these women's control. One thing was certain, though: once Jürgen departed, Elena's vacation would be over. She would move from the comfort of the "First World" tourist hotel back to her one-room shack with no running water and would resume all of her normal daily activities—taking care of her daughter and cooking and washing for an extended family of five. With Jürgen, she also had a break, however brief, from the constant worry of finding enough clients to meet her many financial obligations. It was difficult making ends meet day after day, especially since she also sent 1,000 pesos (U.S.$83) every month to her parents in the countryside to pay their bill at the local *colmado* (small grocer). Besides, with Jürgen gone, who else was going to treat her so well? For a couple of weeks Jürgen showered Elena with gifts and attention, a far cry from her getting dressed up every night, dodging the police, and trying to land clients at the Anchor. Jürgen paid Elena money for her sexual services, but he also treated her—and Elena's family—unlike any other client had before. As Elena described it: "He does not deny me anything. We go to the disco, we play games in the casino, we go to restaurants." He even paid a pawn-shop broker to retrieve a bracelet Elena had placed in hock when money was tight. And he promised to send money via Western Union once he was in Germany. Is this a relationship *por amor* or *por residencia*? I asked Elena. "It is a little of both of course," she replied. She feared that Jürgen might lose interest in her once he returned to Germany. "It's hard to meet good men like this."

Jürgen kept his word; he wired Elena money and kept in touch through faxes. With the money wires, Elena was able to move into a larger cement house located around the corner from the one-room wooden shanty the five girls shared. The new house had a bathroom and a kitchen sink (though it was without a spigot and water lines), which worked well for holding the water they hauled from communal tap stands. The rent increase was considerable, double what she paid previously: an increase from 450 pesos (U.S.$37) to 1,000 pesos (U.S.$83) a month. She could not afford such a surge in rent without Jürgen's support. Elena wasted no time putting her windfall to good use: the same day Jürgen wired money for her to move, she paid the rent and bought a dining room table and four chairs.

Even more surprising than his money wires and faithful fax communiqués was Jürgen's return to Sosúa only two months after his previous visit. Wishing to avoid paying what he called "outrageously high" taxes in Germany, he moved his business address to the Dominican Republic and planned to travel periodically to Germany for work.[5] He explained that with the money he would save in taxes, and the low cost of living in the Dominican Republic, he would not have to work as much as in the past. Within days of his return to Sosúa, he rented a two-bedroom apartment along the main paved road in Los Charamicos (the Dominican side of Sosúa) that cost 3,500 pesos (U.S.$292) a month. The apartment had running water and an electrical generator (for use during daily blackouts). He bought beds, living-room furniture, and a large color TV. Elena, her daughter, and younger sisters moved in immediately and set about furiously cleaning their new home.[6] Her three older sisters came by to help and to fuss in their sister's new home, which had items they could only dream about for their own homes: sinks, a shower, a toilet, an electric stove, and a large refrigerator.

Everyone was very excited, especially Elena. She was living out the fantasy of many sex workers in Sosúa, sharing a household with a European man who supported her and her dependents. Jürgen moved her from a wooden shack at the end of a dirt street that barely had enough room to accommodate a bed, to a modest middle-class, two-bedroom apartment with electricity and running water. He paid for food that Elena and her sisters prepared and had cable TV installed. He also paid for Elena's daughter to attend a private school, and he came home one day with school supplies for her. Occasionally, he took them out to eat at one of the tourist restaurants lining the beach. After observing how much time Elena spent washing clothes by hand, he rented a washing machine. Elena had moved up in the world: eating in tourist restaurants, sending a daughter to private school, and living in a middle-class apartment were clear symbols of her increased social and economic mobility.

A single mother who had been taking care of her daughter and younger sisters with her earnings from sex work for three years, Elena quit sex work soon after Jürgen started wiring her money. Her situation mirrored that of her friend, Andrea, who also had left sex work and moved into a bigger house (with plumbing) thanks to her transnational relationship with a foreign tourist. Once Elena moved in with Jürgen, her new role was unusual in Los Charamicos: She was no ordinary Los Charamicos "housewife." Having a German "husband" and living in one of the few painted concrete apartment buildings that contained an electrical generator set her apart from other Dominican women in Los Charamicos.[7] Sex work, and the transnational relationship it had fostered, transformed Elena's life, as well as the lives of those who depended on her. But for how long?

Breaking Transnational Ties

It was not long before Elena discovered that Jürgen was not her or her family's salvation as she first had hoped. Soon after Jürgen moved to town, Elena found out she was pregnant. Both she and Jürgen were very happy about having a baby. He had a teenage son living with his ex-wife in Germany and relished the idea of having another child. At first, he was helpful around the house and doted on Elena. But the novelty soon wore off, and he returned to his routine of spending most days in the German-owned bar beneath their apartment. He also went out drinking at night with German friends, hopping from one tourist bar to the next. He was drunk, or on his way there, day and night. Elena saw him less and less frequently, and they fought often, usually over money. Eventually he started staying out all night. On one occasion, a friend of Elena's (a sex worker) saw Jürgen at the Anchor talking and later leaving the bar with a Haitian sex worker. Elena knew he was cheating on her, but she did not want to bring it up with Jürgen. Reasoning that men "do these things," she instead focused her anger on the fact that he was not giving her enough money to take care of the household. "I'm fed up. I'm in the house all day, and he's out. He goes to El Batey (the tourist side of town) to drink in the tourist bars, or he is below drinking in the bar. I wanted to go out dancing Saturday night. He did not want to go, and he would not give me the money to go either. And if he does not give me the money, I don't have it." Their vacation days of going to the beach and dancing at clubs had truly come to a close. Elena now had less disposable income than she did before she lived with Jürgen. Back then, she would go out dancing and drinking with her friends—not looking for clients—but just to have fun. Now, without an income of her own, she was dependent on Jürgen not only for household expenses but for her own personal expenses as well.

Eventually, their fights got so bad that he kicked her out of their bedroom, and she started sleeping on the couch. They stopped speaking. She joked about her predicament and her inability to understand Jürgen and his ways: "Here in the Dominican Republic when couples fight, it is the man who ends up sleeping in the street. And with the Germans, it's the man who is in the bed and the woman who is in the street." On more than one occasion I served as interpreter between the two during their attempts at "peace negotiations," after they had not spoken to one another for days. Since Elena does not speak any German or English, she asked me to help her understand why Jürgen was mad at her as well as to communicate her viewpoint to him. In preparation for one of these "negotiations," she briefed me on what she wanted me to explain to him, "I want to know why he is not talking to me? And why he is not giving me any money? He is my esposo and is supposed to give me money. I need to know if he is with me or with someone else. He pays for this house and paid for everything here. I need to know what is going on. You know I was fine living alone before; I'm able to do that. I took care of everything before—this is not a problem. But I need to know what is going to happen." As they were living together, and Jürgen was paying the bills, Elena considered them to be married. To Elena and her friends, Jürgen, as an esposo, was financially responsible for the household, a role she perceived he was not fulfilling.

But Jürgen saw things differently. He felt Elena thought he was "made of money" and was always asking him for more. He asked me to translate and tell her, "I'm not a millionaire. I told Elena last week that I don't like her always asking for money. She did not listen. She asks me for money all day long. I don't want to be taken advantage of." Elena and her sister shopped like most poor women in town by buying food items as they needed them to cook the family's meals, sometimes going to the markets three or more times a day. Therefore, it is not surprising that Jürgen felt Elena was constantly asking him for money—she was.[8] Although they worked through this rough time, and Elena moved back into their bedroom, they fought explosively on many more occasions. Making up resulted in Jürgen's loosening his purse strings. Elena described how they settled one of their many fights: "Everything is fine now. He bought me pizza and gave me money to rent a washing machine. And he gave me money to go shopping. Tonight we are going out." Eventually, however, they fought so often that Elena started sleeping on the couch permanently. When I questioned what she would do if Jürgen left her, she replied, "I worked before in a restaurant back in my home town when Mari's father left me. And I was a domestic for a family. It went fine there. I could do that again. My older sisters could look after Mari and the new baby, and I'll get them a smaller house."

One day, without warning, Jürgen packed his bags and left for Germany for business. Elena knew this day would come; she knew that Jürgen had to go to Germany to work. But she did not expect their relationship would be in such disarray and that he would depart without leaving her money (although he did pay a couple of month's rent and left some food money with her younger sisters, who turned it over to Elena). In Jürgen's absence, Elena took her daughter out of private school, since the tuition soon became over-due, and she started working part time at a small Dominican-owned restaurant. Once Jürgen returned to Sosúa from Germany a couple of months later, they split up for good. Elena moved out of their apartment and back to the labyrinth of shantylike structures on dirt paths off the main road. Her economic and social mobility was short lived. She had not accumulated any savings or items she could pawn during her time with Jürgen. He had never given her enough money at any one time so that she could set some aside for savings. And all the things he bought for the apartment were *his* things, not hers. When they vacated the apartment, he took all of the furniture and the TV with him.

Today Elena is still living in the same conditions she had before she met Jürgen. Upon his return to the Dominican Republic, Jürgen lived for a while longer in Sosúa with another Dominican woman, also a sex worker. Elena had her baby, a boy, and Jürgen initially gave her money from time to time to help care for him. Once Jürgen moved out of Sosúa for good, he stopped all financial support. After a couple of years went by, Jürgen visited Sosúa to see his son. During this visit, he denied paternity of the boy, insisting "There is no way I could have a son this black." Elena never returned to cruising Sosúa's sex tourist bars for clients, and she has made significantly less money in a series of tourist-related jobs such as restaurant and domestic work. Her older sisters helped her take care of their younger sisters, and Elena still sends what money she can to help out her parents[9]—though she sends less than she did in her sex work days.

A Fantasy Falls Short: Holding Foreign Men To Different Standards

Elena's relationship with Jürgen dramatically changed her life: they had a child together. But her social and economic location remained as marginal as ever. In many ways Elena was better off financially before she met Jürgen. Even though she appeared to have all the material trappings that accompany "marrying" a foreign tourist, Elena ended up returning to the same conditions of poverty. Iron-ically, when she and Jürgen fought, and he withheld money from her, she was less economically independent than she was as a sex worker, when she could earn on average 500 pesos (U.S.$42.00) per client. Despite other sex workers' aspirations to achieve what Elena had, Elena's relationship with a foreign man was clearly far from ideal. Jürgen turned out to be an undependable father and a volatile alcoholic who slept with other women, thus putting Elena, and possibly her baby, at risk for acquiring AIDS.[10]

Yet Elena and her friends were quick to overlook Jürgen's faults, his alcoholism and infidelity, and they continued to describe him as an *hombre serio* (good man). Dominican sex workers often dismiss foreign men's imperfections and instead describe them in idealized terms—versions of the type of men they always wanted to marry. This romanticized construct contrasts with the women's described perceptions and failings of Dominican men, particularly their drinking and womanizing. It was only toward the end of Elena's and Jürgen's relationship, when his drinking was so obviously out of control, that Elena's friends finally admitted that, like the Dominican men they constantly criticized, Jürgen was trouble.

THE TOWN

1. SOSÚA: A TRANSNATIONAL TOWN

When I first traveled to Sosúa, to interview Dominican women selling sex in its bars and nightclubs, I quickly learned that Sosúa is not just a beach town with a sex trade but a site of interaction—at times contentious—between an unlikely group of neighbors. Almost all are migrants to this town on the north coast: Dominican migrants from throughout the country; Haitian migrants; an expatriate resident community of Germans, and an assortment of other Europeans and Canadians; elderly Jewish European "settlers" (refugees from Nazi persecution) and their descendants; and, of course, a constant stream of tourists, generally from Europe. With such a diverse community, what started out as a project on sex tourism expanded into a study on globalization and the changes, opportunities, and inequalities it has engendered within one tourist town. I ended up interviewing a wide range of individuals—Dominican and foreign—who live in or vacation in Sosúa. What I heard were descriptions of a place that varied wildly and were often contradictory. Sosúa, many things to many people, is a contested site in which individuals seek, to different degrees, to reinvent or to improve the conditions of their lives. One fundamental feature, however, supports the town's social and economic life and affects all Sosúans: sex-for-sale by Afro-Dominican and Afro-Haitian women to foreign white European and Canadian men.[1]

Even before they arrive, the migrants and tourists imagine the town and what it can provide them in dramatically different terms. Sosúa offers sun and beaches for tourists and inexpensive, Afro-Caribbean sex workers for white foreign sex tourists.[2] A safe haven for European Jews fleeing Nazi persecution in 1941, it is now a refuge for criminals on the run from authorities in their own countries. For foreigners seeking a more privileged lifestyle and tranquility, Sosúa is a place to retire. And for those valuing anonymity, it is a place to launder stolen or illicit money. For Dominicans, it offers not just employment but also the hope of economic and social mobility. Yet many Dominicans also refer to it as a modern-day Sodom and Gomorrah. These multiple images are both real and imagined, rooted in the material and the ideal, reality and fantasy. And for the thousands of poor women and girls who have flocked there since the early 1990s to work in its sex trade, Sosúa is a stepping stone to migration—through marriage to foreign tourists—off the island.

This book compares some of the many images that draw people to Sosúa with their actual experiences there. To understand how one town could be imagined, described, and experienced in such divergent ways, I consider why many perceive it as a place to better themselves or the conditions of their lives—what I call Sosúa's "opportunity myth." Despite the wide array of perceptions about it, Sosúans agree that the locale represents a space of transformation—no matter how remote the possibility to improve one's life actually is.[3] Sosúa's power to act as a transformational space is bound up with its transnational ties. These transnational connections separate and distinguish Sosúa from other Dominican towns. In Sosúa we find networks of individuals and capital, networks linked together through tourism and sex tourism, through new marriage-based migration circuits, through foreign investment in Sosúa, and through foreign residence there.

What can the experiences of residents and travelers in one tourist setting tell us about globalization?[4] What happens when forces of globalization touch the ground and affect particular lives in one particular place (Sassen 1998)?[5] What happens when towns such as Sosúa become deeply enmeshed within the globalized economy and connected to distant places—both through economic relationships as well as personal ones? What role does the sex-tourist trade play in shaping social and economic life in Sosúa? And how is this role different from the conventional tourist trade? The connection between "large structural forces" in the globalized economy and their effects on individuals is often difficult to discern, but in this book I seek to reveal these connections by examining two transnational processes that result from globalization and that affect all Sosúans: tourism / sex tourism and migration. These transnational processes, and the transnational linkages that result, affect individual lives unequally—depending on hierarchies of race, class, citizenship, mobility, gender, and sexuality.[6] By ethnographically examining Sosúa's tourist and sex-tourist trade, and the migration into and out of Sosúa, this research contributes to what Sarah Mahler and Patricia Pessar identify as "the need to anchor or ground transnational processes in particular places and histories" (2001: 444)[7] and thus helps make visible some of the effects of globalization. Since the centerpiece of this book is real people's experiences in a real place, the cultural production and transnational practices that occur in Sosúa do not take place by "free floating people" in an "imaginary 'third space' " (Guarnizo and Smith 1998 on Bhabba 1990 and Soja 1996). Instead, I spotlight the on-the-ground experiences of Sosúa's Dominican migrants, foreign tourists, and foreign residents, as well as consider how they "imagine" Sosúa before they get there. I also examine how Dominicans "imagine"—and in some cases experience—life off the island, in Europe or Canada. With so much attention paid—both in academic scholarship and in the media—to anything associated with "globalization," ethnographic accounts of how people cope with the effects of a globalized economy help bring this otherwise overused (and often misused) concept into focus.

With its constant influx of Dominican and Haitian migrants for work in the sex and tourist trades and of European tourists for play, as well as a large foreign-resident community living there year-round, Sosúa has become a transnational sexual meeting ground. I am particularly interested in how the transnational process of *sex tourism* has quickly and flamboyantly changed daily life in Sosúa—especially for Dominican women—as well as informed Dominican and foreign perceptions of Sosúa and Sosúans in different ways than has *tourism*. Since Sosúa has become known as a place where tourists can buy sex, Sosúa and Sosúans have experienced monumental changes. Because sex tourism has played a critical role in the town's transformation, I see it as a space inextricably tied up with transactional sex—it has become a "sexscape" of sorts. I use the term *sexscape* to refer to both a new kind of global sexual landscape and the sites within it. The word *sexscape*[8] builds on the five terms Arjun Appadurai has coined to describe landscapes that are the "building blocks" of "imagined worlds": "the multiple worlds which are constituted by the historically situated imaginations of persons and groups spread around the globe" (1990: 4). He uses the suffix -*scape* to allow "us to point to the fluid, irregular shapes of these landscapes" (with such terms as *ethnoscape, mediascape, technoscape, finan-*

scape, and *ideoscape*) as he considers the relationship among these five dimensions of global cultural flows (1990: 6–7). Sex-for-sale is one more dimension of global cultural flows, and Sosúa is one site within a global economy of commercialized sexual transactions. Although a strict application of Appadurai's terminology to the global landscape of sexual transactions would describe Sosúa as merely one point, or node, within a single global sexual landscape / sexscape, I will, for convenience, refer to it as an individual sexscape.

Sexscapes link the practices of sex work to the forces of a globalized economy. Their defining characteristics are (1) international travel from the developed to the developing world, (2) consumption of paid sex, and (3) inequality. In a sexscape such as Sosúa there are differences in power between the buyers (sex tourists) and the sellers (sex workers) that can be based on race, gender, class, and nationality. These differences become eroticized and commodified inequalities. The exotic is manufactured into the erotic—both privately in consumers' imaginations and quite publicly by entire industries that make money off this desire for difference.[9] Let me be clear: these differences, between sex workers in the developing world and sex tourists traveling from the developed world, are essential to distinguish sexscapes in the developing world from red-light districts (or other sites where paid sex is available) in the developed world. So too are the radiating effects of consuming practices—of paid sex—which undergird social and economic life in sexscapes. Within sexscapes, the sex trade becomes a focal point of a place, and the social and economic relations of that place are filtered through the nightly (and daily) selling of sex to foreigners. In contrast, the sex trade in red-light districts in the developed world—such as in Frankfurt, Rome, or New York—by no means defines social and economic life outside of these districts. Nor do the female citizens of these places necessarily become associated with sexual availability or proficiency. As Altman notes in his book *Global Sex*, although sex is "a central part of the political economy of all large cities," few cities can base their economies on sex (Altman 2001: 11).[10]

When sexscapes emerge within a globalized economy, globalized hierarchies of race, class, gender,[11] citizenship, and mobility create undeniable power differentials among the actors in these geographic spaces, which, in turn, give them unequal opportunities.[12] In Sosúa, there are very different and often uneven opportunities for foreigners and locals, and men and women, while race and age also play a role.[13] The asymmetries and inequalities that result from the mix of differences in Sosúa reveal the "unevenness" Appadurai describes in his discussion of modernity as "decisively at large, irregularly self-conscious, and unevenly experienced" (1996: 3). In this sexscape, the buyers eroticize these differences—particularly gendered and racialized differences—as part of their paid-sex experiences. Meanwhile, the sellers often struggle to capitalize on these differences. One way is through their "performance of love" (this idea of pretending to be in love is detailed in chapter 3).

Since Sosúa both offers sex-for-sale and houses an economically powerful foreign expatriate community, foreigners are more likely than Dominicans to find what they are seeking there. (And if they cannot find what they seek, they can always leave—unlike Dominicans.) While sex tourists can pay to fulfill their racialized sexual fantasies, expatriates can buy a life of comfort at a cheaper cost than in Canada or Europe. Sosúa emerges as a kind of border town / transnational space in which many imagine that their dreams for better lives will be attained. I pay attention to a range of individuals' experiences (Dominican and foreign) in Sosúa while I foreground sex workers' experiences. Possibilities for economic mobility do open in transnational spaces such as Sosúa but possibilities only for a few. Many foreign residents reinvent their daily lives, installing pools and hiring domestic help, while Dominicans—not just sex workers—only rarely make significant improvements to their economic status in Sosúa's tourist economy, even though they imagine their prospects otherwise. Although most foreigners in Sosúa are from the working to middle classes, they have sufficient resources to travel internationally or even to move permanently overseas if they so desire. Meanwhile, Sosúa's sex workers have limited resources and face numerous legal constraints to migration off the island.

This ethnography of "Sosúa-as-sexscape" builds on and offers new twists on familiar themes in transnational studies. First, it showcases globalized hierarchies at work in one particular transnational space as a result of particular transnational processes—tourism, sex tourism, marriage migration, and migration. Second, it examines the processes by which transnational spaces distribute opportunities and inequities to the individuals who work and live within them.

Third, it expands the notion of "transnational social fields"—what I will refer to here as transnational networks—to include those who do not actually move and whose transnational ties might be episodic at best, and unrealized at worst. Fourth, it allows for a fine-grained account of women's paid sexual labor in a particular setting where global capital is at work, a site where women workers have a fair degree of control over their working conditions. Finally, it stresses the importance of the social work of the imagination by considering how neocolonial race-based fantasies and stereotypes inform Sosúa's sex tourists' (and foreign residents') expectations and experiences in Sosúa-as-sexscape, as well as how economic fantasies of an easier life in an imagined Europe inform Sosúa's sex workers' expectations of what foreign tourists can offer them.

Sosúa as a Transnational Space

Before I elaborate on how both sex and love are commodified in Sosúa, let's look at how the place is imagined and experienced. So many foreigners (tourists and expatriate permanent residents) move into and out of Sosúa that Dominicans often see it as a town outside of the Dominican Republic. With no place to buy a plate of Dominican rice, red beans, and chicken in downtown Sosúa at Dominican prices, the town indeed looks and feels "un-Dominican." Instead, Sosúa's streets, lined by German beer gardens and kiosks selling European newspapers, remind passersby that many non-Dominicans now live, own businesses, work, and vacation there.[14] Time and time again I heard that Sosúa is not the "real" Dominican Republic, and Dominican friends urged me to visit towns in the countryside to see "true" Dominican culture. As a banana plantation for the United Fruit Company in the early part of the twentieth century, and a sanctuary for European Jews at the beginning of World War II, Sosúa has long been an economic, social, and cultural crossroads between the local and the foreign. Known now both for its beaches and for its sex bars, Sosúa's development into an inexpensive tourist and sex-tourist destination is the latest phase of its encounters with the "outside."[15] Tourism and sex tourism merely have sped up and intensified Sosúa's engagement in the global economy.

This book explores what migrants and visitors seek in Sosúa, why they believe Sosúa will deliver these things, and what in fact they

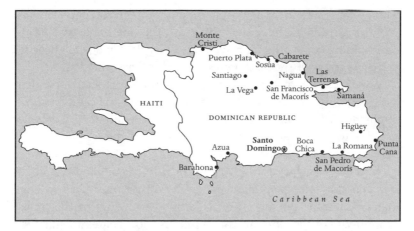

Map 1. Map of the Dominican Republic

find there. Poor Dominican women, for example, establish new internal migration patterns by migrating from throughout the Dominican Republic to work in Sosúa's sex trade. Once there, many hope to meet and to marry European or Canadian men who will sponsor their migration off the island. Poor Dominican women (and men) also migrate to Sosúa to work in its tourist restaurants, hotels, bars, and shops. Like prospectors searching for gold, Dominican migrants imagine that once in Sosúa "anything could happen," and it has the reputation of being a town in which Dominicans can get rich quick. It is this fantasy of what *might be* that keeps so many new people arriving everyday. Meanwhile, some foreign tourists and sex tourists fall in love with living in a Caribbean "paradise" and move to Sosúa permanently. Although Dominican sex workers and other Dominican migrants usually end up disappointed and no better off economically than when they first migrated to Sosúa, foreign tourists and residents usually find what they are seeking.

Dominicans imagine Sosúa's tourist and sex-tourist trade differently. I am interested in how the Dominican migrants there strategize for the future regardless of the outcomes. These migrants attempt to circumvent asymmetries of power to turn Sosúa into a space of opportunity, rather than a space of exploitation and domination, and are engaged in an ongoing struggle to wrest some of the profits and control away from the foreign owners who have taken over Sosúa. With German citizens and other foreign nationals controlling much of the foreign-tourist industry, a tension between possibilities introduced by globalization, on the one hand, and locals' constraints, on the other, is played out every day on Sosúa's beaches and in its souvenir shops, restaurants, hotels, bars, and discos.[16]

When looking at how a globalized economy affects individual lives, we must explore how these individuals imagine capitalizing on opportunities opened by global linkages, not whether they actually are able to do so. We also must consider how these opportunities might appear to be open to all, especially in transnational spaces such as Sosúa, whereas, depending on race, class, gender, and citizenship, they are open only to a few.[17] And we must acknowledge that citizenship—not just capital—empowers many in the global economy. Globalization can enrich not only local elites and (already capitalized) foreign investors in the developing world, but also cash-poor foreigners who create expatriate communities of relative privilege. In Sosúa, where Europeans and Canadians of the working and lower middle classes can reinvent themselves and their lifestyles—in large part because of their citizenship and accompanying mobility—while those from the same classes in the Dominican Republic cannot, those who have greater access to visas and mobility can take better advantage of an increasingly interconnected world. Sosúa's transformation by tourism into a transnational revolving door—with foreigners coming and going while Dominicans stay behind—is the larger context in which Sosúa-as-sexscape emerges.

The few instances in which sex workers migrate to Europe as the girlfriends or wives of European tourists propel the fantasy for others that "anything could happen," even though these few cases of actual migration that were known to the women I interviewed ended in eventual return and downward mobility. With only a handful of women regularly receiving money wires from clients in Europe—and a rarer few actually moving to Europe to live with their European sweethearts—success stories of women who are living out this fantasy nonetheless circulate within the community of sex workers like Dominicanized versions of Hollywood's *Pretty Woman*.[18] Sosúa and its tourists represent an escape.[19] The women dream of European men "rescuing" them from a lifetime of poverty and foreclosed opportunities.[20] And just as Richard Gere's character (a Wall Street takeover whiz) represents the fantasy of unbridled commodity consumption, so too foreign tourists promise the possibility of economic stability as well as new ways of consuming—and maybe, even of romance, better treatment, and greater gender equity in the household. Thus, women and girls migrate to Sosúa ready to meet their "Richard Gere," and Sosúa's opportunity myth goes unchallenged.

What's Love Got to Do with It?

Beyond the transaction of sex for money, complex politics of relationships are at work in the encounters between Sosúa's sex workers and sex tourists. As they represent themselves as sexually desirable and available to both attract and to anchor sex tourists to their own lives and futures, they also deploy love strategically. This role-playing is not without costs, however, as sex workers find themselves both exploited and exploiters in a cascade of customers, suitors, boyfriends, and partners.

PERFORMANCE AS STRATEGY

Dominican sex workers' strategies to get ahead (*progresar*) through Sosúa's sex trade with foreign tourists—successful or not—can be viewed as examples of what Michael Smith and Luis Guarnizo (1998) label transnationalism "from below."[21] Their strategies often hinge on their performance of love. Of course the sex trade in any locale relies on the charade that sex workers desire their clients and enjoy the sex.[22] Yet in Sosúa's sexscape some sex workers also pretend to be *in love*. Sex workers candidly admit that their relationships with foreign clients are por residencia, not por amor. In this distinction there is a highly strategic element to Sosúan sex workers' (and resort workers') use of sex and marriage. With so many financial demands on them as single mothers (nearly every sex worker I met was a mother), and so few well-paying jobs available to them, Dominican sex workers in Sosúa who perform well at being in love have much at stake.[23] Keeping transnational ties open is a daily task for some sex workers. Many send faxes to four or five foreign clients at the same time with whom they have simultaneous ongoing relationships (it costs under U.S.$1 to send or receive a fax at Codetel, the national phone company).[24] For some, dropping by the Codetel office to see if they have received any faxes is a daily ritual. Those considered lucky receive faxes instructing them to pick up money at the Western Union office in downtown Sosúa. Others receive word that their European or Canadian clients / boyfriends are planning a return visit.

The most envied women receive "letters of invitation," essential to obtaining a tourist visa to visit the men in their home countries.

Whether these encounters between foreign tourists and Dominicans emphasize the "exotic" (First World tourists' seeking to observe, interact with, and take photographs of the "authentic Other") or the "erotic" (First World tourists' seeking to have sexual relations with the dark-skinned "authentic Other"), international tourists often "seek in the margins of the Third World a figment of their imagination" (Bruner 1996: 157). But in Sosúa, Dominicans too have "imaginings" about Sosúa's opportunities, the tourists, their money, and the tourists' lifestyles back home in Europe. Consequently, the fantasies are often two way. In this economy of desire based on difference, Dominican sex workers and foreign sex tourists forge new practices and meanings of "love" that grow out of the tourist and sex-tourist trades. Sosúans (both sex and other workers) and, increasingly, foreign sex tourists and tourists, understand that many relationships that begin in Sosúa are strategic performances by Dominican citizens for visas.

SEX WORKERS AS EXPLOITED AND EXPLOITERS

Without these transnational connections—faxes, money wires, clients' return visits, and the possibility of traveling to or moving to clients' home countries—Sosúa's sex trade would be no different from sex work in any other Dominican town. Sosúa's sex trade also stands apart from many other sex-tourist destinations in the developing world because it does not involve pimps or the coercion of women into selling sex, and therefore it allows sex workers a good deal of control over their working conditions.[25] I do not suggest that these women do not risk rape, beatings, arrest, and HIV infection; the sex trade can be dangerous, and Sosúa's trade is no exception. However, Dominican women are not trafficked into Sosúa's trade but usually are drawn to it through female social networks of family and friends who work or have worked in it.[26] These female-based social networks can act both as a buffer against men who try to make money off of some stage of women's sexual labor in Sosúa, as well as a way for women to make money by persuading their friends to join them in Sosúa. In these cases, sex workers earn a one-time kind of "finder's fee"; unlike pimps they do not get a cut of their friends' nightly earnings with clients. The absence of pimps in Sosúa is critical to sex workers' lives.[27] Without them, Sosúan sex workers keep all their earnings, essentially working "freelance." They decide how many hours they will work, with whom, and for what price. Sosúa's sex trade allows women more choices than they would have in other sites.

In light of the debates over whether sex work can be anything but exploitative, ethnographic accounts of Dominican women's experiences in Sosúa suggest that there is a wide range of experiences within the sex trade, some beneficial and some tragic. Women enter sex work for diverse reasons and have greatly varying experiences within it. Even within Sosúa, sex workers' conditions in the sex trade are highly divergent. In Sosúa there are Dominican and Haitian sex workers; women who work with foreign or Dominican clients; women who receive money wires from foreign clients; women who receive financial help from local Dominican *clientes fijos* (regular clients); women who live with or are separated from their children; and women who have AIDS, or have been raped or battered in the sex trade. These differences in experiences are crucial to shaping a woman's capacity for choice and control in Sosúa's sex trade.

The debate about how scholars, activists, and sex workers understand women's sexual labor centers on issues of agency and victimization, as well as economic empowerment and powerlessness. Some assert that women are forced to choose sex work because of their race, class, nationality, colonial status, and gender and do not have a "choice."[28] To them, all forms of sex work are exploitative and oppressive, which is why they usually employ the terms *prostitute* and *prostitution* rather than *sex worker* and *sex work*. The latter terminology recognizes that selling one's body is a form of labor that— under certain contexts—women can *choose*. While grappling with the thorny issue of whether sex work is inherently oppressive, Anne McClintock's warning against conflating agency with context in discussions about sex work is helpful: "Depicting all sex workers as slaves only travesties the myriad, different experiences of sex workers around the world. At the same time, it theoretically confuses social *agency* and identity with social *context*" (1993a: 2–3). Rather than lumping all sex workers in all places together as victims with no control over their lives, I suggest a nuanced understanding of women's room for maneuvering within the sex trade.[29] Within the context of Sosúa, the sex trade is a story not simply of women who use sex work as a survival strategy but also of women who try to use sex work as an *advancement* strategy. Marriage and migration off the island are the key goals of this strategy. These women see Sosúa's sex trade and marriage to foreign tourists as a fast track to economic success—a way not just to solve short-term economic problems but to change their lives (and their families' lives) through migration overseas, in the long term.

In her research with Filipina domestic workers in Hong Kong, Nicole Constable has been careful not to focus solely on "success-ful" forms of resistance to the neglect of considering "accommoda-tion, passivity, or acquiescence adequately" (1997: 10). Rather, she heeds Lila Abu-Lughod's caution not only to look for "hopeful con-firmation of failure—or partial failure of systems of oppression" but also to "respect everyday resistance not just by arguing for the dig-nity or heroism of the resistors but by letting their practices teach us about the complex workings of historically changing structures of power" (Abu-Lughod 1990: 53). Like feminist ethnographers who explore larger structural forces that contribute to poor women's oppression while also highlighting how these women try to improve their lives, my aim is to consider structures of inequality in sex workers' lives and their creative responses to them.[30] I see, in fact, a great deal of what Sherry Ortner (1996) calls "intentionality" in these women's use of the sex trade.[31] Their creative strategizing, the ways they attempt to use the sex trade in Sosúa to move beyond daily survival, presents an important counterexample to claims that *all* sex workers in *all* contexts are powerless victims of violence and exploi-tation. These women, local agents caught in a web of global eco-nomic relations, try to take advantage (to the extent that they can) of the men—and their citizenship—who are in Sosúa to take advantage of them. In Sosúa's bar scene, European sex tourists might see Do-minican sex workers as exotic and erotic and pick out one woman over another in the crowd, as a commodity for their pleasure and control, but Dominican sex workers often see the men, too, as readily exploitable. The men all are potential dupes, essentially walking visas, who can help the women leave the island—and poverty.

Despite this distinction between sex work as an advancement strategy and sex work as a survival strategy, there nonetheless re-mains a tension between highlighting the efforts of marginalized women to get ahead and considering the local and global forces that constrain them. Far from documenting "failures" of "systems of oppression" (Abu-Lughod 1990) at work in Sosúa's sex trade, this book catalogs many more stories of sex workers' disappointment with Sosúa, its tourism, and foreign men. Sex workers' relationships with foreign men inevitably fall short of mutual exploitation since white foreign male sex tourists are better positioned than Afro-Dominican female sex workers to leave Sosúa satisfied with their experiences there.[32] Sex workers in Sosúa are at once independent and dependent, manipulating and exploited. I write about women who are content with what they have achieved through sex work, as well as those who have suffered humiliation and abuse.

SEX WORKERS' ROLLER COASTER LIVES

Despite sex workers' strategizing, a recurring story seems to unfold: most sex workers in Sosúa end up just getting by, rather than improving their own or their children's futures. Why are there so few "successes" of women's use of the sex trade? Dominican women's migration strategies cannot work, for example, unless the European or Canadian clients follow through on their promises of visa sponsorships and marriage. At any time these foreign men could stop sending money wires or decide to withhold help in the visa process.[33] Since the late 1980s, when Europeans began vacationing in Sosúa in significant numbers, only a modest number of European men have married Dominican women, let alone sponsored their migration to Europe. But nearly every sex worker recounts stories in which foreign men break their promises to Dominican women. Sex workers' experiences with foreign men (such as Elena's with Jürgen) often fall short of their expectations. Their international and interracial relationships do not prove an antidote to the perceived financial irresponsibility and sexual infidelity of Dominican men, which sex workers often decry.[34] And as I write in the chapters that follow, relationships with local Dominican men can sometimes bring unanticipated rewards.

Particularly striking about women's participation in Sosúa's sex trade is the impermanence of their "successes" and "failures." As recounted in the preface, Elena's economic mobility while she lived with Jürgen was short lived. And in later chapters, I write about women who enjoy surges of income, from either regular money wires or increased work with multiple clients. As unpredictably as foreign men begin sending money wires, they stop sending them. Moreover, the women themselves move in and out of sex work. Kamala Kempadoo also has observed that commercial sex work is not always a "steady activity" but might occur in conjunction with other income-generating activities. It also can be an activity that women (and men) take up for short periods or as part of an "annual cycle of work" (1998: 3–4). In Sosúa's sex-tourist trade, women engaging in paid commercial sex with foreign tourists do not simultaneously work in other income-generating activities.[35] Only a few women I met in 1993 were still working in Sosúa's sex trade in 2003. Most have long since returned to their families in towns and cities throughout the island. Those who have stayed in Sosúa have moved on from sex work; some have married Dominican men, while others still look to foreign men for resources and visas. I could never have predicted back in 1993 that some of them—who had no ties to men overseas and who were not actively seeking to establish them— would eventually marry foreign men and move to Europe. And of course the reverse has happened: women whose relationships with foreign men seemed fairly secure have experienced the dissolution of these relationships, resulting in the women's return migration from Europe to the Dominican Republic and downward mobility.

As women have gotten older and left the sex trade, they still might try to parlay relationships with foreign tourists and expatriate residents in Sosúa into solutions to their financial crises. Years after Elena left the sex trade, foreign men have still figured in her income strategy. However, following her many—and unforseen—disappointments with Jürgen, she no longer has any illusions that these relationships will supply anything other than economic security. Nor does she leave her economic future up to chance. Ultimately, Elena has made ends meet through her own pluck, intelligence, resourcefulness, and willingness to work hard. Since Jürgen abandoned her and their son in 1995, she has made money working in restaurants, dancing in Bachata contests, and trying her hand at the lottery. Everything changed for her (and her family) once again in the spring of 2001 when she met and legally married (in the Dominican Republic) another German man. She spent the remainder of 2001 preparing the paperwork to move, with her children, to Germany. Yet by the following spring of 2002, her new husband had stopped visiting the island and wiring money. The most recent times I have seen Elena, in January and July of 2003, she dismissed him entirely. Not only did she not miss him, since she had never loved him; his odd insistence on marrying her immediately—during only his second visit to the island—had convinced her that he was "crazy." She sees him as unreliable as Jürgen, though for different reasons: "He had to get married right away, I never understood why. He is just crazy." But this time around she was prepared for anything; she entered into the relationship keenly aware of foreign men's unpredictibility and unreliability.

What's Sex Got to Do with It?

In the bars and discos, sex workers and sex tourists all know what is for sale—sexual acts, culminating in men's "sexual release." It is these sexual acts to which women attach a price and for which men pay.[36] The commodity here is not just the "aesthetic illusion" that Anne Allison (1994) describes Japanese hostesses as providing, or on which strip shows are based, but rather one in which women deliver an actual "good" by physically touching—what Wendy Chapkis calls "commodified touching" (1997: 6)—and in most cases, sexually arousing and sexually satisfying their male customers. Whereas the Japanese hostess-clubs' customers ultimately expect and indeed pay for their hostesses to remain sexually unavailable while selling the illusion of sexual fulfillment, sex tourists in Sosúa desire, demand, and pay for real—not imagined—sex. At the same time that Sosúan sex workers try to get men to fall in love with them, they also must deliver the expected and agreed upon "sexual goods." While Jürgen vacationed in Sosúa (before the couple moved in together), for example, Elena stayed with him every night in his hotel. They might have been doing all the things travelers do on vacation, going to the beach, eating in restaurants, and going out dancing, but Elena was expected—and was paid—to supply sex to Jürgen when he wanted it. It is here that the sexual contract in Sosúa also diverges from what is for sale in Japanese hostess clubs. Part of what customers buy, explains Allison, is precisely what they cannot have. Paying outlandish prices for drinks and a few snacks, accompanied by hostesses' sexual banter and flattery, allows these Japanese salarymen to display their prestige: the more expensive the woman, the more off limits she is. As these men leave these high-class clubs alone, they can take satisfaction in the prestige of their conspicuous consumption. The working- and middle-class European and Canadian sex tourists in Sosúa are not in search of a similar public display of prestige and satisfaction. Rather, they fly to Sosúa for private satisfaction: to experience sex acts in the privacy of hotel rooms.

It is worth noting, of course, that European men get on a plane to buy sex that they just as easily could buy in their home towns and cities (even from women whose "home" is in the same sites the men travel to). A number of studies have come out in recent years that document that more consumers from the developed world are traveling to the developing world to buy sex.[37] This observation begs the question, why travel so far to buy sex? Sex has become a currency of and for money, transnational negotiations, and migratory desires. Why are these particular desires transacted "through sex," and what does it mean that the sex trade is escalating throughout the world? Obviously, each specific sexscape has its own selling points and attracts particular kinds of consumers for particular experiences with paid sex. Susanne Thorbek, for example, sees several explanations for sex tourists' interest in Thailand and Thai women: the dissolution of communities and increased loneliness; the long work day and little time for a social life; and the view that sex is a commodity "like any other" to which "the white man feels he has a right" (2002a: 39). She also sees the sex tourist to Bangkok as the "quintessential postmodern man" who "avoid[s] fixation and keep[s] the options open" (Thorbek 2002a: 38) as he seeks sexual encounters without emotional involvement and desires "something different without commitment but still safe" (Thorbek 2002a: 39).

Precisely what is being transacted in sex-tourist exchanges—beyond the act of sex—is elusive and depends on the individual and the setting in which he buys sex.[38] Beyond discussions about specific sex tourists in specific sites, it is difficult to pinpoint why more individuals are traveling to buy sex at this particular moment of globalization. Sex-tourist destinations do, however, share certain characteristics: women's poverty in these spaces in the developing world leads to their participation in the sex-tourist industry (in some cases requiring women to migrate internally or internationally); second, global economic inequalities have resulted in more sex-tourist destinations in the developing world; and, finally, inexpensive travel opportunities have permitted more—and less moneyed—tourists to circulate the globe.

I contend that part of Sosúa's appeal to sex tourists lies in the overall experience Sosúa provides as the backdrop for their sexual transactions. European consumers of paid sex have an array of choices in Europe (what Elizabeth Bernstein refers to as "the fungibility of choices")—including Afro-Caribbean women—and the prices are often just as low there as they are in some sexscapes in the developing world (Bernstein 2002). Consequently, sex tourists' experience in the environment in which they are buying sex is significant. Just as important as cheap prices for sex in Sosúa is the experience that *everything* is cheaper than at home; thus foreigners, able to afford nearly anything they desire, can enjoy "feeling rich." Even though they might find sex workers in their home towns (or other European cities) who charge cheap prices for sex, there will be other sex workers whose services they could not afford. And, of course, an array of goods and services always will be out of reach for them in Europe, reminding them that they cannot get away from the spending limits of their *real* social and economic selves. Sex tourists in Sosúa, on the other hand, can *play at* being "big men." Their relatively low social and economic status back in their home countries is inverted; their money goes farther, they have much more of it compared to most Dominicans in town, and they are sexually and romantically pursued by multiple young, beautiful Dominican women. Sex is but one more commodity they can purchase—even "in bulk," since they can afford to have sex with several different women on each day of their vacation. Susanne Thorbek sums up the privileges that travelers from developed countries now can enjoy: "The increase in the male demand for paid sex is logical in the sense that privileges which were formerly restricted by class, race, and gender are now available to everybody; there is no need to be rich to exploit women in very poor countries" (Thorbek 2002b: 2).

In 2003, as tourism in Sosúa slumped and there were fewer tourists walking around the town (and spending their money there), another appeal of Sosúa as a sexscape became apparent. Return tourists can enjoy the smallness and familiarity of Sosúa. Over the years, these returnees get to know the owner-operators of the small hotels, lunch shacks, restaurants, bars, and nightclubs they frequent. Similarly, the male strip club regulars who Katherine Frank interviewed in the United States often referred to the television show *Cheers* in describing the atmosphere of their favorite clubs, where they were known by the dancers, bartenders, and waitresses (Frank 2003: 180). The actual places in Sosúa might not be grand—in fact, as fewer tourists visit Sosúa, many businesses are fraying around the edges—but what they offer is warm hospitality by owners who know their customers and go out of their way to make them feel at home. Since German tourists often frequent German-owned establishments that serve

German food and beer, and British, French Canadian, and Dutch tourists also tend to go to bars or restaurants owned by fellow countrymen, these tourists know they can have conversations, in their native language, with the owners and other customers. And, of course, returning sex tourists can look for their favorite sex workers, with whom they might have been corresponding.

What's Marriage Got to Do with It?

Sosúan sex workers' transactional use of marriage is an ages-old story. What is new is how marriage-as-transaction operates in a globalized world where legal crossing of national borders requires passports and visas. In Sosúa's sexscape, marriage between Dominicans and Europeans and between Dominicans and Canadians emerges as an economic strategy as well as a legal route to securing the papers necessary to migrate off the island. Within what Constance Clark calls "the politics of border crossing," her research on so-called mail-order-brides vividly underscores how marriage to foreigners is often the only viable option for legal migration for citizens of certain countries (Clark 2001). For example, young Chinese women are able to gain the exit visas and passports that most Chinese spend years waiting for—or never get—by marrying foreign men from Japan or Singapore through marriage introduction agencies (Clark 2001: 105).[39] Research on marriage-as-transaction, such as Nicole Constable's work on marriage introduction agencies, throws into relief Western "culture-bound assumptions about what constitutes a 'good' marriage." It also demonstrates that the Western, white, and middle-class feminist critique of marriages based on traditional division of labor does not consider the calculus of women who have "worked in fields or a factory for subsistence since childhood" (Constable 2003: 65). For them, marriage, even those that take the most traditional forms—and are not based on "love"—can be a vacation from back-breaking work and daily financial crises. With their own work loads lightened (Constable describes how, for example, working-class or rural Filipinas' workdays may involve "a combination of hard work in shops, factories, or rice fields combined with domestic chores and responsibilities for an extended household" [2003: 66]), their material comfort improved, and the possibilities to remit money back to their families expanded, marriage for migration and economic security can be good enough. Love may not be missed.

Indeed, although some Dominican sex workers ideally might hope for love and greater gender equity in the household (as an alternative to Dominican machismo) within marriage to foreign men, most regard these marriages strictly as business transactions.[40]

Since Sosúan sex workers do not see marriage to foreign men as ending other romantic and sexual relationships, they know they still can share love and engage in sex they enjoy with other partners. Throughout the book I recount stories of sex workers who maintain relationships—with Dominican and foreign men—while they are married to foreign husbands. Lauren Derby's description of the "complex and contradictory structure of the Dominican family" as "characterized by concubinage, serial unions, female-headed households, de facto polygyny" helps explain why Sosúan sex workers did not conceive of marriage as either restricting their sexual lives or as permanent (Derby 2000: 217). Nor do they necessarily imagine living their lives out in Europe (I recount stories in later chapters about women who return from Europe over their European partners' protests). Of course, migration through marriage is not a possibility for all. Gays and lesbians can not legally marry, older women have a more difficult time finding foreign partners through the sex trade or marriage introduction agencies, and men do not have the same opportunities as women through marriage agencies.[41] Despite these limitations, the prospect of marriage, at least for young sex workers engaging in heterosexual relationships in Sosúa, dangles the possibility of a legal and expeditious exit from the Dominican Republic and its hardships.

Sexscapes

The proliferation of sex-tourist destinations—such as Sosúa—throughout the developing world reflect global capital's destabilizing effects on less industrialized countries' economies, in which the globalization of capital not only shapes women's work options in the developing world but also forces them into insecure—and possibly dangerous—work.[42] In sexscapes we see the tremendous effects of global capital's disruptive and restructuring activities: its redirection of development and local employment into the tourist and sex-tourist industry, especially women's work and migration choices; its creation of powerful images, fantasies, and desires (both locally and globally inspired) that are inextricably tied up with race and gender;

and its generation of new transnational practices from which foreigners extract more benefit than locals.[43] By examining hierarchies within transnational spaces, we see the people, particularly women, whom Saskia Sassen (1998) describes as left out of the "mainstream account" of economic globalization: those who keep houses and hotel rooms clean, food hot, and tourists sexually satisfied.[44] The growth of the sex-tourist trade in the developing world and poor women of color's participation in it are consequences not only of the restructuring of the global economy but also of women's central role in the service sector of tourism, a "hospitality" industry (Sinclair 1997; Momsen 1994; Swain 1995; Kinnaird and Hall 1994; Crompton and Sanderson 1990; Enloe 1989). Women perform the majority of this kind of "service-oriented" labor, and since they often are paid less than men, their relatively cheap labor has assured that destinations—such as Sosúa—are affordable for even the most budget-conscious travelers. Yet much of the scholarship and discussion in the media about globalization do not consider the starring role women play in opening up more and cheaper vacation possibilities for those traveling from the developed world to the developing world.[45]

RACE AND SEXSCAPES

As sites in the developing world become known as sexscapes, sex-for-sale can come to define these countries—and the women who live there—in the North American and European imaginations. Although I argue throughout the book that Dominican women—and Sosúa—have become associated in Europe (particularly in Germany) with sexual availability and proficiency, these associations are not as well known in other countries. Nor is the Dominican Republic's reputation as a sex hot spot as widespread as that of other sexscapes, such as Thailand. In her description of the "libidinalization of Thailand," Annette Hamilton points to the "public image" of the "alluring, very young woman" as the "central icon for the quintessential Thai experience," which cements the "Western identification of Thailand with sex for sale, or 'play-for-pay'" (Hamilton 1997: 145).[46] These associations between nationality, race, and sexual prowess draw sex tourists to sexscapes in the developing world, where they not only buy sex more cheaply than in their home countries but can live out their racialized sexual fantasies. Sexscapes often depend on racial differences between the buyers (sex tourists) and the sellers (sex workers). Sex tourists' fantasies about particular women in a particular place often arise out of associations between nationality and race which are rooted in colonial racist discourses, and, more recently, are fueled by media depictions and Internet discussions and photos.

Sex tourists' girlfriends or wives (or ex-girlfriends or ex-wives) might not travel with them to these sexscapes, but they are there, nonetheless, as imagined points of contrast. Misogyny among these foreign male travelers directed toward Western women "back home" can play a role in the men's racialized sexualization of women as "Other" in the sexscapes to which they travel. Hamilton describes a "profound misogyny" expressed by Western sex tourists toward Western women in her research in the sex trade in Bangkok (1997: 151), as does Jeremy Seabrook, who also writes about the sex trade in Thailand. In his interviews with Western male sex tourists, they told him they traveled to Thailand because Western women were not as compliant or as feminine as Thai women. They came to Bangkok to "escape into the fantasy of men-as-men and women-as-women, an uncomplicated distribution of roles which provide a refuge from life" (1996: 36). In the Dominican Republic it is also common for European men to seek long-term relationships with Dominican women as a break from the "demands" of "liberated" European women. They have fantasies not only of "hot and fiery" sex but also of relationships that reflect more "traditional" understandings of gender roles than they might have in their relationships with European women. As Sosúa's sex workers appropriate their foreign clients' misogynist comments about European women as a way to distinguish themselves as better and more exciting lovers, they too take part in perpetuating racialized and sexualized stereotypes.

These associations between nationality, race, and sexual prowess have been fueled not only by sex tourists and sex workers but also by various commercial enterprises that cater to and perpetuate these associations. In Thailand, for example, brothel owners or sex-tour operators might include fees for foot massages in their bill for sexual services because, as Seabrook describes, Western men perceive Thai women as being "tender," "a quality conspicuously absent from the sex industry in the West" (1996: 3). He observes: "Men feel particularly cherished by what they experience as the compliance, ea-

gerness to please and considerateness of Thai women" (1996: 3).
Indeed, "in the early stages of their contact with Thai women,"
Seabrook writes, the men describe themselves "as being over the
moon, being on cloud nine, walking on air, and wondering what they
have been doing, wasting their life until now" (1996: 3). Although
these sex tourists' racism and their stereotypes about Asians inform
their expectations and even their experiences, they "rarely see [that]
this idealisation of 'Oriental' women is racist" (Seabrook 1996: 3).

Contemporary Western associations between nationality, race,
and sexuality often have evolved from colonial notions of race, gender, and sexuality in which white Europeans were set in opposition
to the darker "natives" they colonized. Commenting on the "tension in the sexual politics of colonial states," Ann Stoler lists the
racist dichotomies that ran through colonial discourses in Southeast
Asia: "Native instinct and white self-discipline; native lust and white
civility; native sensuality and white morality" (Stoler 1997b: 35). Because such colonial discourses of desire not only were about "a
racialized sexuality and a sexualized notion of race" but also were
"productive of, and produced in, a social field that always specified
class and gender locations," Stoler recounts, colonial authorities
enacted policies that first permitted and then disallowed concubinage between Asian women and European men (1997b: 34). Although sexscapes are characterized by racial differences between
buyers and sellers, at times buyers' racialized desires only go so far. It
is one thing to have an Afro-Dominican girlfriend on vacation but
another entirely to bring her home to meet family, friends, neighbors, and coworkers.[47]

These racist hierarchies shape not only clients' desire in sexscapes
but also opportunities and working conditions within sex workers'
communities. Kempadoo has written about Curaçao, for example,
where white European women (often Dutch) and light-skinned migrant sex workers from Columbia and the Dominican Republic work
under better conditions for higher pay than darker-skinned Afro-
Caribbean women. Such "colonial racist hierarchies" are a "trend
evident throughout the Caribbean" and are "reasserted through this
structuring of the inferiority / undesirability of 'blackness' and superi-
ority / privilege of 'whiteness'" (1998: 130).[48] Kempadoo's observation that "the 'brown-skinned girl' constitutes a mainstay of the
Caribbean sex trade" (1998: 131) is also evident in Fusco's research in

Cuba with *jinetcras* (whom she describes as women who "exchange a range of favors, including sexual ones") (Fusco 1998: 151). Within Cuba's own colonial racial history, "the *mulata* has stood for illicit sex,"[49] and more recently, as a "tropicalist cliché," a "national symbol that the country's tourism campaigns simply take advantage of" (1998: 155). One Cuban patron at a chic Havana café explained to Fusco the appeal of the Afro-Cuban woman as exotica to be purchased and experienced in this newly opened sexscape: " I'll tell you one thing. No one comes to Cuba for ecotourism. What sells this place is right on the dance floor—rum, cigars and *la mulata*" (Fusco 1998: 152).

Dominican and Haitian Women's Race. Few of the Afro-Dominican women I interviewed in Sosúa's sex trade identified themselves as *negra* (black), a term typically reserved in Dominican Spanish for Haitians (del Castillo and Murphy 1986; Franco 1989; Moya Pons 1998; Torres-Saillant 1995, 1999; Sagás 2000; Howard 2001; Simmons 2001). Rather, Sosúa's sex workers—who range in skin color—privilege their Spanish ancestry over their African ancestry as well as a mythic Indian past by describing themselves using a variety of terms, such as *morena, india,* or *india clara*.[50] Commenting on how Dominicans downplay their African descent, Silvio Torres-Saillant notes that since "blacks and mulattos make up nearly 90 percent of the contemporary Dominican population," some "would contend, in effect, that Dominicans have, for the most part, denied their blackness" (1998: 126). By inventing a Taino Indian identity, Dominicans are able to "maintain a real and symbolic distance from anything Black, especially Haitians" (Simmons 2001: 92). Indeed, David Howard observes that Dominicans generally do not use the term *mulato / a* to describe their ethnicity (Howard 2001: 8) and that historically the Dominican elite "emphasized strong European heredity and 'purity of blood' " (2001: 8). The "mulato" dictator Rafael Trujillo, who ruled the Dominican Republic from 1930 to 1961, went to great lengths to cover up his African ancestry—literally by using skin-lightening creams—and by commissioning biographies that claimed his parents were "pure" French and Spanish (Howard 2001: 9). Trujillo's hatred of Haitians is well documented and was most violently clear in the massacre he ordered in 1937 of Haitians—and Haitian-Dominicans—living within Dominican borders.[51]

Ernesto Sagás explains Dominican elites' "obsession" with issues of race: "Dominican elites, faced with the inescapable fact that their country shares the island of Hispaniola with Haiti, have erected barriers of prejudice and racism to distance themselves from their poor, dark-skinned neighbors. The same elites have also found race a useful political tool in thwarting challenges to their status" (Sagás 2000: 1). Thus an ideology of *antihaitianismo* has emerged in the Dominican Republic. It scapegoats Haitians both as an ideological method of political control directed at Haiti and Haitians, but it also marginalizes "Afro-Caribbean members of Dominican society, who tend to be poor" by "intimidating them from making demands or otherwise participating in politics" and thus maintains a "narrow status quo" (Sagás 2000: 4).

In Sosúa's sexscape, racial hierarchies cut in two important directions. One set of hierarchies plays out within the encounters between the group composed of white foreign sex tourists, tourists, and foreign residents, on the one hand, and the Afro-Caribbean people in Sosúa, on the other. But many of the temporary visitors remain unaware of another set of hierarchies between Haitians and Dominicans—some do not even know that some of Sosúa's inhabitants are Haitian. Instead, they are likely to see what Sagás aptly terms a "racial mirage" of a tropical paradise and racial harmony (2000: 2). Yet Haitian sex workers and Dominican sex workers rarely socialize or live together. This is due in large part to the racism of Sosúa's Dominican boardinghouse owners, who generally refuse to rent rooms to Haitians—men or women. Haitian sex workers are thus forced either to cluster together in the one or two boardinghouses that will rent to them, or they rent their own houses, usually in neighborhoods where other Haitian migrants live. Since few speak Spanish fluently—and I never met a Dominican sex worker who spoke Creole—language barriers also keep these two groups apart. Dominican racism also plays a large role. As the Dominican Republic's poorest inhabitants, Haitians migrate to the eastern part of the island for menial and back-breaking work, most notably in the sugarcane fields. The conditions in which Haitian sugarcane workers live eerily and tragically resemble slave quarters during colonial times.[52] With Dominicans now moving to Europe, and marrying and having children with white Europeans, a third racial hierarchy has emerged within Sosúa's sexscape. These children represent new challenges to conceptions of race and *Dominicanidad* (Dominicanness).

Foreign and Dominican Men. In the next chapter I discuss Sosúa's foreign-resident community, particularly the gossip and the scapegoating that occurs both within and among different national communities. But here I first introduce the men in Sosúa's sexscape and make clear that not all foreign men travel to Sosúa to buy sex; nor did I meet many "sexpatriates," a term Seabrook uses to describe people who move permanently to Bangkok because of the sex industry (1996: 1). It is difficult to use descriptors that would apply to all foreign men who enter Sosúa, although some patterns emerge. Germans are the largest group of travelers, sex tourists, and foreign residents in Sosúa, and many—but not all—of them hold working-class or lower middle-class status back in Germany.[53] Seabrook's description of male sex tourists in Bangkok's sexscape as "'rednecks,' racists, know-nothing adventurers, out simply for fun" (Seabrook 1996: 39) could describe some sex tourists in Sosúa, but by no means all. Hamilton also provides an unflattering portrait of Thailand's "sexpatriates," to whom she refers as "the Bangkok Old Hands," many of whom have written novels and short stories in which they recount their experiences with Thai women. Although the "Old Hand" often writes that he "truly understands" "real life" in Thailand and that his time in Thailand has been transformative and given him an opportunity to "discover the primal pleasures which only untrammeled access to feminine sexuality" could offer him, Hamilton suggests that the other side is that "many such men are in fact 'losers' who couldn't make it in their home environments" (Hamilton 1997: 151).

In Sosúa, I met many "losers" similar to those Hamilton describes and often found it uncomfortable to interview some sex tourists, especially when they were drunk. Despite my best attempts to interview foreign men when they were sober (by hanging out, for example, in the bars and restaurants on Sosúa's beach in the morning), it was often difficult to find foreign men who were not yet drunk. In the following chapters, I recount how rude foreign men can be to Dominican women—all Dominican women, not just those who are sex workers—and how their behavior has offended women throughout Sosúa, in its supermarkets and cafés, not just its sex bars and nightclubs. I must point out, however, that far from observing exclusively Seabrook's and Hamilton's picture of the "losers" in Bangkok, I also met sex tourists who were sober and polite—at least to me, a white, blond researcher from the United States[54]—and I interviewed sex workers who reported being treated well by some clients. In fact I grew fond of some of the return sex tourists whom I got to know over the years. Their kindness to their girlfriends and their children, as well as their embrace of Dominican culture, makes it impossible to dismiss all of Sosúa's sex tourists (and sex tourists turned foreign residents) as unfeeling cads. The danger for sex workers, as I explore in chapter 5, lies in the unpredictability of these foreign men. No sex worker really knows how she will be treated once she and a client are behind closed doors. Men who might treat sex workers well— buy them drinks and appear attentive and polite—in the public space of bars and nightclubs, can turn verbally abusive or physically violent in private.

Dominican men in Sosúa's sexscape typically earn less than Dominican women migrants who work in the sex trade. This produces a kind of inversion of gender relations and ideologies in Sosúa's sexscape, in which Dominican women become the breadwinners and Dominican men try to siphon money off their girlfriends' earnings. This inversion challenges understandings of how masculinity is constructed and enacted in Latin America and the Caribbean, where traditionally honor and manhood long have been associated with protecting and financially providing for one's family.[55] Contrary to these myths of manhood, Dominican men who draw some of this money from their Dominican girlfriends in Sosúa—even women who have sex with other men for a living—are not seen as any less macho. In the context of Sosúa's tourist and sex-tourist trade, reliance on a woman is recast as macho. New meanings of masculinity emerge in Sosúa that allow men to be *tígueres* (tigers),[56] the ultimate Dominican machos, while earning far less than the women in their lives—or in some cases without earning at all.[57] A tíguere, Christian Krohn-Hansen argues, is "a type who acts according to the situation, is cunning, and has a gift for improvisation. . . . The image of the *tíguere* represents both an everyday hero and a sort of trickster" (1996: 109). Although sex workers harshly criticize men who sponge off of fellow sex workers' hard-earned money and call them *chulos* (pimps), these men—this new brand of tígueres—at the same time are admired by the other migrant men in town. In the process, while men try to reap the benefits, women assume all the stress, risks, and real dangers associated with the experience of migration to Sosúa and with its sex trade.

What Is "Transnational" about Sosúa?

Sosúa—its international tourist, sex-tourist trade, and foreign-resident community—can be seen as a product of globalization. Its transnational features result from global flows of people, money, and imagery linked to notions of paradise, racialized bodies, and sex. The recent flurry of research on transnational processes reflects social scientists' attempts to understand the effects of globalization, described by Anthony Giddens as "the intensification of worldwide social relations which link distant localities in such a way that local happenings are shaped by events occurring many miles away and vice versa" (1990: 64). Research on transnational processes has critically analyzed a variety of global issues such as cultural production and reception, economic asymmetries and linkages, identity formation, and nation-building projects (Glick Schiller, Basch, and Szanton-Blanc 1994). The term *transnational,* however, has been tossed around loosely in this scholarship, and there seems to be little consensus on how to define the term and what qualifies as transnational research.[58] For example, whereas Edward Bruner doubts that "there are any spaces in today's world that are not in some sense transnational, or to phrase it more cautiously, that could not profitably be approached from some transnational perspective" (1999: 462), other scholars more narrowly have delineated what is—or is not—transnational. Much anthropological and sociological work on transnational processes has grown out of migration scholarship, for example, and discussions on transnational migrants' ties to their "home" countries.[59] Participants in a 1990 conference on transnational migration, and the 1992 book that grew out of it, produced a definition of transnationalism clearly focused on migration: "We have defined transnationalism as the process by which immigrants build social fields that link together their country of origin and their country of settlement" (Glick Schiller, Basch, and Szanton-Blanc 1992: 1–2). In fact Glick Schiller later shifted from using the term *transnationalism* to *transnational migration* when speaking about migration as a transnational process.[60] Transnational migrants, she writes, "literally live their lives across international borders" (1999: 96). The women I write about here might not live their lives across borders, but they try to maintain relationships that span borders.[61]

My own research is informed by migration scholars' groundbreaking work on transnational migration, especially since I am concerned with Dominicans' internal migration to Sosúa—and their hope for international migration out of Sosúa. Migration scholars pay particular attention to the flow of people, goods, and ideologies through transnational social fields and the effects of these flows on the cultures of both sending and destination countries. These empirical and theoretical foci are particularly well suited to exploring the multiple forms of movement into and out of Sosúa (by foreign tourists and expatriate foreign residents) and their impact on competing notions of Sosúa's and Sosúans' authentic "Dominicanness."

Transnational migration scholarship is also significant for this study because the largest cities to the smallest rural villages in the Dominican Republic have sent migrants to the United States— particularly to New York—since the mid-1960s (Levitt 2001; Georges 1990; Grasmuck and Pessar 1991; Guarnizo 1994; Duany 1994). No scholar studying anything "Dominican" can ignore the role migration has played both on the island and within Dominican communities in the United States. The past few decades of Dominican migration to New York and the transnational cultural and economic flows between these two places have led many Dominicans to look *outside* the Dominican Republic for solutions to economic problems *inside* Dominican borders.[62] So adept are Dominicans at migrating off the island, that Sørensen even refers to Dominicans as "natives" to transnational space (1998).[63] The quest for a visa—to Canada, the United States, or Europe—is virtually a national pastime. Juan Luis Guerra, a Dominican musician, captures this preoccupation with *fuera* (the outside)[64] and the visas necessary to get there in his hit song "Visa para un sueño" (Visa for a dream).[65] Whereas tourists can enter the Dominican Republic without a visa (and in the 1980s and early 1990s, it was even possible for U.S. citizens to use a driver's license instead of a passport), Dominican citizens must jump through hoops to travel abroad and often undertake elaborate and dangerous schemes to do so.[66] As the benefits of working abroad can prove transformative for extended families left behind (through remittances), a variety of legitimate means to get fuera, as well as scams, abound. Some are so desperate to get off the island that they willingly risk their lives. Dominicans perish in *yolas* (small boats or rafts used to travel to Puerto Rico),[67] and two stowaways in the landing gear storage area of an airplane were crushed to death when the plane's wheels were lowered while landing in Puerto Rico. Professional line-waiters are paid to hold places in the visa line at the U.S. consulate in Santo Domingo, and there is a lively industry in false papers, including passports and visas, some of which cost thousands of dollars.

This preoccupation with getting fuera plays a significant role in shaping sex workers' expectations that Sosúa's sex trade with foreign tourists might be an exit from the island. As a transnational space, Sosúa represents a land of opportunity within the Dominican Republic and a point of departure to other countries. Many often migrate internally to Sosúa; it is the closest they can get to the "outside." Sex tourism links these two forms of migration in a powerfully gendered and racialized way. Consequently, when women move to Sosúa to enter into sex work, they are able to see themselves as taking the first step toward entering another country with more and greater possibilities. To make sense of the transnational processes of migration and tourism at work in Sosúa, I take up many "transnational" threads. In sum, I use the term *transnational* throughout the book in several interrelated senses: I examine what makes the town a transnational space, who engages in transnational practices in Sosúa (successfully or not), and who participates in transnational migration into and out of Sosúa. I also write about the new transnational networks this migration produces.

Rethinking Transnationalism "from Above" and "from Below"

Out of Sosúa's tourist and sex-tourist trade, and Sosúa's foreign-resident community, new "transnational social fields"—what I will also refer to as transnational networks—and migrations emerge.[68] Although most migration scholarship (Glick Schiller, Basch, and Szanton-Blanc 1994; Goldring 1998) views "transnational social fields" as created through migration, I argue these connections exist even when Dominican sex workers do not leave the island. Most Dominican sex workers (or resort workers) will never actually visit Europe or Canada, let alone move there, but they maintain links with European or Canadian men (or women in the case of male resort workers) through fax, phone, money wires, and their foreign partners' return vacations to Sosúa. These European and Canadian businesses, recreational, and personal networks link cities and towns in Europe and Canada with Sosúa. These transnational networks now include Dominicans. In addition, the creation of new migration circuits between Europe (and Canada) and Sosúa—no matter how many or how few individuals actually travel along them—facilitate these transnational practices. Thus new transnational networks that connect Sosúa with places in Europe (and Canada) develop not only through migration of Dominicans and Europeans (and Canadians) to one another's countries but also through encounters between them in tourism and sex tourism in Sosúa, and most recently through various forums on the Internet (a theme I address in chapter 6).

By looking at these transnational networks and the flights of imagination and fantasy that flourish through them,[69] I highlight ways in which gender, race, and nationality are mutually constituted within transnational contexts. For example, through Internet discussions and photographs of Afro-Dominican women (sex workers and nonsex workers), along with media stories (especially in Europe) on Sosúa's sex tourism, a nation's women (and, to a lesser extent, men) have become associated with sexual availability.

To understand the long-term implications of Dominicans' incorporation within European and Canadian transnational networks, scholars need to rethink their conceptualization of the scope of transnational relationships without, as Smith and Guarnizo warn, stretching conceptualizations of transnationalism so far as to run "the risk of [it] becoming an empty conceptual vessel" (1998: 3–4). First of all, we must acknowledge that persons who do not themselves move across borders can become incorporated within transnational social networks and live within a transnational social field (Basch, Glick Schiller, Szanton-Blanc 1994; Glick Schiller, Basch, and Szanton-Blanc 1992; Mahler and Pessar 2001). Second, we must address the issue of differential power held by the various actors within the transnational social field, a power delimited not just by differences in class, gender, and race but also by the relative power of the states in which they hold citizenship rights. For example, German citizenship and its accompanying benefits in the global economy facilitate unimpeded travel and tourism, as well as migration and resettlement. Germans face no barriers in establishing homes or businesses in the Dominican Republic and moving back and forth between Germany and the Dominican Republic, if they resettle. And male German sex tourists hold much more economic power in Sosúa—even those who have little economic power in their home countries—than the Dominican women from whom they buy sex. These differences make it clear that any discussion of transnational processes and contexts has to examine the question of relative degrees of power of the various actors.

To differentiate the freedom that citizens of powerful states enjoy to travel and to establish transnational social fields from the restricted ability of citizens of weak or impoverished states to do the same, I expand the use of the terms *transnationalism from above* and *transnationalism from below* popularized by Smith and Guarnizo (1998). They distinguished between the interactions and strategies of political leaders—transnationalism "from above"—and the quotidian border crossing and personal and familial interactions of impoverished people—transnationalism "from below." I include in the term *transnational from above* the transnational connections made by middle class and wealthy persons who are citizens of states central to the accumulation and deployment of capital. And I see Dominican women's creative use of the sex trade, with its intimate access to European and Canadian citizens, as an example of transnational strategizing "from below." Even though these poor women might not be equal in resources to their foreign clients, they strategize and plan a better life for themselves nonetheless. However, while poor Afro-Dominican women consistently face constraints due to their country's marginal position in the global economy, white European and Canadian citizens of the working and lower-middle classes clearly benefit from their country's position in the global economy as they travel or move to a new country. Aiwha Ong's (1999) distinction between "mobile" and "nonmobile" subjects applies to European and Canadian citizens in Sosúa. Her notion of "flexible citizenship" captures the advantages these travelers enjoy in the global economy. While Dominicans carry passports, for example, that designate what Ong refers to as "inflexibility," Europeans in Sosúa can revel in their "flexibility." She explains, " 'Flexible citizenship' refers to the cultural logics of capitalist accumulation, travel, and displacement that induce subjects to respond fluidly and opportunistically to changing political-economic conditions. In their quest to accumulate capital and social prestige in the global arena, subjects emphasize, and are regulated by, practices favoring flexibility, mobility and repositioning" (1999: 6). Those who carry European and Canadian passports have an edge over Dominican citizens in successfully fulfilling their transnational imaginings. Despite their dreams—and work strategies—Dominicans usually do not strike it rich in Sosúa, nor are they able to use it as a way station to get beyond the island.

As working-class and lower middle-class foreign citizens set up businesses and build their "dream" houses, they transform themselves from workers far from retirement with a heavy tax burden, to privileged neocolonials in a state of quasi-early retirement. Whereas in Europe or Canada they might not be in the socioeconomic position to capitalize on the opportunities—and inequities—opened by globalization, they realize tremendous benefits in the Dominican Republic. In Sosúa, foreign citizens who are not flush with money can take up residency and find social mobility. They sell their cars and residences in Europe and Canada and open T-shirt shops, bars on the beach, or other tourist-dependent businesses to have an income stream every month. Many are younger than retirement age—in their forties—but describe their move to Sosúa as a kind of early retirement. Their money goes much farther in Sosúa than in other "retirement spots" in the developing world. "The very rich do not come here to vacation or to live," asserted a middle-aged German woman. She "looked to retire in Thailand or Tunisia, but it was not as easy or as cheap to build a home as in Sosúa." Another German expatriate, from Liepzig, also "looked everywhere to retire—Haiti and Hawaii" but found that he could live well in Sosúa "without millions." In Sosúa he could "build a nice house and open a small business, but not work too much. . . . No one in Sosúa wants to work." They might not be moneyed, and thus still have to work for a living, but many expatriates find an improved quality of life. One female bar-owner on the beach boasted, "Although life is not a holiday here—you must work to earn a living—it still is better than life in Germany. Look, I can walk out of my house and drop into the sea. This is very nice."

Globalization at Work

This book ethnographically examines how globalization has effected a dramatic transformation of a Caribbean beach town into a "sexscape" with unequal opportunities for its Dominican residents, on the one hand, and foreign residents and tourists, on the other. Understanding Sosúa's allure—its opportunity myth—helps elucidate why so many individuals, both Dominican and foreign, imagine that migrating to Sosúa might change their lives. The imagining of alternative lives, often fueled by the global circulation of media images, spurs many Dominicans and foreigners to leave their current lives, either temporarily or permanently. With a deteriorating economy and few secure, income-earning possibilities, poor Dominicans migrate to Sosúa to cash in on the tourist boom. They bank on the myth of endless opportunity in tourist spaces where vacationers spend their money, and they imagine that in this "non-Dominican" town they will make much more money—a windfall of sorts—than they could working in other "Dominican" towns. They arrive in search of a better life. So do the foreigners who take up residence in Sosúa. Yet even though the imagination allows individuals throughout the world "to consider a wider set of 'possible' lives than they ever did before" (Appadurai 1991: 197), the attainability of these fantasy lives depends on who is doing the imagining and where. The "local" becomes central to discussions about the "global" because transnational practices, such as faxing a German client or receiving money wires, are "embedded in specific social relations established between specific people, situated in unequivocal localities" (Smith and Guarnizo 1998: 11). Unlike working-class and lower middle-class Europeans and Canadians who realize in Sosúa their dreams of an early retirement and lives of comfort that otherwise would not have been affordable in their home countries, Dominicans who migrate there are much less likely to fulfill their aspirations. At the very least, their gains, relatively speaking, are on a much smaller scale than the significant socioeconomic leap foreign residents can make in Sosúa.

Even though I take seriously the impact the global transmission of media images of European middle-class comfort has on Dominican women's imagination, and consequently their migration and labor choices, I proceed with caution.[70] Overemphasis on the global circulation—not only of media images but also of people, capital, ideologies, commodities, and technology—at times offers too facile a perspective on effects of globalization. In the following chapters, I make clear that poverty and the responsibilities of single motherhood are the most decisive factors that inform Dominican women's choice to work in Sosúa's sex trade over other labor options. Although transnational spaces seem to promise endless possibilities and to blur divisions between the center and the periphery, the majority of sex workers' experiences in Sosúa suggest a different dynamic. Transnational spaces not only are sites of new economic, cultural, and sexual possibilities but also are locations which can reproduce existing inequalities.[71] Sex workers in Sosúa might exercise more control over their working conditions than they would in factories, in private residences working as domestics, or in other sex-trade sites, but their decisions and actions constantly collide with those of sex tourists. As one savvy sex worker, Ani, put it, sex workers (and other Dominican migrants hopeful of striking it rich off the tourist economy) who come to Sosúa often end up disillusioned: "They hear they can make money, and meet a gringo, so they come to Sosúa. Some women enter sex work because they want it all so fast. They come with their big dreams. But then they find out it is all a lie."[72]

No matter how persuasively media images condition sex workers' fantasies, a gap remains between their boundless imaginations and the constraints of their social and economic realities. Their short- and long-term sexual encounters with foreign men illustrate Marianna Torgovnick's assertion that despite all the scholarly fuss about the "crossing and recrossing of things," little critical attention has focused on the "social and economic facts" behind these global flows. She reminds us that celebrations of global flows can be *short-sighted*:

> The problem is one of sprezzatura, of carnivalesque rejoicing, of celebrating the crossing and recrossing of things, of believing that contact and polyphony are inherently liberating. Certainly I understand, and even share, the impulse to enlist in Marshall McLuhan's global village. And I'm all for having fun and for the carnivalesque moment. I agree, utterly, that traces of the West exist as part of non-Western realities and (as I suggest above) vice versa, and that this mixture will yield unpredictable (and maybe hopeful) results. . . .
>
> The essence of the carnivalesque is that one cannot tell male from female, rich from poor, black from white: those differences, ordinarily so crucial, do not matter for the duration of the carnival. Everything is freer there, everything is possible. But carnivals do not last. And the interpenetration of third and first world is not just festive. Behind the festivities are social and economic facts we should not forget. (1990: 40)

These global economic inequalities facilitate the development of both expatriate communities and sexscapes throughout the developing world. The failure of the majority of Dominican sex workers, or resort workers, to leave Sosúa with foreign husbands (or wives), visas, or fattened bank accounts underscores that even in transnational spaces not everything is possible and that the differences between male and female, rich and poor, black and white—and, I add, Dominican and foreign, sex worker and sex tourist, and resort worker and resort client—are all the more pronounced. Sosúa's sexscape offers fulfillment of dreams to only a few. Europeans and Canadians on vacation truly escape: norms of behavior and responsibilities of "home" are suspended. Some foreigners (those who move permanently to Sosúa) enjoy more than just holiday carousing and escape from their daily routines; they are able to exercise class, race, gender, and citizenship privileges not available in their home countries. But sex workers and other Dominican "workers" in Sosúa, cannot suspend their racial, class, gender, or immigration status. Ultimately, it does not matter what consumption possibilities the media depict and how much individuals fantasize about them: living out fantasies means having access to required resources, particularly the right passport. Otherwise, citizenship trumps transnational desires every time.

Sosúa and the experiences of individuals such as Elena who live and work there force a reevaluation of the opportunities within transnational spaces. As the next chapters demonstrate, only a lucky handful of Dominican sex workers make gains in Sosúa. And vacations must come to an end. Most male clients, upon returning home, do not continue to communicate by fax or send money or gifts to the sex workers they might have helped financially during their vacation in Sosúa. With every client who returns home, sex workers' dreams of getting off the island leave with him. Meanwhile, sex workers remain in Sosúa hoping that their "ticket" is on the next plane full of European tourists, ready not only to have sex—but also to feign love—for a shot at leaving the island.

Fieldwork

This book is based on field research I conducted in Sosúa in the summer of 1993, 1994–1995, the summer of 1999, and January and July of 2003. I owe a great debt to the Dominican AIDS outreach and education nongovernmental organization CEPROSH (formerly known as COVICOSIDA), particularly to its health messengers (mensajeras de salud). These peer educators, composed of sex workers and former sex workers, lead presentations to sex workers living in Sosúa's bars and boardinghouses. They teach AIDS prevention as well as women's health and safety issues. They let me accompany them on their charlas (talks / presentations) and generously introduced me to their colleagues and friends involved in the sex trade. As my research assistants, three of the health messengers were invaluable in helping set up interviews with sex workers.[73] Because sex workers move often among various bars and boardinghouses, it would have been difficult for me to locate women for follow-up interviews without the research assistants' help.

While making daily rounds with the health messengers to the bars and boardinghouses, I had the opportunity to speak informally with hundreds of sex workers. We not only went to bars and boardinghouses in Sosúa but also to those in nearby towns: Cabarate, to bars for tourists; Sosúa Abajo, to bars for Dominicans; Montellano, to bars for Dominicans; and Puerto Plata, to bars for both Dominicans and tourists. I met women (and girls) in many stages of sex work: I spoke with some women on the day they arrived for the first time in Sosúa, observed women change their living and working arrangements while in Sosúa, and said good-bye to many others who left Sosúa and sex work. I even saw off a handful of sex workers who traveled to Europe to live with clients-turned-boyfriends / husbands, and greeted fewer still who returned for vacation—or for good after their marriages failed. I observed many aspects of the sex trade in Sosúa. At night I hung out in the bars where women met clients; during the day, I spent time with women when they were not working but were relaxing in their rooms, doing their wash, running errands, or going out to cafés and restaurants. I conducted in-depth interviews, with a tape recorder rolling, of fifty sex workers and kept track of these women's lives, conducting as many follow-up interviews as possible. I continue to correspond, via fax, telephone, and e-mail with some of these women, particularly the peer educators who have access to e-mail at the CEPROSH office in Puerto Plata.

I used surveys during initial interviews to gather information on women's work, education, family, and reproductive histories.[74] I also asked questions concerning sexual abuse and violence in and out of sex work; where the father(s) of their children were, whether they were employed, and whether they contributed money to their children; whether they had family members in New York or elsewhere abroad and whether they had ever sought to migrate there; and whether they had worked overseas in the sex trade or other industries. Also, I inquired into whether they received faxes or money wires from foreign clients. Since many studies on sex work do not address the network of individuals who gain from sex workers' labor, this book includes interviews with individuals who facilitate and benefit from the sex trade: clients; bar, nightclub, and boarding-house owners; hotel personnel; and taxi drivers.[75] I also interviewed a variety of Dominican, Haitian, North American, and European individuals living and working in Sosúa.[76]

Sosúa is not a "sending community" in any traditional sense, and consequently doing field research in a space that internal migrants use as a way station to external migration ensures difficulties with follow-up interviews, particularly with those who actually make it off the island. Because none of these internal migrants are originally from Sosúa, when they return from Europe or Canada—whether to visit or to stay permanently—they often never return to Sosúa but to their home communities. Consequently, although fieldwork in a migrant transnational town offers rich opportunities to see forces of globalization "touching the ground" (as I noted in the opening of this chapter), it also guarantees methodological headaches. Yet I never lacked for research possibilities. When I left the bars, night-clubs, or boardinghouses, my fieldwork did not stop. Because tour-ism is the most important business on the north coast, most of the people with whom I spoke are involved in some way with the tourist industry. At the very least, nearly everyone in Sosúa has an opinion about the town's reputation as an international sex-tourist destina-tion. Unlike the Japanese scholars and informants who discouraged Anne Allison (1994) from studying what transpires in hostess clubs, Sosúans often encouraged my research on account of their concern and amazement over how quickly tourism—and sex tourism—has transformed life in Sosúa.[77]

As forthcoming as so many people were, I also must admit that doing fieldwork in a tourist environment was frustrating. Turning down street vendors one after the other, every day, can be exhaust-ing, as well as discouraging for the anthropologist who wants to be "in the field," not "on vacation." Perceived by some as a tourist, and by others as one more expatriate who has come to live in paradise, I could not get away from my own part in constructing this transna-tional space. What other foreigners in Sosúa assumed was "familiar" to me was in fact "strange." I had expected the world of the sex workers' community to be new territory but so too were the experi-ences of tourists, sex tourists, and foreign residents. What I found overcommercialized, noisy, and intrusive, many foreigners found charming and amusing. I write this not just in the spirit of the postmodern "confessional" but also to add my perceptions and experiences in Sosúa to a range of contradictory images of Sosúa that I present in the next chapter. These themes—the subjectivity of what constitutes "paradise," the multiple, conflicting images of Sosúa, and the hypercommodification of everyday life in a tourist town (including gendered, racialized, sexualized bodies)—help elucidate the myths of opportunity which emerge in this transnational space.

2. IMAGINING AND EXPERIENCING SOSÚA

A visitor is as likely to find a menu that lists coq au vin and weinerschnitzel as he is to happen upon the rowdy Latin American pastime of watching a cockfight. On the west side of town, called Los Charamicos, the Latin community lives and plays in a tropical hodge podge of markets, merengue music, and laughter. On the other side of the beach, packaged-comfort resorts, attractive guest houses and waterfront cafes lure hordes of European and Canadian vacationers each year. . . . I am used to the anomalies that appear around every corner of Sosúa—menus made up of an entertaining jumble of Spanish, English and German; sleek Cherokee Jeeps parked next to motor scooters in desperate need of mufflers; and the coincidental fact that this haven from Nazi oppression is now a prime vacation spot for non-Jewish Germans.
—LAURA RANDALL, "Golden Cage"

In the style of promotional travel literature, the passage above from American Eagle's in-flight magazine speaks glowingly of Sosúa's "international flavor." What the writer does not mention, however, is that the "jumble" of things Dominican, German, and from elsewhere also translates into mistrust, mythmaking, and sometimes animosity between the diverse groups of individuals living in Sosúa as well as within them. With new ways of living comes backlash. In Sosúa there is an ongoing battle between the local and the foreign, between the status quo and dynamic change, and between the respectable and the shameful. James Clifford could be describing Sosúa when he writes about "contact zones," "those transgressive intercultural frontiers," where "stasis and purity are asserted. . . . against historical forces of movement and contamination" (Clifford 1997: 7).[1] Transnational spaces, sites where, as Michael Kearney writes, there is "a diffusion of cultural traits gone wild," provide endless opportunities to study constantly shifting, fluid, and contested terrains of culture, identity, and beliefs (1995: 557). This chapter explores the disdain many Sosúans hold for Sosúa as well as for one another—especially for sex workers. Gossip becomes sport in Sosúa, where, in the midst of rapid changes, residents search for both explanations and scapegoats.

Sosúa's History as a Transnational Space

Women in the sex trade, in particular, have become flashy symbols of all that has gone awry with Sosúa's transformation from a quiet farming community into a commercialized, tourist hot spot. Sex workers embody Sosúa's transformation, real and imagined, from a safe, "authentic" Dominican town into a dangerous, decadent hybrid space. Although the opportunity to make money has taken many new forms as a result of tourist development, sex work with foreign tourists has been the most controversial. Dominican and Haitian women who crowd the tourist bars every night have been at the center of a firestorm: they have been the subject of community meetings, articles in the local newspaper, and many conversations among residents concerned for the town's future. Under pressure from the business community (comprising both Dominicans and foreigners), and concern throughout the Dominican Republic about the country's reputation as a sex capital, the police have closed down the bars and nightclubs on several occasions since 1996. Residents are divided over whether tourism brings more harm than benefit. Tourism has brought new economic opportunities, but it also has ushered in profound social change over which residents express a range of attitudes, from ambivalence to excitement to outrage. While some Dominicans and foreign residents in Sosúa eagerly embrace tourism and its changes, others express nostalgia for a pretourism past. Even some of the tourists grumble that Sosúa is "too commercial" and not as "authentically Dominican" as it used to be. Sosúans report that the changes that have accompanied foreign tourism and sex tourism have created an "anything goes," lawless environment and led some to view Sosúa as a re-creation of the "wild, wild West." Runaway tourist development, lax regulations for foreigners seeking residency (including criminals on the run from authorities in their home countries),[2] a weak judicial system, and the local police's abuse of authority all contribute to a climate of insecurity. This climate fosters corruption and violent crime, and it places sex workers who engage in illegal work at great risk of being victims of crimes as well as scapegoats in gossip.[3] For some Dominicans and foreign residents, however, they see the foreigners hiding out there as the real criminals. When several Sosúan residents (Canadian, German, and Dominican), for example, knocked on the door of their new neighbor, a German nightclub owner, they were greeted with profanity—and a gun. Referring to him as a "thug" and a "mafioso," they described feeling powerless and knew that their pleas for him to turn the club's music down after 2 a.m. would go unheeded. Still other Dominican Sosúans assert that recently released Dominican criminals, attracted to Sosúa because of its tourist trade, are the ones who make it a dangerous town.

Since most of the voices throughout this book are those of sex workers, this chapter focuses, instead, on the views of residents and visitors toward Sosúa, tourism, Dominican culture, and women in the sex trade. How do the experiences people have in Sosúa compare to their fantasy images? Drawing on interviews with foreign tourists, and Dominican and foreign residents, this chapter examines how the tourist and sex-tourist trades have transformed the town's physical, cultural, social, and economic landscape.

SOSÚA AS FOREIGN ENCLAVE

Enclaves, as historian Catherine LeGrand notes (1998) are rarely seen as local territory, but rather, as spaces constructed and controlled by foreigners.[4] From its early days as a banana plantation for the United Fruit Company and then as a settlement for European Jewish refugees during World War II, to its present-day incarnation as an international tourist destination, the space known as Sosúa has been shaped by foreign control or influence. Because of tourism's far-reaching changes, the Dominican and foreign residents often see contemporary Sosúa as un-Dominican. Even the "Dominican-ness" of its Dominican inhabitants is called into question. A Dominican resident of nearby Puerto Plata who works in Sosúa elaborated on how he believed Sosúans are different from Dominicans: "Here instead of going to church like other Dominicans, people go to the disco. They don't care about anything, just money." Others described their embarrassment when traveling in other parts of the country and telling fellow Dominicans they are from Sosúa, since, as a young souvenir vendor affirmed: "People outside of Sosúa think that the only people who live here are tígueres and *putas* [whores]." A middle-aged Dominican woman who had grown up in Sosúa was also "embarrassed now about what Sosúa has become." After an idyllic childhood when she used to play in the middle of the main street because "there was so little activity," the changes brought about by tourism have been too much for her. She expressed a hatred of Sosúa now and reported that she never goes out, opining that her "country was not ready for tourism." She worried that Sosúa will become "so bad that it [will be] like another Puerto Rico—with a lot of crime and drugs because of tourism" and that eventually "tourists will leave our island to vacation on another Caribbean island." One Canadian business owner would not hire Sosúans to work in his store but preferred to bus Dominicans in from Puerto Plata, thirty miles away, explaining that "anyone that chooses to live here, or puts up with all the noise, trash, prostitution, and general seediness is not the type of person I want working for me." It is little wonder that many Dominicans and foreigners who seek "authentic" cultures insist that Sosúa is not the "real" Dominican Republic.

Signs of foreign influence are found throughout contemporary Sosúa. The sound of large passenger planes ferrying visitors to and from the island punctuates daily life. Billboards along the main highway advertise nightclubs, restaurants, and hotels in English, German, and French, while supermarkets are stocked with imported goods. Real estate for-sale signs are usually in German, since Germans are the largest foreign-national population living in Sosúa, and a German journalist chose Sosúa over other sites in the Caribbean to start a German-language weekly publication, *Hallo,* because of the sizable community of German-speaking residents living on the north coast.[5] A German bakery, bookstores that specialize in German-language magazines and newspapers, and bars and restaurants with German beers and cuisine all make it possible for the German community to reproduce its lifestyle—but in a warmer climate. Postcards are even sold in German-owned souvenir shops that read, "Welcome to the DDR: the Deutschen Dominikanischen Republik." An article in *Express* (a daily newspaper published in Cologne) unabashedly celebrates a kind of German neocolonialism in Sosúa: "After Columbus and the Spanish colonizers, the Germans are the new masters on the island" (Heikhaus 1995a). As the "new masters" on the island, the German residents (and sex tourists) exercise a privilege that reflects what Sara Friedrichsmeyer, Sara Lennox, and Susanne Zantop call the German "imperialist imagination" (1998). This term refers not only to fantasies of nationhood and Germanness before the "formation of Empire," and to the "myths

1. Newsstand with German-language publications in El Batey

and legends that emerged in Germany alongside European expansionism," but also to those fantasies that "are in some ways operative in the minds of many Germans even today" (1998: 20).

The inequalities between foreigners and Dominicans illustrate Mary Louise Pratt's writing on "contact zones": "A 'contact' perspective emphasizes how subjects are constituted in and by their relations to each other. It treats the relations among colonizers and colonized, or travelers and 'travelees,' not in terms of separateness or apartheid, but in terms of copresence, interaction, interlocking understandings and practices, often within radically asymmetrical relations of power" (Pratt 1992: 7). Inequalities in this contact zone are abundant. "As a German," a fifth-time returning sex tourist told a German journalist, "you can do here whatever you want" (Heikhaus 1995a). The foreign residents, however, generally do not see themselves as particularly privileged but rather as hard workers who practice frugality in order to live in a Caribbean paradise. As one

German woman in her fifties who owned a restaurant on the beach with her thirty-three-year old daughter explained, their restaurant did not bring in "a lot of money," so they needed "to be careful, find the right markets, cook [their] food, and not waste money." "My friends come here to visit from Germany and think it's an easy life," she complained. "But you can't live rich here." Nonetheless, she is able to maintain a certain "standard" of living that she conceded is considerably more comfortable than most Dominicans' living conditions in Sosúa. She justified the differences in living conditions between expatriates and Dominicans: "We have a standard. We can't live like Dominicans do. But they are used to living another way." She even suggested that there are biological differences between Germans and Dominicans, "We get hot and need pools. They can stay cool in a small house with a tin roof."

TWO COMMUNITIES IN ONE: EL BATEY AND LOS CHARAMICOS

Although in the bars, at the nightclubs, and on the beach there is a great deal of social interaction between foreigners and Dominicans, the spaces in which the two groups live are radically different. Divisions between foreigners and Dominicans, and owners and workers, is reflected in Sosúa's physical geography. A beach divides the town into two communities: El Batey and Los Charamicos.[6] I have often heard them referred to as the First and Third Worlds—the modern and the traditional—a dichotomy around which travel guide books (such as the source of this chapter's epigraph) base their romanticized observations of this town. The housing, sanitary conditions, and availability of water and electricity are strikingly worse for Dominicans in Los Charamicos. Even though the whole island experiences electrical blackouts and water shortages, Los Charamicos residents blame the lack of water on the north coast on the big tourist hotels, which they believe the state water company supplies because of bribes the hotels pay.[7] And whereas foreign-owned hotels and restaurants—along with many foreign residences—have backup electrical generators and water-shortage tanks, these are so costly that they are out of reach for even most middle-class Dominicans.

The separation between the two communities began in 1941 with the arrival of the first European Jewish refugees. The Jewish colony settled northeast of the beach in El Batey, while Dominicans who

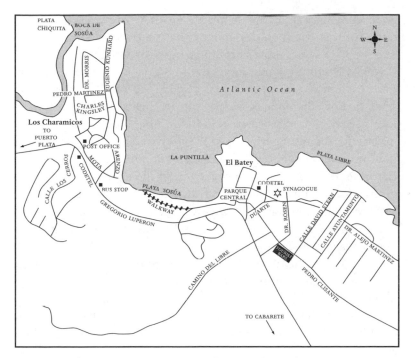

Map 2. Map of Sosúa's two communities: El Batey and Los Charamicos

migrated to Sosúa to work on the Jewish settlers' dairy farms settled in Los Charamicos, southwest of the beach. The two communities remain distinct to this day. For example, national Dominican newspapers are not sold anywhere in El Batey, and non–Spanish language publications cannot be found in Los Charamicos. Perhaps the most telling sign that Sosúa, or more precisely, El Batey, is not "Dominican," is the absence in the downtown area of colmados—an essential feature of every Dominican community.[8] These stores, however, are on nearly every block of Los Charamicos.

With real estate prices skyrocketing in and around Sosúa, the economic gap between the foreign-resident and Dominican communities is widening. Few Dominicans can now afford to live or open businesses in Sosúa's "gringo community," El Batey. Yet tourists do not often frequent the spaces in which Dominicans can afford to start businesses, such as off the main street in Los Charamicos or in Dominican communities—mainly rural—surrounding Sosúa. Although Dominicans make money by working in the foreign-owned establishments in El Batey, the big money that tourism is reputed to bring to local communities, money that motivates Dominicans to migrate to Sosúa, is more likely to be made by foreign owners.[9]

When Dominican migrants arrive in Sosúa, they generally live in Los Charamicos and work in El Batey. Except for a few cheap pensions in Los Charamicos, where young backpackers stay, foreign tourists stay in hotels located in El Batey. The foreign-resident community, for the most part, lives in El Batey and in condominium and housing developments farther to the east of Sosúa, along the road to Cabarete, the next major tourist town on the north coast (internationally known for its near-perfect conditions for windsurfing). The large resorts, known as "all-inclusive" hotels, are also located along this road.[10] One large complex that houses thirteen all-inclusive hotels, Playa Dorada, is located just on the outskirts of Puerto Plata, the third-largest city in the Dominican Republic. Even though they might not be staying in Sosúa, tourists come into Sosúa from all of these places, to go to the beach, shop, dine, drink, and to pick up sex workers. The availability of sex workers in Sosúa has become its most known feature that draws certain tourists while keeping others away.

JEWISH REFUGEES AND DOMINICAN MIGRANTS IN THE 1940S

Although in the 1930s the United Fruit Company owned a failing banana operation in Sosúa, the first significant growth in the town's population came at the beginning of World War II. With sanctuary offered by the Dominican dictator Rafael L. Trujillo, about 600 European refugees settled in Sosúa.[11] While attending an international conference on refugees in Evian-Les-Bains, France, in July 1938, Trujillo's delegate announced that the Dominican Republic would be willing to issue 100,000 visas to European Jews. The Dominican Republic was one of a few countries that offered sanctuary to Jews fleeing Nazi persecution. Historians have suggested that Trujillo's gesture was an attempt to rehabilitate his image in the international community following his orchestration of a massacre in October 1937 of an estimated 20,000 Haitians in towns along the Haitian border (Corten and Duarte 1995; Derby 1994). The offer also reflected his interest in whitening the Dominican population.

Trujillo donated 26,000 acres of land for the settlement (Crass-weller 1966), which he had bought from the United Fruit Company in 1938 for U.S.$50,000 (Eichen 1980). In 1939 the Dominican Republic Settlement Association (DORSA) was founded in New York, and its representatives were sent to Europe to issue visas. The following is an account from an unpublished memoir by Otto Papernik,[12] an Austrian, about his selection as a Sosúa settler from a refugee camp in Bayonne, France:

> One day the news spread that an American and his wife were coming to the camps to select some people for an agricultural settlement . . . Hardly anybody knew where this country [the Dominican Republic] was located. . . .
>
> The American, a Mr. Trone and his wife told us from the beginning that they had only fifty visas and that he was ordered to select people with professions and good health but not older people or people with children because there were no facilities at this new settlement, called Sosúa, for those people. There was a small hospital, and barracks would be used to sleep in and whoever was selected would have to consider himself a pioneer.
>
> Naturally, everybody tried to be in this group but since we were 296 they could only take those they thought best fitted the jobs. When they came to me and asked for my profession and I told them cabinet maker, who could build furniture but also houses (I had built two) he was very impressed. They right away accepted me.[13]

In my interviews with original settlers, they stressed that this "pioneer" spirit was needed to carve a community out of Sosúa. Felix Koch, a radio operator from Vienna who had been a refugee in Luxembourg, described what he found when he arrived with his brother in 1941: "It was a jungle here. There was no road, electricity or running water. The only thing here was wood, so the first thing we did was to make barracks. There were 20 barracks in all, some for married couples and others for single people. This was in the beginning, and we did not know how to live there yet. Not one person was living here." Another Jewish refugee-turned-settler, Luis Hess, came to Sosúa before the other settlers to work as an interpreter employed by DORSA. He also stressed the early lack of development: "Most Europeans could not adapt to the climate and a very primitive life. It was a wilderness. And we were not used to working in fields with a machete, most of us were from cities. No one had ever farmed before."

2. Synagogue in Sosúa

Yet Felix Koch emphasized that despite the "primitive" conditions, "We were very happy. We would do anything we could here. We were in a safe place, safe from persecution." The Jewish settlers eventually built a community complete with a schoolhouse, medical facility, synagogue, and movie house. In fact, the meat and dairy cooperative they started, Productos Sosúa, today is one of the country's most successful industries and sells its products throughout the country.

RECENT MIGRATION TO SOSÚA

Present-day Los Charamicos is a town of new and old migrants. New migrants—pushed and pulled by both economic forces and media images—are joining migrants of a previous generation. Sex workers make up the majority of the single women who are new migrants. Few women who are not planning to enter the sex trade migrate to Sosúa alone. Male migrants either migrate alone or with their families. Shanties have been built in the spaces behind the original wooden houses that line the main road, creating a labyrinth of dirt paths. The area is so overbuilt in relation to its infrastructure that most families in Los Charamicos rely on communal tap stands

3. Wooden house along main road in Los Charamicos

for water and draw electricity from the main power lines by dangerously running scraps of wire from their houses. The lack of living space, the virtually inoperative water and electrical systems, the noise and environmental pollution, and the expense of buying all foodstuffs at inflated prices make living in Los Charamicos difficult.

Luisa, a middle-aged Dominican schoolteacher, had grown up in Sosúa. Her parents had owned and farmed land in Los Charamicos, but they sold the land years ago, leaving no space even for a small garden. She was saddened that because so many people arrive every day to find work, she now saw more unfamiliar people than people she does know. Luisa and other Los Charamicos residents who are not recent migrants take great pride in distinguishing themselves from the new migrants. Pretourism residents point to increased crime as the signal change from the "old days." They also insist that none of the *ladrones* (thieves) are from Sosúa. "Old time" residents view the new migrants, especially sex workers, as on a quest for easy money, introducing crime and irrevocably changing their previously tight-knit community into a town—as Luisa recounted—of strangers. One old-time resident, a watchy-man (security guard) at an apartment complex, explained: "I've been here forty years. The people who are *de aquí, de aquí, de aquí* (from here)—are not ladrones."

Ani, a sex worker, speculated as to why "of course everyone says the thieves are not from here." As Ani saw it, "Thieves can't steal in a place where everyone knows them. So if you want to steal you go to Boca Chica [a tourist destination five hours away on the south coast of the island], and the thieves from there come here."

FIRST FOREIGN TOURISTS AND
FIRST DOMINICAN ENTREPRENEURS

International tourism began slowly, with the docking of cruise ships off Sosúa's shore and the construction of an international airport between Sosúa and Puerto Plata in the early 1980s. Up to this point, visitors to Sosúa had been wealthy Dominicans who built magnificent vacation houses in the hills overlooking the beach along with upper middle-class Dominicans who owned modest apartments for weekend getaways from Santiago, a city two hours away. Canadians comprised the first foreign tourists and foreign residents and consider themselves to have "discovered" the serenity of this then uncommercialized beach town. They dominated as tourists, foreign investors, and business owners until the late 1980s, when new transatlantic flights opened the Caribbean to more arrivals from Europe. Canadians and other nationalities are now outnumbered by Europeans, especially Germans, as tourists and as business owners.

Able to take direct flights from Europe, tourists began pouring into Sosúa. Although there was a lull during the first Gulf War when all air travel dipped significantly, tourism has continued to fuel the Dominican economy.[14] As a result, the process of making money in Sosúa has changed rapidly. For example, beach vendors (Dominican and foreign) who pay rent to a beachfront association have replaced some of the first Dominican entrepreneurs, such as women who had set up charcoal-burning stoves on the beach to cook lunches for cruise ship visitors. Arturo described how he used to help his mother when he was a young boy: "In the old days my mother would cook for the tourists on the beach. There was nothing there—no cafés, no restaurants or bars. I walked around the beach selling my mother's food." Juice bars, German beer gardens, and pricey restaurants (by Dominican standards) have replaced informal entrepreneurs such as Arturo's mother.

Moreover, although some of the beach vendors are Dominican, business in Sosúa is now dominated by foreigners, especially the more profitable and capitalized ventures. In fact, a walk through downtown El Batey reveals that foreigners own and operate most of the businesses that cater to tourists. Even back in 1986, before the recent spate of foreign-owned commercial development, a study on the spatial dynamics in Sosúa between the formal and informal sectors found that foreigners already owned around 75 percent of all formal-sector establishments (Kermath and Thomas 1992). With Sosúa offering overcrowded and expensive living conditions in Los Charamicos and an informal sector eclipsed by a foreign-dominated formal sector, it becomes important to ask why Dominicans keep arriving. Part of the answer lies in Sosúa's "opportunity myth."

Dominican Imaginings of Sosúa

To understand the allure of Sosúa for Dominicans in other parts of the country it helps to examine what the place represents to different people, as well as the economic realities of the Dominican economy. Almost everyone in Sosúa has an opinion about its development. Some see it as a modern-day Sodom and Gomorrah where foreign influence destroys Dominican culture and replaces it with decadent—and possibly dangerous—aspects of European and North American cultures, bringing not only sex-for-sale but also the spread of AIDS. Sosúa's image as a dangerous, morally bereft, and corrupt town is juxtaposed, for Dominicans, against its image as a place where fortunes are made. With tourism comes jobs, primarily in the service sector: Kitchen and wait staff, domestic service, grounds keeping, and other assorted positions that maintain restaurants, stores, and hotels.[15] Although these jobs pay wages only slightly higher than the same jobs pay in other parts of the country, jobs in Sosúa offer contact with foreigners that can prove more valuable than their wages. Working with tourists offers an array of economic, social, sexual, and romantic opportunities not generally available to all Dominicans in other parts of the country. In the next chapter, I further examine how resort workers try to capitalize on their access to foreign tourists. Workers seek jobs with a high degree of interaction with tourists because the payoff can be marriage and migration off the island. While the image of Sosúa as boomtown emphasizes the opportunities that can accompany tourist development and modernization, the depiction of Sosúa as morally and culturally bankrupt focuses on the costs of development. Both visions have a basis in myth and in reality.

The commodification of nearly everything in Sosúa has angered Dominicans who have witnessed their small town overrun by foreign investors, travelers, and expatriate residents who have decided to stay. Yet others are thankful for the tourist trade and even for sex workers who attract tourists to Sosúa rather than to other beach resort areas on the island.

Many bemoan the costs of "development." The commercialization, increasingly violent crime, corruption, drugs, and sex tourism have prompted worries over the loss of Dominican culture and a peaceful way of life. While hitching a ride with a young Dominican driving a pickup truck from a rural community about one hour from Sosúa, I asked what he thought of Sosúa. His comments express several themes that Dominicans frequently use to characterize this location: "It's a place of a lot of diseases, like AIDS, and tígueres and putas. You know, corruption." Like many Dominicans from other towns, he avoids Sosúa. "I don't like going there. You can get in a lot of trouble, because the police don't respect Dominicans." Like the sex workers, he is afraid of arrest: "I don't go to the bars and discos where the police find people to arrest." In fact, he mentioned that "lots of Dominican men get arrested for no reason—like for having long hair." He said he avoids being mistaken by the police as a *sanky-panky* (a young man who escorts female tourists around town),[16] by making an effort to look nice whenever he visits his friends there. His concerns about putas, tígueres, and Sosúans with AIDS reflect a preoccupation with the town's moral character. Throughout Latin American history, spaces of modernity, such as newly developed urban centers, and mining or railway outposts, have been represented as places of vice, lawlessness, and contamination.[17] Not surprisingly, sex workers, fixtures in spaces occupied mainly by male migrant laborers, often have been the target of law enforcement, church censure, and public health and safety campaigns.[18] Long blamed for the spread of sexually transmitted diseases, sex workers today are castigated throughout the world as vectors of the AIDS virus (de Zalduondo 1991).

In this space of conflict and change, residents see sex workers not only as a source of disease but also as a primary cause of moral and cultural decay. They often blame "putas" for Sosúa's downfall: its unregulated development, trash in the streets, drugs, and crime. In

4. Trash on street in Los Charamicos

fact, "old-time" residents often use the term *ladrón* (thief) inter-changeably with *prostituta* (implying that prostitutas are ladrones but not necessarily the reverse). Consequently, women perceived to be sex workers—and men perceived to be sankies—live under police surveillance and risk arrest any time they are in public spaces. This process of deciding who *is* and who is not a sex worker—or a sanky—leaves all Dominicans, especially those who are black and poor, vulnerable to the police.

THE ANCHOR

When the Anchor was the focal point of the sex trade in the early 1990s (before it burned down),[19] it helped create an atmosphere of an open-air "sex market" in downtown El Batey. With sex workers and their clients spilling out into the street in front of the bar, and music blaring until the early morning, business owners and residents pres-sured both the club's owner and the police to control the flow of people outside the bar as well as the music. In response, the An-chor's owner (a Dominican man) built a large wall to semienclose the previously open-air bar. And periodically, the police went from club to club demanding that the music be turned down. Usually, however, the clubs were at full volume once again by the next night.

Music at the clubs was loud. One could feel the bass beat shaking floors and walls blocks away.

In the Anchor's heyday (before the police shutdowns started in 1996), the blocks closest to the bar were completely transformed at night from a quiet shopping and restaurant district by day. It was a spectacle: sex workers and sex tourists everywhere, stopping traffic (Dominican women and foreign men crisscrossed the street, hopping from bar to bar). *Motoconchos* (motorcycle taxis) clogged the corner by the Anchor, delivering women from their boardinghouses in Los Charamicos and picking up women and their clients to bring them to the men's hotels (or, sometimes back to the women's rooms). Meanwhile, street vendors hawked jewelry, Haitian stone carvings, and woven baskets. With all of this activity happening within just two short blocks, it did get quite crowded. In the midst of all the partying and confusion, male tourists complained of having their wallets lifted. One scam tourists often reported was that a woman would grab a man's genitals with one hand while taking his wallet from his pocket with the other.

Between the petty theft, crowds, noise pollution, and visible sex trade, the Anchor became the main symbol of Sosúa's sex trade and target of residents' anger. Responding to the community's criticism, the Anchor's owner told me that the atmosphere in his club was very "controlled." His description of his club, however, bore little resemblance to its nightly activities: "We have things here other than women—music, folk dances, and an information center on Dominican culture." Pointing to a corner in the back of the club, he told me, "I even have an idea about a museum."

Once the police began closing the bars in 1996, the sex trade, which had visibly dominated all economic and social life in downtown El Batey, was forced behind bar and nightclub walls. With the Anchor—and another open-air club across the street—both out of business, and few sex workers and sex tourists hanging out in the streets, it might have appeared that the sex trade was over following the bar closings. But as sex workers living in Los Charamicos, sex tourists drinking in El Batey, and AIDS educators at CEPROSH (a Dominican AIDS-education organization) assured me, the sex trade in the late 1990s was as lively as ever—it just was not as public. New nightclubs and bars—none open-air—became the center of the sex trade, although no single establishment replaced the Anchor as "the" place to go. Rather, the trade seemed dispersed among different dancing clubs, bars, and casinos.

In Los Charamicos, sex workers—especially in the Anchor's heyday—seemed to be everywhere. So many women living in Los Charamicos were involved in the sex trade that parents could not possibly shield their children from it. Children on their way home from school inevitably passed groups of sex workers who were out running errands, some of whom were only a few years older than the children attending school. Ani, a sex worker, has seen many families leave, especially those that had been living in Sosúa before the tourist trade and the most recent waves of Dominican migration it precipitated. She reasoned, "Most families, if they have the money, live in other places. Here all life is the tourists and their money." For Ani, Sosúa is a "jungle" compared to the "family towns" outside. As she saw it, "Sosúa has only two kinds of people—prostitutes and business owners." In nearby Puerto Plata, in contrast, Ani believed, "there is another way of living" where "the night life is more mixed —it does not revolve around the tourists." Rather, there are restaurants, clubs, and casinos that cater to Dominicans. "So a woman [who might be a sex worker] could say she works in a disco and no one would know otherwise. You can lie." But in Sosúa, where all the businesses revolve around the tourists, "everyone knows what you do." Even so, "there are so many sex workers that people are used to it here."

TOURISM AND AIDS

Sosúa is also closely associated with AIDS. The pickup driver's views expressed a widely held belief that sex between tourists and local Dominicans (not just for money) is spreading the virus: "Having sex with the tourists is dangerous." His fears are not unfounded. Whether through casual or paid sex, tourists engaging in unsafe sex have made tourism an HIV-transmission vector in the Dominican Republic (García 1991; Koenig et al. 1987). In response to the threat of AIDS transmission to Dominicans working in the tourist industry, CEPROSH conducts seminars and theater presentations on safe sex for resort employees and high-school students, as well as for sex workers. There are similar successful education programs in Europe which, for example, target tourists and individuals working in the tourist sector. A European Community AIDS-prevention project for travelers and migrants, AIDS & Mobility, has taken particular interest in the links between vacation behavior and AIDS transmission (van Duifhuizen and Broring 1993; Hommes and van der Vleugel 1993). A number of European studies have demonstrated, for example, that individuals on vacation are much more likely to engage in "risky" behavior than when they are at home (Conway, Gillies, and Slack 1990; Ford and Inman 1992; Hawkes 1992; Pasini 1988). Drinking alcohol to excess, taking drugs, eating unhealthy foods, staying out late, and buying sex or practicing unsafe sex are all examples of how people on vacation might cut themselves free from their normal routines.

Whereas tourists possibly "let loose" on vacation in Sosúa, Dominicans describe monitoring their behavior. Just as the pickup truck driver carefully chooses what he wears and where he goes out, another young Dominican, Juan, altered his sexual behavior with tourist women because of the threat of AIDS. One of the early entrepreneurs on the beach, Juan, described precommercialized Sosúa in idyllic terms, free of crime, sex tourism, and disease: "I set up a bar on the beach in the late 1980s. I realized there were no places to drink. I did not pay rent. I had no competition. I started out with five chairs, and then six months later I had twenty. I was there about a year and a half, until the Casa Marina Hotel [a large, all-inclusive] paid me to leave." He described romantic relationships between Dominicans and foreigners as inevitable: "You spend time together, and after a few days you started falling in love. I went to discos and restaurants with women I met. After three weeks you were in love. It was a very beautiful time. There were not as many putas and ladrones." The threat of AIDS became a wake-up call for him to change his lifestyle, and he began to see tourists differently: "Now, I'm tired of tourists. They've changed; there are more Germans. I was in an environment I liked. I really liked this life. Then came AIDS. And I said 'stop.' I liked the tourist women, but I wanted to marry and to stay healthy."

Today, Juan says he is done flirting with tourist women. He is married to a Dominican woman, has two children, and rarely has any interactions with tourists. He owns a colmado in Los Charamicos where his clientele is Dominican. Both AIDS and the rate at which Germans have moved into Sosúa and dominated its money-making ventures have curbed Juan's zeal for tourism and tourists.

Although entrepreneurs such as Juan could make money in the informal economy by working long hours during the early phases of Sosúa's tourist trade (in the late 1980s to early 1990s), start-up capital is now just as important as hard work. Dominicans who cannot compete with German investment capital have become embittered.

TÍGUERES, FAST MONEY, POLICE, AND CORRUPCIÓN IN SOSÚA

Besides seeing Sosúa as a place of disease, Dominicans also criticize it for attracting individuals who migrate to Sosúa in search of "fast money" (*dinero rápido*). Many Sosúans associate making fast money with laziness, greed, or illegal activities. Both putas and tígueres are seen as willing to go to any lengths to make money. Almost all motorcycle taxi drivers are called tígueres (I never saw a woman driver), especially those who make extra money by acting as "guides" for tourists looking to buy sex. I have seen motorcycle taxi drivers walk into boardinghouses where sex workers live, with foreign male customers in tow, at all hours of the day and night. Not surprisingly, some sex workers are friends with these drivers and benefit from their access to foreign tourists. Yet sex workers, like Ani, also deride tígueres as self-serving and untrustworthy: "A tíguere is a person who thinks he knows everything. Like a tiger, he is aggressive and ferocious. He is not afraid of anything. In other places [i.e., outside of Sosúa], tíguere is not only a negative term, because they will defend others. Look out for them. But here, they are not really tígueres; they are bandits."

One of the first words used by residents—and many Dominicans from other parts of the island—to describe Sosúa is *corrupt*. As a catchall term, *corrupción* captures Sosúans' unease with the locale's rapid transformation from a small agricultural town into a tourist destination. They identify several sources of corrupción: government corruption, the failure of political institutions (including the police), and the sex trade. In fact, the name Sosúa is often used as a synonym for corrupción because it boasts both a local police force notorious as one of the most crooked in the country and a thriving sex trade. The police force causes anger and fear in the community, not just because Dominicans fear unfounded arrest but also because they believe these officials commit crimes themselves or extort bribes from criminals to ignore their transgressions.[20] The local citizenry's distrust of the police—often referred to as *mafiosos* by Dominicans and foreigners—reached new heights when the police were implicated in the murder of a money changer (a street dealer in foreign currency) who Dominicans believe knew about police involvement in an illegal deal. Pedro, a friend of the money changer, explained in hushed tones that the money changer's family was terrified of speaking out. He recounted how the money changer's brother was almost run down by some men in a jeep: "Everybody knows it was the police." Los Charamicos residents held a funeral march through the streets and placed candles outside their doors at night both as a remembrance as well as a sign of protest.

The police systematically extort money from prisoners, many of whom they arrest on false charges. Poor Dominican Sosúans feel powerless in the face of such misuse of authority. It is common knowledge that the Sosúa police make more money from bribes than from salaries.[21] This racket makes sex workers profitable targets for arrest. Whether sex workers are working or not, they can be picked up by the police and held indefinitely in jail (as Elena's story in the Introduction describes). I spoke with many sex workers who have been arrested while out shopping and running errands. Such a wide-ranging assault on sex workers inevitably results in the imprisonment of many women who are not in the sex trade. Luisa (the middle-aged school teacher I mentioned earlier in this chapter) explained that the police arrested her cousin, who is not a sex worker, late one evening in Los Charamicos. They approached her just as she was putting her key in the door to her house after a night out with her boyfriend. They accused her of being a sex worker, carted her off to Puerto Plata, and threw her in jail. Her family reported her missing to the police, but the officer who processed the paperwork following her arrest had misspelled her name, and the police could find no record of her arrest. Her family thought she was dead. A few days later, following the jailed woman's pleas to the police to contact her family, she was released, but only after the family paid the standard 500 pesos (U.S.$42.00) bribe. By branding any woman at any time a *puta*, the police terrorize the female population of Sosúa.

Not only women are fearful. Men are also at risk for random arrest, which helps explain why the driver of the pickup was so careful when visiting friends in Sosúa. A young employee of one of the long-distance telephone companies felt helpless, for example, when her brother was arrested as he locked up the small souvenir stand they own together. She explained, "He was leaving our store at 10 p.m., and the police took him and put him in jail. He said he was leaving a business he owned, but who knows what they thought. . . . I don't know if they thought he was a sanky. He was in jail for a day, and, of course, we had to pay them money to get him released." In Sosúa any Dominican—Luisa's cousin, this souvenir vendor—can be harassed and even arrested for alleged transgressive sexual behavior. By indiscriminately labeling women putas and men sankies at any time, the police justify their harassment, incarceration, and extortion of the citizenry.

Foreigners' Imaginings of Sosúa

When I first came here, I had invested all of my savings, U.S.$8,000, with a Dominican business partner in a fourteen-room European-style hotel. I had imagined myself in a cream linen suit and Panama hat, sitting under a big ceiling fan and with a parrot on my shoulder. As I waited with my business partner for our first guests to come downstairs for dinner, he turned to me and said, "They will be down in an hour." "How do you know that they will be here in an hour?" "Because that is all that they paid for." At first I did not understand. When I realized I had just bought a hotel where married men brought their mistresses and prostitutes, I could not believe it. (*Joseph came to Sosúa in the early 1980s from Canada. He sold his share in the hotel and now owns a successful gift shop.*)

Three years ago my husband and I sold our cars and condominium in Canada. We wanted a break, from everything—the cold, work. So we came here, but our money is running out, and our business never really got off the ground. We are moving back to Canada. (*Anne and her husband moved back to Canada in the spring of 1995.*)

I moved here because the sun and warm air are good for you. I could not take the cold weather in Germany. (*Ingrid lives on a shoestring budget selling time-shares.*)

I used to live in South Africa and returned to Germany for a while. I read articles in Germany about how cheap it is to live in Sosúa, so I came here to retire early. (*Susanne owns a bar on the beach that serves German beers.*)

PARADISE

The stories above help illustrate why foreigners decide to move to a beach town in the Caribbean. They come to Sosúa because of an image they have of island life. Some take great risks, especially financially, in their decision to move. Others, particularly those who arrived in the late 1970s and early 1980s, before Sosúa and the north coast were developed, have made a windfall of profits. But most who moved to this beach community, in this early period of tourism development, arrived in Sosúa to improve their quality of life, not to make their fortune. According to a Canadian who settled in Sosúa in the early 1980s: "People used to come here 'to be,' not to make money. It was very existential. It was really wonderful here before. You could get stoned on the beach and wake up there the next morning. This was back in 1984—can you imagine doing that now? You probably would be robbed and killed."

The image of life on a Caribbean island conjures up scenes of palm trees, tropical drinks, and cool breezes. In short, foreigners come to live in paradise. Yet if there is one thing I learned from living in a setting some would call "idyllic," it is that people define "paradise" differently. One place cannot fulfill the dreams of all who arrive. As Sosúa has changed, so has the level of happiness of its inhabitants—both foreign and Dominican.

"SO-SEWAGE"

The commercialization, crime, police corruption, and sex tourism that have accompanied tourism development in Sosúa have disappointed, frustrated, and frightened foreign residents who came to the Dominican Republic seeking a peaceful, safe life. Many Canadians came to Sosúa after living on other islands, such as Jamaica, where violent crime threatened their island retreat. For many of these first expatriates to Sosúa, it is no longer a paradise. Some even refer to it as "So-sewage." The unchecked development, sex bars, loud music from the discos, trash in the streets, and general seediness have deterred many "old-time" foreign residents from walking through downtown Sosúa, especially at night, when the sex workers

5. Sosúa beach

have been everywhere (especially in the 1990s). One old-timer has a business in downtown Sosúa but lives in Puerto Plata. He explained why he moved out of Sosúa: "I loathe what Sosúa has become. I have very little reason to go there anymore at night. In the past ten years, I've been there at night no more than six times." He used the imagery of Sodom and Gomorrah to talk about Sosúa. "Maybe I'm not a good person to talk to, because I've not seen Sodom and Gomorrah in full swing. With Sosúa the way it is, Puerto Plata seems like 100 miles away, which is why I moved there."

This theme of paradise lost runs through the language of many foreign residents as they seek to scapegoat the sources of contamination "spoiling" their "discovery." "My lovely Sosúa," lamented a Canadian resident, "it's being ruined." In tourist encounters, the local population often blames the "undesirable economic and social developments" on the tourists (Urry 1990: 59), and certainly Sosúans harshly criticize tourists and sex tourists. But two other groups receive much criticism: sex workers (by Dominican and foreign residents), and German tourists and residents (by Dominican, Canadian, and fellow German residents). Such finger-pointing is sport in Sosúa. Gossip about sex workers and German tourists and residents has united, on some levels, Dominican, Canadian, and U.S. foreign residents, and Jewish settlers (many of whom consider themselves Dominican, especially if they married Dominicans and raised children on the island). For these critics, Sosúa, as a transnational gateway, is being destroyed by its most recent arrivals.

THE FANTASY OF ISLAND LIFE

Yet there are many who love Sosúa: tourists who come back for all their vacations, and foreign residents who happily moved to an already commercialized Sosúa. Susanne (I opened up this section with a quote from her) had vacationed in Sosúa five times before deciding to move there permanently. A German hairdresser, however, had never been to Sosúa, or to the Dominican Republic, before moving there. He bought a hair salon located in El Batey after seeing an advertisement for it in a magazine in Germany. To many such as this hairdresser, Sosúa is still a paradise—they sell their houses and leave their jobs to start a new life "in the islands." A real estate developer who sells land in the Dominican Republic to people in the United States over the telephone, sight unseen, discussed the appeal of owning property and possibly moving permanently to a Caribbean island: "They have a dream of owning a place in the Caribbean. They give me the money and I supply the dream. I'm selling more than just property—I'm selling fantasies." The land he sells is on the north coast, to the east of Sosúa, and is, for now, commercially undeveloped. But he does not tell the buyers over the phone, none of whom have built on their property yet, that most of this land is already home to many Dominican residents, whom he called "squatters."

Like the sex workers and other internal migrants who take on great risks by coming to Sosúa to fulfill their dreams, foreigners also take their chances at starting new lives and making a living in Sosúa. Yet often, just like the sex workers and other migrants, they do not win big. Isabelle, a French Canadian, quit her job in Canada and sank her savings into a restaurant deal with a Canadian friend. While vacationing in Sosúa, her friend had seen a for-sale sign on one of the dozens of restaurants and bars that line the beach. When she returned to Canada, she persuaded Isabelle to buy the restaurant with her. But by the time they called the restaurant owner, it had been sold. This bad news did not dampen their Caribbean dream, nor did the fact that neither of them had ever worked in the restaurant business before. They wired the restaurant owner money, and he bought land and built a restaurant for them in Los Charamicos. They sold their assets in Canada, moved to Sosúa, and opened the restaurant that served both French Canadian and Dominican

cuisine. The prices were set for the tourist market, so local Dominicans rarely ate there. But neither did tourists. With the all-inclusive
hotels providing tourists their prepaid meals in the hotels, indepen-
dently owned tourist restaurants (most of them located in El Batey)
have been hard hit. Tourists in all-inclusive hotels have no need to
dine out. It did not help that Isabelle's restaurant, moreover, was in
Los Charamicos, off the beaten track for most tourists. Most nights
the restaurant was completely empty. A little over a year after she
had first arrived, Isabelle returned to Canada. She unsuccessfully had
tried to sell her share in the restaurant, but she needed to start
working again to pay off her debts and decided to wait in Canada for
a buyer.

Her story is not unusual. The risks she took—wiring money to a
stranger and starting a business she knew nothing about in a place
she had never seen—reflect the degree to which she wanted to make
her new life work. The lure of an idyllic life on a Caribbean island
blurred her judgement, as it has others', and outweighed financial
caution. Every day that she stayed, she lost money. She also was
worn out by living in a place where rapid development had outpaced infrastructure. With her business and her apartment in Los
Charamicos, she experienced greater water shortages, for example,
than her Canadian friends who were living across the beach in El
Batey. "I'm fed up. There isn't any water. I can't live like this." She
left Sosúa for the same reason that many foreign residents have left
and are leaving: Sosúa was not paradise after all.

ANYTHING GOES: CRIME AND INSECURITY
An outbreak of crimes committed against foreign residents in Sosúa
by Dominicans, ranging from armed robbery to rape, also has compromised foreign residents' notions of "paradise." In the winter of
1995, a rash of crimes touched off a wave of panic in the foreign
community. In response, the U.S. ambassador to the Dominican
Republic held a town meeting in Sosúa for U.S. citizens, and many
other foreign residents attended. The audience was filled with fear—
and anger. They had reason to fear for their families' safety, especially those living in the countryside or on the outskirts of town,
where their homes' relative isolation had attracted criminal activity,
some of it quite violent. With no 911-type emergency response available, no ambulances, and only one vehicle owned by the police
force, these foreign residents felt profoundly insecure. "We are being

terrorized," said one Canadian woman after the meeting. "The police are no help, and there is no such thing as a detective. They don't even have fingerprint kits, let alone other techniques to catch criminals. There is nothing to stop or deter criminals. Why not rob houses? It's easy work around here, with no repercussions. I'll tell you, it's made me a law-and-order person."

In another community meeting, composed mainly of foreigners (Canadian, U.S., and German citizens) and a few Dominican business owners (the meeting was in English), people signed a letter to then-president Balaguer that listed two types of crimes: "Crimes against Residents" and "Crimes against Tourism." The letter stressed the potential financial loss to the Dominican economy if the crime wave persisted: "These crimes have changed our lives to the extent that the first individuals who had chosen the Dominican Republic as their new home are leaving or already have left this island. If this tendency continues negative information about this otherwise lovely place will reach Europe and North America and will sooner or later directly influence tourism, which we all know is one of the major income and work sources on the island." The letter also asked for investigations into some of the unsolved crimes committed against foreign residents and for a mediator between the police and the foreign residents and tourists. Members of the foreign-resident community felt they needed to perform police or judicial functions themselves—responsibilities normally met by state agencies in their home countries. "I'll help out any way I can," volunteered a Canadian man who had moved to Sosúa to windsurf. "I want to see things get better. If not, we are going to Australia." The German community also organized community meetings, eventually forming, in 1999, a new German association, the "Internationaler Residenten Club Sosúa." At a meeting I attended in June 1999 (in a Russian-owned hotel), Dominicans were singled out as committing crimes, just as they were in the meetings held by English-speaking residents.[22]

With fear mounting and law enforcement of little help, foreign residents began to arm themselves. A Canadian woman hired a private security guard to watch her house at night. "We have to realize that the police won't help us, just as in any Third World country." An expensive "gated community" stepped up its security by hiring a Bulgarian "chief of security" and a team of security officers. People living nearby said they often heard gunshots, which they assumed was the security force, or the residents, firing their guns into the woods at any sign of trouble. "We are like an armed camp," declared a Canadian living there. "The security guard takes residents to practice shooting their guns in nearby caves. My neighbors are trigger-happy. Who knows who might get hurt—it might even be the guards on their patrols at night."

Other foreigners were ready to take advantage of—and deepen—this climate of fear. A husband and wife team from the United States, self-pronounced security "experts," held seminars on how to secure one's home or business against break-ins. They charged 300 pesos (U.S.$25) just to attend the meeting, which turned out to be a sales pitch to hire them as security consultants. A Canadian who had been robbed in the middle of the night—he had been tied up, blindfolded, and threatened with a machete to his throat[23]—knew he had wasted his time and money when he saw the husband count the money at the door and then leave to buy himself beer.

TOURISM APARTHEID

The tourist resorts reinforce the image of the local population as violent and criminal. It is virtually impossible to enter the gated resorts without wearing an identification bracelet that indicates you are a guest of the hotel. The bracelet system not only alerts the management as to who are paying guests (since the meals are prepaid, as are the drinks at the bars throughout the resort); it also keeps out sex workers and other undesirables. The Italian manager of a German multinational hotel boasted, "We have never had a break-in." With twenty-four-hour security guards at the beach, the bracelet system, and a strict "no sex workers permitted" policy, they believe they have tight security. He assured me that tourists are "protected," indeed shielded from the country and its people outside of its gates. "Here we live in a different world than outside."

A Dominican manager of another foreign-owned resort explained that they hold "briefing" sessions for all their guests when they arrive. "We tell them not to leave the safety of the hotel and that if they do, they can be robbed, or infected with AIDS." The hotel staff who lead the "safety" presentations act as what John Urry terms "surrogate parents" who "relieve the tourist of responsibility or protect him / her from harsh reality" (Urry 1990: 7). Building on what Daniel Boorstin (1961) called an "environmental bubble," Urry's description of how tourists are "isolated from the host environment and the local people," as well as "find pleasure in inauthentic con-

trived attractions, gullibly enjoying the 'pseudo-events' and disre-
garding the 'real' world outside" (1990: 7), sums up the touristic
divisions in Sosúa. By keeping foreign tourists within resort walls,
and locals out, the hotels have introduced a kind of tourism apartheid to Sosúa. The bracelet system might help the management
secure against freeloaders at the buffet tables and open bars, but it
also creates an environment that is segregated by race, class, and
citizenship.

TOURISM: WHOSE OPPORTUNITY?

Despite some visitors' negative experiences, new tourists arrive
every day; a package tour to the north coast of the Dominican
Republic is high on the list of European travel agents' cheap Caribbean beach vacations. Yet the type of tourist who vacations in Sosúa concerns Dominicans in the tourism industry. A Dominican
marketing specialist for one of the largest all-inclusive hotels believes
his country has suffered from the type of tourist that visits, and
might eventually settle in, the Dominican Republic: "Here we get
tourists that have a low intellectual level, as well as little spending
capacity." He is working on attracting a "better class" of tourist
who might spend more money and appreciate Dominican culture
rather than "damage" it. "Tourists who spend money on plays, see
our archaeological ruins, want to know our history—they don't
come here. Instead, we get people who come here to get drunk and
buy sex."

Luis, a Dominican restaurant owner of a restaurant in El Batey
echoed this hotel manager's concerns with the remark that the
"low-class tourism we have is stifling growth." The all-inclusive
hotels have severely affected his business—his restaurant was empty
most evenings. He contended that the "low-class" tourists who vacation at the all-inclusives spend little money in Sosúa; they "hardly
even change U.S.$100 to spend outside of the hotel." He continued,
"Even if the food is not good at their hotel, the tourists do not go
outside of the resort to find a decent meal, as they are low-class and
don't care what they eat." He described how business was different
before the multinational all-inclusive hotels strangled local business,
when "people would change between U.S.$1,000–2,000 and it would
get distributed throughout the town: Some for lodging, food, and
entertainment." But now "not only do the local merchants not get

any of the money, but it never even leaves the tourists' home countries—like Germany or Austria—where they pay for their vacation in advance."

Although development and foreign investment have brought "First World" hotels and services to Sosúa, the local population in Los Charamicos still lives in "Third World" conditions. The most successful resorts in and surrounding Sosúa are foreign owned, and though they do create employment opportunities for the local population, they also squeeze small hotel and restaurant owners—like Luis—out of business. As Luis observed, profits are not invested in the Dominican economy but repatriated to accounts in their home countries. Nor are the hotels making long-term contributions to local communities: rather than paying for improvements to the public water and electricity supplies, the big hotels operate their own electrical generators and independent water systems. This private infrastructure vividly symbolizes how benefits from tourism development often do not reach the local population.

Foreign ownership, repatriation of profits, and the monopolistic nature of all-inclusive resorts diminish the benefits local Dominicans derive from tourism. Foreign firms are present in all four segments of the industry in Sosúa: airlines, hotels, services, and tour operators. In some cases, the same foreign company handles all four components of a tourist's stay. At a hotel owned by a German airline company and located on the highway between Sosúa and Cabarete, 80 percent of the hotel's guests are German, all of whom paid for their airfare, lodging, and food in Germany, according to the hotel's general manager. Tour operators who work for these multinational companies book the hotels and air flights and even determine the package prices. Tom Barry, Beth Wood, and Deb Preusch (1984: 80) capture the control these tour operators exercise over island economies dependent on tourism:

> The capability to direct the flow of the tourist trade puts the tour operator in a powerful position relative to local interests. The tour operator can pressure local hoteliers to drop their rates or face a loss of business. . . . Tour operators contribute to the foreign-exchange crisis in the Caribbean through their prepayment policies. Tourists, particularly those on prepaid tours, spend almost all of their vacation allowance in their home country before ever leaving for the Caribbean. Owing to the transnational

nature of the business, payments for services actually delivered in the Caribbean go directly to the New York headquarters of Sheraton or Hertz, never even passing through agency offices in Jamaica or the Dominican Republic.

With tourist expenditures not circulating beyond the literal walls of the all-inclusive hotels in and around Sosúa, it is difficult for small to midsize tourist businesses that involve either food or lodging to compete with larger multinational operations. Within this business climate of an uneven playing field, Dominican entrepreneurs such as Manuel, who owns a small restaurant in El Batey, not only accused large foreign-owned companies of putting small Dominican restaurants and shops out of business; he also criticized better-capitalized foreign residents: "Germans have the businesses now and they don't want Dominicans here in business. You can count on one hand how many Dominicans are owners here." He complained that even when German entrepreneurs "make a lot of money," Dominicans still do not benefit, because German business owners living in Sosúa expatriate the cash to banks in Germany. Rather, many Dominican suppliers were owed money by German citizens, "because they don't have their money here, but in banks in Germany."

TOURISM: DAMAGING DOMINICAN "CULTURE"
Whether or not Dominican Sosúans see tourism as an economic opportunity or as a threat to Dominican culture generally depends on socioeconomic class and educational background. Those with a high-school education, or more, often lament the disintegration of what they call "Dominican culture" in the midst of a tourist economy which imports goods, managers, languages, and business practices from the outside. Carlos, who has his own sign-painting business, described the tension between the benefits of tourism and the damages: "Some see tourism as a benefit; others with higher social status see it with different eyes, and see the harm." Though most of his business relies on tourism, he nevertheless longed for the pretourist days, when "We used to survive without tourism." With a tourist economy now in full swing, however, he waved his arms. "How many robberies, rapes, drug addicts, prostitutes and other problems have we had? And for what? More money, OK, but money—nothing more. We don't have our culture and our customs, only money." Although Carlos's nostalgia for a pretourism Sosúa assumes that the

Sosúa that existed before was untouched by capitalism and that this culture was somehow "more authentic," his sentiments of loss and powerlessness nonetheless convey the frustration of many residents.

Juan, the beach bar owner turned colmado owner in Los Charamicos, described the changes in "Dominican culture" he has witnessed: "It's a disaster. The prices here are much higher, and now we have diseases like AIDS. And we are beginning to be a subculture, since we take so many things from the tourists like men wearing earrings and ponytails. These are all negative consequences of tourism." Carlos also sees Sosúa's culture as too derivative of the tourists' cultures, and he attributes many of Sosúa's problems to the fact that Sosúa is a town of migrants:

> This has always been a migrant town. This is why we don't have our own traditions. The dominant culture became weaker. The way of dressing, doing one's hair, dancing, or drinking have become ways to copy foreigners. This is bad; we have nothing of our own culture left. In the workplace, foreigners have imposed their way of conducting business, and in the discos you don't hear merengue anymore. And when merengue is played, there are the sanky-pankies who are eager to teach the tourists. They don't really care if they lose their culture. They make their money off of tourists. What else could they do—they don't have jobs or education. Modernization has changed everything.

Us versus Them

> That the native does not like the tourist is not hard to explain. For every native of every place is a potential tourist, and every tourist is a native of somewhere. Every native everywhere lives a life of overwhelming and crushing banality and boredom and desperation and depression, and every deed, good and bad, is an attempt to forget this. Every native would love to find a way out, every native would like a rest, every native would like a tour. But some natives—most natives in the world—cannot go anywhere. They are too poor. They are too poor to go anywhere. They are too poor to escape the reality of their lives; and they are too poor to live properly in the place where they live, which is the very place you, the tourist, want to go—so when they natives see you, the tourist, they envy you, they envy your ability to turn their own

banality and boredom into a source of pleasure for yourself. (Kincaid 1988: 18–19)

SCAPEGOATS

In this town of change, struggle, and uncertainty, a heightened sense of moralism and traditionalism creates divisions among and within various groups. Just as the signs of Sosúa's transformation into a sex-trade destination are so flamboyantly public, so too are its residents' claims to tradition and morality. Everyone seems to know what is best for Sosúa's future. A diverse group of residents lay claim to both a cultural and moral high ground. At times it seems as if everyone tries to "out-tradition" and to "out-moralize" one another—at least in their public discourse. Attempts by the residents and the police to "clean up the streets" by arresting sex workers and shutting down the bars where they meet tourists, for example, are obvious efforts to restore a cultural and moral center that never was. Sosúans who are angered by change often seek out and assign blame for such cultural collisions or, in James Clifford's words, "contamination" (1997: 7). But whom—if anyone—can they blame? The sex workers make easy scapegoats. So, too, do the latest wave of German residents and tourists. Within these assertions of local "purity" and tradition, Dominican and Haitian sex workers and, increasingly, German tourists and residents have become symbols of rapid tourist development and profound social transformation. As Sosúa continues to change, both Dominican and foreign residents focus their anger on these two groups. A recurrent theme within these discourses of morality is the notion that sex workers are "contaminants" who threaten not just the family but also the image of the Dominican Republic and of Dominicans. In chapter 6, I write about the increasing association in Europe—in part due to photos and discussions of Dominican sex workers on the Internet—between Dominicans and sexual availability and proficiency. Assignations of blame and pollution saturate Sosúans' talk of the sex workers in town. The words, at times, echo those used by a police officer in Nawal El Saadawi's novel *A Women at Point Zero* to justify, in the name of community and country, his rape of Firdaus, a sex worker: "You're a prostitute, and it's my duty to arrest you, and others of your kind. To clean up the country, and protect respectable families from the likes of you" (El Saadawi 1975: 62).

But others are also viewed as contagion: Germans have become the latest scapegoats in this period of conflict and change. Domini-can and foreign residents have bigger concerns beyond German economic dominance. Since German nationals have been involved in drug busts, money-laundering, and high-profile murders of a young male transvestite and a female sex worker (which I discuss in chapter 5), residents' concerns now center on foreigners' criminal activities.

Juan (the colmado owner in Los Charamicos) attributes the pres-ence of foreign criminals in Sosúa to the ease with which foreigners enter the country and the restrictions Dominicans face at interna-tional borders: "Tourists who come here are from a very low class, without manners. And criminals can enter without problems. Our government allows this. It isn't important where you are from or what you have done. We don't have a government for the people. For an entrance fee of U.S.$10 you can enter, without being investi-gated, without anything." He blames the Dominican government for "selling" his country to any bidder, which reinforces the Domini-can Republic's history of dependence as a colonial possession. This association between foreigners and "criminality" affects all foreign residents' experiences in Sosúa. Tourists do not simply represent sources of money or visas anymore. They now also represent dan-ger—from AIDS to criminality. The image of the sunburned, photo snapping dupe contrasts with new images of foreign tourists as wanted international criminals, gun-toting thugs, and AIDS carriers. It is possible that Dominican residents might soon characterize Sosúa as a town of putas, tígueres, and European criminals.

Germans, in particular, are not just scorned by Dominicans but by other foreign residents as well. Fears (whether founded or not) that had previously focused exclusively on Dominican burglars and rap-ists have turned to Germans. A Canadian resident showed serious concern about her German neighbors: "With all the craziness in Sosúa, I'm not worried about my daughter's safety with Domini-cans. We have never had a break-in or other problems. I'm worried about the German men who come here." The absence of entry re-strictions has made the Dominican Republic a sanctuary for interna-tional criminals, and Sosúans are increasingly resentful of foreigners reputed to be hiding there (as well as in other towns). Pictures of foreign men arrested by the Sosúan police often appeared on the front page of a now-defunct Sosúan weekly newspaper, *Vocero*, and, like the sex workers, have aroused community fears. Some Canadian women who attended the community meeting held by German-speaking residents also blamed German residents for bringing sex tourism to Sosúa: "If they had not started vacationing here, there would not be as much sex tourism." They saw the German community as "very closed." "We are on the perimeter, they all know one another and stick together." These women perceived the English-speaking and German-speaking communities as so segregated in fact that "if something happened to us [the English-speaking community], they [the German-speaking community] wouldn't help." They also criticized German-speaking expatriates for "exploiting" Dominicans in Sosúa. "We all try to learn Spanish and to give back to the community. But the Germans don't try to learn Spanish." While at the meeting, they pointed out that "when the English-speaking community holds meetings, there are Dominican business owners." "But look who is here. They [German-speaking residents] did nothing to reach out; there are no Dominicans here."[24] Moreover, they were wary of the men who attended the meeting. "Who are these men? They could have been anybody in Europe—bank presidents, or criminals!"

The Genie out of the Bottle: Social Change in Sosúa

In the closing comments of their study on tourism and social change in Papua New Guinea, Deborah Gewertz and Frederick Errington (1991) expressed concern that the construction of an airstrip and a tourist hotel would affect the lifeways of the Chambri. Although the Chambri were happy to sell their crafts to the tourists who visited along a scheduled stop from a tourist ship, would they be as welcoming to all the unforeseeable, and inevitable, changes airplane access would bring? Any process of social change—whether initiated, for example, by tourism, free-trade zones, or missionaries—raises the difficult question of turning back the course of change if it is not what was envisioned.

Throughout the book I explore how tourism has made and re-made Sosúa. It is not surprising, of course, that Sosúa has undergone even more changes since I conducted the bulk of the fieldwork for this book, in 1994–1995. What is surprising, however, is the extent of those transformations. Tourism has been the proverbial genie let out of the bottle—so much so that I am often struck at the staggering amount and rapidity of change. I wrote above that starting in 1996, when a new national government was elected, the Dominican government periodically closed the Anchor and other bars like it. For months, there were fewer sex workers in downtown El Batey. It is difficult to assess the impact the closings may have had either on tourism or on the sex trade. By some accounts, tourism picked up, but this partially can be attributed to the completion of the sewer project in downtown El Batey and Los Charamicos. Initially, following the first round of bar closings, some business owners—those who blame sex workers for "destroying" Sosúa—were hopeful that Sosúa was "turning around." A Canadian resident saw the closings as possibly redirecting its future: "We could not market Sosúa the way it was. Maybe in five years you will never even know that it was a place for sex tourists." These residents' hopes for a new direction were dimmed, however, when after about a six-month lull in the sex trade, Sosúa's nightlife was thriving again. Since then, the sex trade has experienced periodic crackdowns in the form of police arrests of sex workers and bar closures. More recently, the sex trade has moved, as I mentioned earlier and will explore further in the Conclusion, to indoor nightclubs on the outskirts of town.

FINAL WORDS: TOURISM AND
SEX TOURISM IN SOSÚA

Tourism, and its perceived effects on Dominican culture, have led some Sosúans to reclaim a vision of the traditional. Parents and community leaders struggle to raise children to value education and to resist the allure of the tourists' material culture. One woman with two daughters observed, "Now we have our youth hanging out in the streets with the tourists rather than studying." They fear their children will become more attracted to making fast money, by becoming tígueres rather than working hard. As a counterforce to "kids see[ing] sex workers and sankies [sanky-pankies] driving around on *pisolas* [motor scooters]," Carlos (who has the sign-painting business) started a theater and pantomime group "as a form of protest against the government. The government is responsible for the way tourism has developed. For example, they make it difficult for kids in the countryside to study.[25] Why does the government do this? Because they know that an educated population means trouble—they will want more." Carlos hoped that by working with school children in Sosúa, they would not be so easily "seduced by things." "Back in the late 1970s, when tourism was not so strong, people thought more about their culture. Kids were interested in learning about our culture. We were more unified. But with tourism, kids know that tourists have a lot of money, so they leave their culture to get women and money."

While Dominicans such as Carlos criticize tourists and blame them for contaminating Dominican culture, others laud the tourist sector for its job creation. Meanwhile foreigners either romanticize life in a Caribbean "paradise" or fear living too closely to the local population. In this mix of fantasy images, exaggerations, and alternating impulses to idealize or demonize, sex workers have come to symbolize all that is economically possible in Sosúa as well as the exploitation—and, to some, immorality—that tourism brings. It is easy to pin the rapid social changes on sex workers, but they were part of the Sosúan landscape long before the tourists arrived, just as they are part of most Dominican towns. Contrary to popular mythology, Sosúa before tourism was no more of a moral or cultural center than any other Dominican town. Attitudes toward sex workers shifted when the sex trade began to cater to foreign tourists. A Canadian "old-timer" who arrived in the early 1980s commented on the transformation of Sosúa's small brothels with a local clientele into an internationally known commercial business: "There was a place down the road in El Cangrejo [about ten minutes from Sosúa]—a whorehouse. And in Los Charamicos of course there were bars with rooms out back. . . . It is and always has been a part of Dominican culture. But now Europeans have made it into a business venture."[26]

In this era of the "all-inclusive" resorts, the sex trade is one of the most profitable ventures in town, drawing tourists and thus revitalizing otherwise failing businesses in downtown El Batey that cannot compete with the multinational resorts. Furthermore, many Dominicans and foreign residents have made considerable money off of the sex trade. Clothing merchants, bar and nightclub owners, restaurateurs, and landlords in Los Charamicos and El Batey depend on the steady flow of women to Sosúa. Without the sex workers "polluting" the streets, many of their critics would make less money, including the police force.

The dynamic of sex tourism echoes the larger patterns of tourism development in the Dominican Republic, but it is also a focal point of people's fears of change and cultural transformation. Thus, sex workers become the symbol of a "prostituted" country, while they generate significant resources for business owners and investors, as well as for their families and boyfriends. These women, clad in tight Lycra skirts and with bare midriffs, who at times have outnumbered tourists in the bars, serve as scapegoats—an easy and flashy explanation—during a period of intense social change and conflict.

THE TRANSNATIONAL PLAN: LOOKING BEYOND DOMINICAN BORDERS

3. PERFORMING LOVE

"**A**Double Wedding" and "Love in the Caribbean," the news headlines read.[1] The local event in Sosúa had become national news. Two white English female tourists met—and soon married—two Afro-Dominican male resort workers in a shared ceremony. They married two months after they had first met at the all-inclusive hotel in Sosúa where the men worked and the women had been guests. The marriage ceremony took place after the men had been refused entry into England. Even though the men had tourist visas and all the necessary paperwork, when they landed at Heathrow, English immigration officials detained them, questioned them separately, and decided that they were so young, at eighteen years old, that they might have the intention of overstaying their tourist visas and looking for work. But it was also on the issue of love—and its implausibility—that the officials denied the Dominican men entrance. "The authorities concluded that it was not reasonable that two young English women, with less than 15 days to get to know the men, would have sent two tickets to visit England, with no other additional motives," reported a leading Dominican news magazine (Victoria 1994: 45). If officials reasoned that they were not *really* in love, they must have seen the men as pretending or *performing* being in love.[2]

President Joaquín Balaguer issued a statement on the wedding, the media led with the story, and neighborhood gossip in Sosúa picked up on this event. The wedding became symbolic of how the Dominican Republic sells itself through tourism. "There is no way the men love these women," gossiped both Dominicans and foreign residents alike living in Sosúa. "These guys are sankies, they want visas; that's it." By characterizing the men as sankies—essentially male sex workers—Sosúans assumed the men were in the relationships solely for material gain. This assumption is clear in a cartoon from a now-defunct Dominican satirical magazine that lampoons

6. Cartoon on the double wedding, DDT (Declarado Delirium Tremens), 8 December 1994, "The Love of the Little Black One." See page 94 for translation.

Cartoon on the double wedding, DDT (Declarado Delirium Tremens), 8 December 1994, "The Love of the Little Black One."

London: A local and melancholic morning of 1499, two English women, bored to no end, renew their passports before leaving on an adventure toward "El Nacional" (Sorry: toward the Caribbean).

> ENGLISH WOMAN 1: Allison, do you have everything ready? I'm calling Apollo taxi and coming to get you. . . .
>
> ENGLISH WOMAN 2: Yes, I already threw my stuff in the bag. Let's go.
>
> ENGLISH WOMAN 3: Be careful with the Sand Key Pants Kids!

Airport sign: Welcome to the Dominican Republic

> DOMINICAN WOMAN: Welcome to the Dominican Republic, misses, but you're going to have to wait to check in because there is no electricity.
>
> CUSTOMS WORKER 1: The light is back! (Damn, it only lasted four hours!)
>
> CUSTOMS WORKER 2: Good that it's back!

Billboard: Welcome to Sosua
Hotel sign: Sosua, Kingdom of Kings

> HOTEL CLERK: And your family, how are they, Mrs. Pujols?
>
> DOMINICAN MAN: Hi, young ladies. My name is Cupid and I'm a specialist in love.
>
> ENGLISH WOMEN: Sorry, we didn't come for that.

Then a loudspeaker sounds . . .

> LOUDSPEAKER: "We ask our guests to come on down, the activity boys are going to begin their dance spectacle."

And then in English . . .

> LOUDSPEAKER: "We say come on to the people because our boys are beginning the dance class."
>
> DOMINICAN MAN 1: American, look, it's "monkey waist" that I'm giving!
>
> DOMINICAN MAN 2: The dog dance is like this!

the overnight weddings. The cartoon plays up the "predatory" nature of the Dominican men in featuring in the second frame one of the English women's mothers crying "Cuidado con los Sand Key Pants Kids!" [Be careful with the sanky-pankies!]. It is just as illustrative of the presumed naivete of the English tourists, who are portrayed as initially rejecting the advances of the predatory sanky-pankies. This cartoon, and the media frenzy in general that surrounded the tourists' relationship with the Dominican men, inspires myriad questions: Why did these weddings grab national attention? Why were so many Dominicans embarrassed by it? Why are relationships in Sosúa between Dominicans and foreigners, particularly tourists, questioned, doubted, and sometimes even laughed at? Why were the men portrayed as sanky-pankies? And most strikingly, why were these relationships dismissed as mere performances of love and not seen as the "real thing?"

The "real thing," marriage por amor, is understood by Sosúans in the context of Sosúa as "sexscape" as driven by romance and emotional needs rather than strategy and financial needs (marriage por residencia or for a visa).[3] Unlike Linda-Anne Rebhun's research on love in Caruaru, Brazil, where the people she interviewed "expressed confusion over the nature of love and about the changes they had seen during their lifetimes in the definitions of love" (1999: 11), in my interviews with Sosúans they regularly echoed one another's descriptions of relationships based on "real love." Rebhun aptly expresses just how difficult it is to do research on love because of the "slippery nature" of emotions: "now conscious, now unconscious, now openly expressed, now indirectly expressed, and always manipulated" (1999: 11).[4]

In this chapter I am not attempting to determine which relationships were rooted in emotion or which grew out of strategy; rather, I am interested in analyzing why Sosúans drew the conclusions they did about other people's relationships. I cannot possibly measure "real love" in one relationship or another or guess precisely what motivates individuals. My aim is to make sense of why Sosúans described others' relationships as "real" or not. Of course, when sex workers and resort workers told me their own relationships were based on strategy and not on emotion, it took me out of the guessing game. Elena, for example, laughed when I asked if she was in love with the German man (not Jürgen) whom she married in the spring of 2001: "You know how it is. It's not love. My children and I will have more opportunities in Germany." However, it is important to keep in mind the various motivations that could shape self-reporting on love. Positing love could make Sosúan sex workers appear foolish. No matter what they feel for their foreign boyfriends, these women have an incentive to portray themselves as not naive enough to actually fall in love.

Even though sex workers in Sosúa talk about the possibility of marriage por amor, I only rarely heard sex workers describe having experienced this kind of emotion-driven love as opposed to strategy-driven love. (Nanci's love story that I tell here is unusual.) Rather, sex workers' descriptions of what they want in relationships—in marriage or in consensual unions with either foreign or Dominican men—do not center on emotions but on the concern for better treatment in the household (greater gender equity), sexual fidelity, and financial security. For Sosúa's sex workers, choosing to "fall in love" with one man over another is a rational process with serious material consequences. Contrary to the notion of "falling in love" as a kind of elation that comes with losing control of one's senses or wits, for these women being in love—or pretending to be in love—requires alertness, savvy, and determination. Rebhun comments on this idea that in the United States "we tend to believe that sentiment is genuine only if it is spontaneous; conventional, required, manipulated sentiment seems false . . . and its falseness morally reprehensible." But, continues Rebhun, "deliberation and requirement are as much a part of emotion as spontaneity" (Rebhun 1999: 29–30).

Marriage in a Sexscape

This chapter examines the practices and meanings of "love" within the Dominican community in Sosúa that have emerged alongside the growth of the tourist and sex-tourist trades.[5] Specifically, I focus on how resort workers (men and women) and sex workers try to parlay their access to foreign tourists into marriage proposals and visa sponsorships At the discos, bars, and beaches, it is possible for any Dominican to meet—and perhaps to marry—a foreigner. Dominican resort workers, in particular, have many opportunities to spend time with tourists. Love takes on multiple meanings in this tourist setting, and marriage has specific uses. Marriage in a tourist economy—especially in an internationally known sex-tourist destination—often has nothing to do with emotion-driven love or romance.

Below, I recount several women's and men's marriage choices, and though they might describe having experienced emotion-driven love, they chose to marry individuals as a strategy to get ahead (progresar). They use the discourse and practices of romantic love to secure marriage proposals for a visa. After all, why waste a marriage certificate on romantic love when it can be transformed into a visa?

Other scholars have documented poor women's use of the sex trade as a first step to marriage and greater financial security. Kamala Kempadoo writes about migrant Colombian and Dominican women who work in the sex trade in Curaçao's Campo Alegre / Mirage whose work with clients might develop into "close and intimate" relationships that lead to marriage. Women also might pay to acquire Dutch citizenship by marrying, which means that migrant women could stay and work legally as sex workers in Curaçao or travel to Europe without restriction (1998). Sylvia Chant and Cathy McIlwaine also write about the sex trade as a possible route to marriage—and sometimes to migration—between Europeans and Filipina women. Much like the perceptions Dominican sex workers maintain of life in Europe, Filipina sex workers also perceive a better life for themselves and their children in Europe. And like their Dominican counterparts, these Filipina women are locked out of opportunities for legal migration (1995: 248).

Some relationships are not easily described, however. Many relationships that start out as transactional (by one or both parties) can transform into something else entirely. In the sex trade, in particular, the line between love and money can become "very fuzzy," as Yos Santasombat has observed in relationships between Thai sex workers and farang men (white-skinned Westerners) (1992: 15–17, cited in Hamilton 1997). In fact, many sex workers and resort workers in Sosúa hope for romantic love even while they doubt the "authenticity" of the relationships around them. No relationship between foreigners and Dominicans escapes scrutiny. In this context of transnational desires and economic ambitions, these relationships become fodder for the gossip mill. "So are they really in love?" is a common response by both Dominicans and foreign residents living in Sosúa when they hear about a relationship between a Dominican and a foreigner. The possibility of love for migration is almost immediately mentioned, and then either waved away or confirmed. In fact when stories of the double wedding hit the newsstands, Sosúans (both Dominicans and foreign residents) had a field day.[6] Comments flew about how plain and overweight the women were and how handsome and well muscled the men were. Quite simply, I could find no one—in either the Dominican or foreign-resident communities—who believed these relationships were out of emotion-based love on the Dominican men's part. Like the British immigration officials, Sosúans did not believe that these relationships (at least on the men's part) could be the "real thing." Rather, Sosúans understand—indeed expect—that many relationships beginning in their town are strategic performances on the part of Dominicans. Their love-skepticism emerges from Sosúans' knowledge that, in Arlie Hochschild's (1983: ix) language, "active emotional labor" is involved—indeed demanded—in jobs at hotels, bars, and nightclubs. Hochschild sharply observes that "simply having personality does not make one a diplomat, any more than having muscles makes one an athlete"; along these lines, if we focus simply on the exchange of sex for money (or goods) in Sosúa, we will miss "a sense of the active emotional labor involved in the selling" (1983: ix). Sosúans know that many sex workers and resort workers are hard at work selling romance along with the other goods and services they deliver.

With much of any tourist experience relying on fantasy, Edward Bruner's (1999) description of "touristic borderzones" as "performative space[s]" calls attention to the performative aspects of tourist encounters. He writes, "The touristic borderzone is like empty space, an empty stage waiting for performance time, for the audience of tourists and for the native performers" (1999: 158). Tourists on vacation often engage in behavior and activities they would never engage in at home, such as paying for sex or, as Deborah Pruitt and Suzanne LaFont observed in Jamaica, having cross-racial relationships (1995). When I interviewed male tourists in Sosúa, they often told me that they never had paid for sex at "home," but since they were on vacation they thought, "why not?" Chant and McIlwaine also found that some foreign men—who had not intended at the outset to pay for sex—buy sex in Cebu's bars in the Philippines because of "peer pressure." One man boasted to his friends, for example, that he had bought five women in one night (1995: 225). In encounters between locals and foreign tourists, locals often have more practical goals—such as laying the groundwork to receive money wires from tourists once they return to Europe—and might need to "perform" for tourists to achieve them, whereas foreign tourists primarily seek fun and pleasure.

Sex and romance in Sosúa have thus become more than just sites for the production of intimacy, pleasure, and emotional comfort. They have become, in a way, sites of capitalist production and consumption (with Dominicans possibly supplying sex and / or "romantic love" for foreign consumers), which can result in inequalities, discomfort, and sometimes even violence. Sexual exchanges across interracial and international borders can reinforce existing racial hierarchies and inequalities. Karen Kelsky's research with "yellow cabs," for example, suggests that sexual exchanges *not* based on money can also reinforce racial hierarchies and inequalities. The term *yellow cabs* refers to young, single Japanese women who spend their savings on "erotic adventure with a variety of non-Japanese men" in places such as tourist resorts in Hawaii or U.S. military bases in Japan. Although these women might seek to have sex with these non-Japanese men, they will not marry these men, because of ideas of "racial purity."[7]

Relationships in Sosúa por residencia also can be a kind of stage for Dominicans to resist such racial hierarchies as well as inequalities based on gender, class, and citizenship. For example, the strategizing of Dominican women within Sosúa's sex trade sometimes has economically advantageous results. Some clients have paid for the education of their "girlfriend's" children (as Jürgen did for Elena's daughter; see the Introduction) or have helped sex workers get a fledgling business off the ground (such as a clothing store or hair salon). In these cases, sex in a postcolonial context, much like in a colonial context, can be used as a "vehicle to master a practical world (to achieve privileged schooling, well-paying jobs in the civil service, or access to certain residential quarters)" (Stoler 1997b: 44). Because any use of sex between black local women and white foreign men in a postcolonial context is a "crucial transfer point of power, tangled with racial exclusions in complicated ways" (Stoler 1997b: 44, on Fanon 1967: 63), today's sex trade is inextricably linked with a violent colonial history for Hispaniola's women. In the relationships between sex tourists and sex workers, there are similarities to the relationships between the colonizer and the colonized. I do not mean to suggest, however, that Dominican sex workers (or resort workers) are "enslaved" but want to underscore that they stand to lose more—materially—than love gone awry.[8]

Of course not every Dominican worker in Sosúa's tourist economy tries to parlay access to foreign tourists into marriage proposals and visa sponsorships, yet many are perceived as doing so. Sosúans (Dominicans and foreign residents) and Dominicans outside of Sosúa brand as "sankies" a wide range of men who do not trade their bodies for money. For example, young, good-looking Domini-can men who have migrated to work in Sosúa's hotels, bars, and beaches often are glibly referred to or derided as sankies.[9] Male resort workers, particularly "activity directors"—the resort position held by the two young men who married in the double wedding— often are talked about as sankies.[10] By referring to male resort workers as sanky-pankies, Sosúans see these men as prostituting themselves as well as sacrificing love for migration. The term is now loosely used throughout the Dominican Republic to refer to Domin-ican men who hit on tourist women—especially women older than they.

Female resort workers, too, undergo public scrutiny and risk being stereotyped as putas but usually from Dominicans outside of Sosúa, as Sosúans know that most of the women who clean, wait-ress, and cook in the hotels and other tourist businesses are from Sosúa, Puerto Plata, and other nearby towns. Sosúans also know that women who enter the sex trade are not from Sosúa but migrate from towns throughout the island (to protect their families left behind). However, to Dominicans outside of Sosúa, women's claims of working in Sosúa's hotels and restaurants can appear as "cover stories" for working in the sex trade. In fact, most of the sex workers I interviewed concealed their participation in the sex trade from their families and neighbors by creating "cover stories" about work-ing in Sosúa's tourist hotels and restaurants.

History of Migration off the Island: "Headaches" for Dominicans Wishing to Migrate

The automatic eyebrow raising and speculation of Sosúans that suggest relationships between foreign tourists and Dominicans are por residencia result from the virtual impossibility of leaving the island legally without family members to sponsor migration. Re-sponses to an Internet posting to the message board of a Dominican electronic newspaper in English, *Dominican One*, underscores just how difficult it is for Dominicans to enter the United States. Arnold queried, "Hi, I would like for my Dominican girlfriend to visit me in the United States for two weeks some time in the next year. How much of a big pain is this? She told me I needed to write her an invitation letter and she needed to get a passport. How hard is this and any headaches anyone here foresees?" (31 March 2000). Two responses explained it would take a near miracle for Arnold's girlfriend to obtain a tourist visa: "No, no headaches. It just won't happen! Jesus Christ could not get a visa if he were Dominican! That is about how difficult it is" (31 March 2000); and "Hahahahaha-hahahahahahaha" (2 April 2000, from within the Dominican Republic). A third response hinted that the Dominican girlfriend might overstay her visa and that Arnold should not trust her motivations: "Want some good advice from someone who knows, don't bring her to the U.S. 'You will be sorry,' move to the Dominican Republic with her instead" (2 April 2000). Arnold's innocent question revealed him to be a novice about the difficulties facing Dominicans who want to travel or migrate to the United States.

Understanding why Dominican resort workers and sex workers might feign love and use marriage—or are perceived as feigning love and using marriage—as a way to get off the island demands a brief discussion of the island's migration history. The past few decades of migration from the Dominican Republic to New York and the transnational cultural and economic flows between the two places (Georges 1990; Grasmuck and Pessar 1991; Guarnizo 1994) have informed a diasporic mentality in the Dominican Republic. There is little doubt that families with relatives in New York have benefited as one of Eugenia Georges's (1990: 196) informants sums up: "In the Dominican Republic there are three kinds of people: the rich, the poor and those who travel to New York." And of course, there is a fourth group: families who rely on remittances sent from family members abroad.[11]

Dominicans started using migration as a means to social mobility following the isolationist years under the dictator Trujillo (from 1930 to 1961), who restricted migration off the island. After Trujillo's assassination in 1961, restrictions on migration both in the Dominican Republic and the United States loosened. Sherri Grasmuck and Patricia Pessar argue that following the 1963 revolution, migration was "politically induced" by an "extremely unrestrictive immigration policy favored by the United States" which operated as a "safety-valve for political discontent" (1991: 31). During these years of political unrest, Dominican migration to the United States increased from 900 immigrants on average annually, to 9,000 a year (Pessar

1995a). Many of these early migrants had progressive ties and left disillusioned, or fearful, after socialist Juan Bosch was overthrown by a U.S.-backed military coup in 1963. Out-migration to the United States significantly increased and complemented the model of economic development of the newly elected president, Balaguer, during his presidency of 1966 to 1978. (Leader of the Reformist Party, Balaguer was reelected in 1986 and remained in office until 1996.) Hurt by the Balaguer government's policy of keeping food prices artificially low, rural producers migrated to urban centers, where unemployment grew. Out-migration to the United States continued at an average rate of 12,000 a year during this period (Grasmuck and Pessar 1991). Following the deterioration of the national economy after 1974, and a rise in landlessness from the splintering of many smallholdings, both migrant and nonmigrant households experienced economic insecurity (Safa 1995a). Migration permitted many families to hold on to a "middle-level status," while other nonmigrant families fell into poverty in the midst of a troubled economy (Georges 1990).

Without ties to New York or elsewhere, economic mobility is difficult—even for middle-class families—and, often, families end up just getting by and surviving. Low salaries are an obstacle to mobility for all classes, other than for the wealthy. Schoolteachers and office workers, for example, earn under 4,000 pesos a month (U.S. $333.00). Consequently, many professionals with university degrees consider themselves both middle class and part of los pobres at the same time. A social worker identified with two classes simultaneously: "My wife, a schoolteacher, and I have been working as professionals for twenty years. But do we own a house? Or a car? We Dominicans work until we die." He also recounted his parents' downward mobility: "My parents, who own a butcher shop, are old and should not be working. But they work every day, my father cutting meat and my mother stuffing sausage. They used to be middle class, but now with prices rising every day they are pobres."

At the time this book went to press, prices for basic foodstuffs, cooking gas, and gasoline continued to rise—while salaries remained the same. Two events in the spring of 2003—the collapse of a bank, Baninter, and the cost of hosting the Pan American Games—exacerbated an already deteriorating economy. Baninter's main owner, Ramon Báez Figueroa, was arrested for allegedly running a "bank within a bank" for more than a decade. The bank is reported to have lost $2.2 billion, a figure equal to 13 percent of the country's GDP. In the process, the peso has depreciated dramatically and the country's credit rating has been downgraded (*Economist*: June 14, 2003).[12] In the midst of rising prices and a falling peso, the Dominican government (under President Hipolito Mejia) spent $175 million to host the Pan American Games in August 2003. Even though the Dominican government banned protests, demonstrators took to the streets to protest against the millions spent on athletic fields and facilities (Gonzalez August 8, 2003: 1). As the Rev. Rogelio Cruz led a demonstration carrying the "torch of hunger" through Santo Domingo's poorest neighborhoods, the security chief for the games declared his troops would "rip the heads off" or "break the necks" of any protesters while President Hipolito Mejia said he should be beaten (Gonzalez August 10, 2003:11).

In this context of limited economic mobility and extraordinary obstacles to legal migration off the island, it becomes clear why Dominican migrants in Sosúa, most of whom do not receive remittances from family overseas, work so hard to establish transnational relationships with the tourist population. These transnational romantic ties act as surrogate family migration networks to access a middle-class lifestyle and its accompanying security. Without family members in New York or elsewhere to sponsor their legal migration, Dominicans who seek to migrate need other means of getting fuera.[13] Marriage to citizens of other countries is one surefire strategy.

Suspicious Love

On account of the obstacles to legal migration just discussed, Dominicans consider the workers in several occupations as under suspicion for "performing" at being in love with tourists for money and visas: male sanky-pankies, male resort workers and activity directors, female resort workers, and female sex workers.

SANKY-PANKIES

One of the first groups of Sosúans who were reputed to "perform" at being in love with tourists were the sanky-pankies. Those first called *sankies*, in the mid-1980s, were young men in their late teens and early twenties who worked on the beach renting jet skis, beach chairs, umbrellas, and the like. Their trademark was bleached dread locks, as well as tanned and toned bodies. Sankies were known for wooing white, female, middle-aged tourists. In this early stage of Sosúa's tourism development, many of the female tourists were French Canadian and Canadian. These men did not work for cash, as did female sex workers, but for gifts, meals, and other expenses at the discretion of the female tourists. Much like the "romance tourism" Pruitt and LaFont describe between Jamaican men and tourist women which unfolds through a "discourse of romance and long-term relationship" (1995: 423), sankies' skills often included treating the tourist women as "girlfriends." Romantic dinners, moonlight strolls, and lessons in dancing merengue at the nightclubs can be part of encounters between tourist women and *sankies*. But money also changes hands. French Canadian female tourists have described giving their Dominican "lovers" money (even though they did not ask for any) and clothes, as well as paying for meals and drinks (Herold et al. 1992). Female tourists do not perceive that they are "paying" for sexual services, however; they recount that "they fell in love with the men and the men fell in love with them" (Herold et. al. 1992: 8). Similarly, Jacqueline Martis observed that men working in the sex trade in Saint Martin or Curaçao (with female tourists) were jockeying to "hook up with a woman who would take care of them and take them away from the island." They, like the sankies, "wanted to think of themselves as having a romantic liaison, not as prostituting" and thus referred to themselves as "players" (1999: 211–12).

Few of these "original" sankies remain in Sosúa; they were successful at marrying female tourists and migrating to Canada. Sosúans report that most of these marriages ended in divorce, after the men received their citizenship. Today, there are a few high-profile men—allegedly some of the "original" sankies—who have returned from Canada. Now, in their late thirties and early forties, their profitable (and capital-intensive) motorcycle rental and beach equipment businesses stand as examples of what one can achieve through marriage and migration off the island.

MALE RESORT WORKERS / ACTIVITY DIRECTORS
In light of the desperation some Dominicans feel to leave the island, and the difficulties they face in order to do so, it is easy to see why Sosúa's foreign tourists are a gold mine. Contact with foreigners distinguishes Sosúa's employment opportunities from those in other parts of the country. The actual jobs might be the same—waiting

tables, bartending, or tending a cash register—but the chance to meet foreign tourists is a fringe benefit of working in the tourist sector, an investment of sorts, in the employees' future. The job of activity director, coveted by young Dominicans who seek either short- or long-term relationships with foreigners, perhaps best epitomizes the sexual or romantic promise of Sosúa. Usually young, energetic men (although there are some activity directors who are women) with self-taught skills in several languages, activity directors organize events for hotel guests, such as exercise classes, dance contests, and volleyball tournaments. Their reputation for romantic and sexual entanglements with female hotel guests is why Sosúans often call them sankies. As mentioned earlier, the two young Dominican men involved in the double wedding were both activity directors. One of the English women recalled how her soon-to-be husband greeted her and other guests with whom she was having a drink: "Hi. My name is Pablo and my job is to make your vacation fun" (Victoria 1994: 44).

Hotel management, keenly aware of how highly valued these positions are, take advantage of willing young Dominicans. Some activity directors work for no wages during their "trial period," which might last a month or longer. The offers for dinner and nightclubbing, as well as gifts (some even continue to receive gifts from abroad long after tourists have returned home), showered on them by hotel guests give them the opportunity to elect to work for free and even continue to endure low wages later on. A Dominican manager at one of the largest all-inclusive hotels on the north coast smiled when I asked about the activity directors. "They have more contact with the guests than other staff," he said and laughed. "Thus, they are privileged." Norberto, the other young activity director who married in the double wedding, described getting many visa promises from hotel guests. But when, at the end of their vacation, the two English women promised that they would send airplane tickets so that Pablo and Norberto could come to England and meet the two women's families, Norberto "did not have many illusions because there are many who say the same thing, but then nothing happens." "But," he added, "when I saw the ticket had arrived, I was convinced this thing was serious" (Victoria 1994: 44).

Hugo, another activity director, left school at age fifteen in Puerto Plata, where he lived with his family, to begin working in the resort complex at Playa Dorada, about twenty miles outside of Sosúa. "We are the heart of the hotel," he explained, "Without us, it would die; we keep the guests happy." Hugo has met a lot of women while working at the hotel: "We meet people all day. They come to us for everything, so we meet a lot of women from all over the world. I have many girlfriends in lots of countries. They send me things and come back on their vacations to visit me." This close contact can pay off. Hugo married a woman from England whom he met when she was a guest staying at the hotel. However, "things did not work out." "My wife," he complained, "always wanted to know where I was going whenever I left the house." To make matters worse, he could not find a job. After living in England for nine months, he returned to the Dominican Republic. Now divorced, he is disillusioned with both living overseas and marriage. He is happy to be back at the hotel, meeting "a variety of women" who "spend their money on me."

At the time we spoke, he was not looking to marry—or to migrate off the island. Unlike his coworkers, he knew firsthand how difficult it is for Dominicans who are not fluent in English to live and to work in Europe. "You know everyone wants to go fuera—that's what I thought a few years ago. But it's a lie; it's not easy there. Sure you can make a lot more money there, if you can find a job." Hugo, like the female sex workers who have lived in Europe (whose stories I recount in chapter 6), has no more fantasies about life fuera. Yet it is unclear what caused him greater unease: marriage and monogamy or the experience of migration. "I don't want to be married—I can't go home to one woman in the house. I need to be free and loose, Dominican men are *machista*; we don't like to be reined in." Some migration scholars have documented threats to men's authority in the household through the migration process (Kibria 1993; Pessar 1996). Since men and women experience migration differently (Hondagneu-Sotelo 1994), marriage to foreign citizens presents even greater challenges during the migration process (a dynamic I analyze further in chapter 6).

FEMALE RESORT WORKERS AND SEX WORKERS

Consuelo, a twenty-four-year old sex worker, walked around Los Charamicos clutching a pocket German-Spanish dictionary wherever she went. Having it with her at all times functioned as a marker of prestige, allowing her to show off her envied ties to Europe. "I'm trying to learn German. I'm moving to Germany in the next few weeks to live with a German man I met here," she elaborated. She also was in the Codetel office at least once a day, sending or receiving faxes or telephoning Germany. She was able to pay for the calls with the money her German client-turned-boyfriend wired to her. Months later, she was still in town, running around making arrangements by fax and phone as urgently as if she were leaving the next day. Some of her coworkers dismissed her preoccupation with going to Germany as folly. Ani had known her for years, since they had worked together in a bar in Boca Chica.[14] "She was the same there—determined to get to Europe. She only sought out clients she thought could get her there." Ani laughed, "But look, she's still here. It does not work that way—it is not easy."

If it is "not easy" to get to Europe (or elsewhere off the island) by meeting foreign men, why do Dominican women such as Consuelo try so hard to do so? Sosúa as a tourist enclave operates much as urban spaces have in step migration. Consuelo, for example, sees migration to Sosúa as the first step toward marrying a foreign tourist, the only legal way she knows to obtain a visa to travel overseas. Without family in New York, women have a greater chance to get overseas by marrying a tourist than they do of obtaining a visa—legally—to the United States. In some ways, hanging out in the tourist bars in Sosúa is a better use of their time than waiting in line at the U.S. Consulate in Santo Domingo. Marrying a tourist can be seen as hitting the jackpot. This, in part, is why so many women who have never worked before in the sex trade decide to do so in Sosúa. Carla, a sex worker, illuminates why Sosúa draws women from throughout the country: "We come here because we dream of a ticket." But without a visa, Dominicans cannot use the airplane ticket Carla describes.

Mari and Andrea: "No, it's not love." The words *romance* and *love* are noticeably absent from female sex workers' and female resort workers' discussions of the "ideal" relationship with foreign tourists. Sex workers and resort workers are looking for hombres serios, not the loves of their lives. Fidelity, financial security, and a good future for their children characterize the tops of their wish lists. This is not to say that they do not also *hope* for romance. One Valentine's Day the tourist bars were abuzz with a striking mix of commercial and romantic desires. The sex workers were wishing one another a happy Valentine's Day, and many expressed hopes that they might find romance that evening. Some had gone to the hair salon earlier in the day, while others put on their best outfits and took more time than usual with their makeup. One sex worker, who had stopped going to the bars because at the time she had been receiving large money wires from a client in Europe, reappeared to celebrate Valentine's Day. She explained that she wanted to hang out with her friends and maybe fulfill her dreams of "romance."

The hopeful pursuit of romance I witnessed on Valentine's Day was rare because, in sex workers' narratives, economic imperatives usually outweigh romantic dreams. There is an expected tradeoff of emotion-driven love for financial mobility. Both sex workers and resort workers candidly admit that they sacrifice romantic love for a better future. Mari, for example, has used both waitressing and the sex trade (when she was younger) to meet foreign men. As a waitress she met and married a German man and lived in Düsseldorf for a year and a half. Surprisingly, she returned to Sosúa because she hated Germany and, as she put it, did not "love him." Back in Sosúa, this time working in *promoción* (passing out flyers to tourists for clubs and restaurants), she met a Dutch man, in his fifties. Still married, Mari planned to return to Germany to see her husband and then "take the train to Holland." I reasoned that since she had opted to leave Germany and return to the Dominican Republic, it was possible that she was looking for romantic love, not just a visa to live in Europe. After all, she had expressly said she did not love her German husband. I was wrong. She and Elena shook their heads, frustrated by my naïveté and carefully spelled out for me that Mari did not love either of these men. These relationships, they made clear, "are not really about love." Rather, "they are about thinking of your family and your future." Because the Dutch man appeared to have more resources than the German man, along with the fact that he treated her well, Mari believed he would make a better husband. (In the Conclusion I recount what happened when her German husband showed up in Sosúa.)

Another sex worker, Andrea, spent the night with her Dominican boyfriend—the man she "really loved"—on the eve of her departure for Germany to marry a German man who had been a client. When I dropped by the next morning to wish her well before she left for Germany, her Dominican boyfriend was still asleep. Stepping outside onto her porch (she lived on the second floor of a house her German boyfriend had been paying for), she explained she could not lie about her feelings for her soon-to-be husband: "No, it's not love." Yet with images of an easier life for her and her two daughters compelling her to migrate, she put love aside—at least temporarily. She went to Germany, married, brought her girls over, and settled into a new life.

Although Andrea's friends who remained behind in Sosúa saw Andrea as living out their dreams, her marriage was far from ideal. Four years later she was still in Germany, but she was trying to get a divorce. Much like Mari, Andrea had met another German man who had a better job—and more money. They planned to marry as soon as her divorce came through. I found out about Andrea's new pursuit from her cousin in Sosúa, to whom she sends money every month. Her cousin was puzzled when I asked if Andrea was in love with her new boyfriend. "This new guy has more money." For Andrea, who wanted her children to grow up in comfort and to get a good education, love takes a backseat to financial concerns. Besides, a network of female family members, such as this cousin and her two children, depend on Andrea to send remittances. In this sense, her successful performance of being in love is directly tied to her family obligations. After all, she was lucky enough to get off the island. Now she is expected to (and willingly does) help out the other single mothers in her family, her parents, and her good friends, including Elena. She has even sent new sneakers, jeans, and belts to a circle of her closest friends (all sex workers). With so many expectations and demands on Andrea, there is considerable pressure on her to keep her relationship afloat, no matter what.

Considering the benefits for family and friends, it is easy to see why Andrea's friends, while sporting new fashions from Germany, perpetuate the fiction that marriage in Europe is without significant conflict. However, as I recount in chapter 6, life in Europe can be isolating for Dominican sex workers. Yet stories of women's migration, such as Andrea's, still manage to persuade women into thinking that tourists will be their ticket off the island. Like Dominican migrants' sanitized narratives during the early years of migration to New York, so too migration to Europe by sex workers has been greatly romanticized. Because migrating to Europe is a relatively new phenomenon, not many former sex workers such as Mari, or resort workers such as Hugo, have returned to Sosúa to dispel the myths and gossip of an easy and fantasy-filled life allá. Instead, sex workers and resort workers imagine lives of material comfort for themselves and, in the case of the sex workers and female resort workers, for their children.

"Love" in a Global World: New Transnational Courting Practices

Part of a day's work for sex workers who are interested in getting off the island—or at least in receiving money wires—is keeping in contact with clients who are back home in Europe. Faxes and telephone calls are the primary ways they communicate. And Codetel has assumed a starring role in the unfolding drama of these relationships. At the Codetel office in Los Charamicos, accordion files contain received faxes filed under first or last names or a slew of other identifying characteristics. There are faxes for "Juana at Hotel Paraíso" or for "Carmen at the Anchor." The senders might have met the recipients at these places or believe that these women work there all the time. Usually written in English or broken Spanish, these faxes document that romantic / sexual encounters are a by-product of Sosúa's tourist trade.[15] Indeed, some days the files are literally bursting with faxes. Judging by one of the customer bases for fax services one is most likely to see inside the Codetel office in Los Charamicos—groups of young Dominican sex workers teasing one another about their "boyfriends"—sex tourism generates a good portion of the faxes in the files.[16] In contrast, the Codetel branch on the other side of the beach, in El Batey, is filled mainly with foreigners: tourists phoning home and residents sending personal or business-related faxes (they have phones in their homes). Cell phone use is on the rise, and during my visits to the nightclubs in 2003, cell phones were a visible accessory—nearly everyone (men and women) sported one on his or her person. Whether the phones work is another thing entirely; many Sosúans buy minutes for their phones through phone cards, rather than keep ongoing accounts.

Unlike the love letters sex workers send their clients, the faxes sex workers receive usually convey some kind of news: when to pick up a money wire or details about the men's return visits to Sosúa. It is not possible to receive incoming calls at Codetel, so sometimes transnational "couples" use faxes to arrange times that the women

7. Western Union office in El Batey

will call the men from Codetel (usually paid for by money wires sent by the men) or to arrange times that men will call the women at a neighbor's house.[17] Some sex workers have become adept at capitalizing on the communication resources available to them, and, as a result, novices at navigating this transnational terrain come to them for advice.[18] Sex workers who are literate, and have a proven track record of receiving money wires or faxes from clients, are at the top of this hierarchy. Elena, for example, has given out a lot of advice, and she has even helped compose letters and faxes for women who were uncertain about what to do with the addresses, fax numbers, and telephone numbers clients gave them. She helped Carmen write a letter to a Belgian client who had sent her a money wire and then abruptly stopped corresponding with her. Carmen came to Elena because, at the time, Elena was living with Jürgen and was experienced, indeed successful, at transnational courting. Elena's advice was simple and centered on Carmen's performance of "love": "You have to write that you *love* him and that you miss him. Write that you cannot wait to see him again. Tell him you think about him every day." Following Elena's guidelines, Carmen composed the following letter that I helped her translate into English (his English was better than his Spanish):

> Dear—
>
> I have been thinking of you every day and have been waiting for a fax to hear how you are. I got your money wire, thanks. But I still want to see you.
>
> Please send me a fax at the following number—, and if possible, a fax number where I can reach you.
>
> I miss you very much and think of you all the time. I love you very much. I wait to hear from you. I hope you come to visit again very soon.
>
> Many Kisses,[19]

Carmen never heard from this client again.

Since women always can enlist the help of more literate friends, being able to read and write is not a critical skill in transnational courting. Sensing which men are not already married and are likely to continue corresponding and to return for future vacations (the most certain first step to receiving an invitation to visit Europe or Canada), often proves a more valuable—and elusive—skill. While sorting through all the pictures and letters of her European clients, Nanci, for example, commented on which ones seemed the most serious about keeping in touch. She pronounced several too "young" and thus not likely to follow through on the relationships. Nanci had honed her ability to detect which transnational suitors were worth pursuing during her four years in Sosúa. She had been receiving money wires on and off from five or six European men at the same time. Her many and varied transnational ties were envied and difficult to replicate, yet many tried. Stashed away in a spare pocketbook, Nanci kept a bundle of letters and faxes.[20] She also had photos—photos of the men back home and photos of her with the men during their vacations in Sosúa. Taped to her wall were photos of at least fifteen different foreign men. Several of them had returned to Sosúa to see Nanci and expressed interest in bringing her to Europe and marrying her (in chapter 6 I recount her experience of marrying one of these foreign men and moving to Germany).

Of course, even those sex workers who are veterans of transnational dating cannot easily predict their European clients' actions (or inaction). Yet some seem to assess better than others the characters of the men. Nora, who has never received an international fax or letter, kept a German client's business card among her valuables. Even though he promised he would fax her, he had not responded to the numerous faxes she sent him. Nevertheless, Nora clung to the card as if it were a winning lottery ticket. She could not seem to throw it away. In contrast, many of her coworkers quickly move on to cultivating new relationships when faced with their clients' lack of communication.

Conclusion: Marriage, "Papers," and Suspicious Love

It is not only in Sosúa's tourist economy that marriage solves obstacles to migration from one country to another; marriage also secures migrants' futures once they are in new countries. In the Spanish movie *Flores de otro mundo* (Flowers from another world [1999]), for example, an Afro-Dominican woman works in Madrid for four years as a domestic, during which time she is often stopped on the street by the police. Without the right papers, she explains to her Spanish boyfriend with whom she and her children are living, she cannot get a good job. An outsider, especially someone whose dark skin makes her unable to conceal her "otherness," cannot, she cries, "break into the circle." The only solution is a wedding. Although this woman eventually falls in love with her Spanish boyfriend, and he with her, she initially moves in with him to bring her children to Spain from the Dominican Republic and to begin the application process for Spanish residency. Love was not on her agenda; her children were her only concern. As she put it, "It doesn't matter what happens to me."

Similarly, the rush to marry in February and March 1997, in cities that are popular migration destinations in the United States (New York City, Los Angeles, Boston, and cities in Texas), demonstrated the central role marriage plays in many migrants' settlement strategies.[21] Fearing that new punitive immigration legislation would prevent them from obtaining citizenship in the future, thousands lined up for licenses and wedding ceremonies. Witnessing this marriage frenzy, a reporter for the *New York Times* questioned the newlyweds' motivation:

Rarely has love been so suspect in New York City as in the last few days, with young men and women of foreign origin being stopped by imperfect strangers and asked whether it is their hearts or their wallets that are going pitter-pat. The reason for this is simple: at marriage bureaus across town, there are suddenly crushing lines of couples looking to sprint down the aisle. No one can swear why this is happening. But common sense suggests that illegal immigrants by the thousands are racing to marry American citizens in the hope—a misguided hope, some experts caution—that they can stave off deportation after a toughened immigration law goes into effect on April 1. (Haberman 1997: A32)

As the reporter suspected, some of these marriages of course were not for love but for residency. I spoke with a Dominican woman in New York who had overstayed her tourist visa and paid $5,000 to a Dominican-born man with U.S. citizenship to marry her. "It's a lot of money, but it's the only way I can stay here." The ceremony itself was bittersweet: "I was very depressed going through the ceremony. It was sad to have such a special ceremony with someone you do not love. But I need my papers for my daughter's future." As a single mother, she is lonely and hopes one day to marry a man for love. But for now, she has a husband solely for documentation purposes. He has kept his end of the agreement by showing up for the ceremony and their meetings with immigration officials. Her cousin was not so lucky: a Puerto Rican man disappeared shortly after she paid him $2,500 (a down payment on his $5,000 fee) to marry her. These two cousins in New York are in the position to "buy" a marriage and thus secure their legal status in the migration process. Unlike sex workers and resort workers in Sosúa, when these cousins pursued marriage strategies, there was no hope or pretense of emotion-driven love or romance on their part or on the part of the men they were marrying. Their performances of love were only for the INS.

Sex workers and resort workers who feign love for an opportunity to get off the island are banking on the outcome that their marriages and migration will translate into mobility for them and their families. Because sex workers have been traveling to Europe to live with European boyfriends only over the past ten to twelve years, this migration por residencia is still a relatively new phenomenon. It remains to be seen how many of these relationships last. These Dominican women and European men may or may not formally marry, move the women's children to Europe, or have children together. Stories abound of the failed marriages of men gossiped about as sankies who married Canadian women and migrated to Canada in the early and mid-1980s. Some of these men's pasts have become legendary—inspiring young men to hang out at their businesses—particularly since they are so visibly successful (especially in the business of renting motorcycles, a particularly macho enterprise). Their performances of love paid off. Similarly, the double wedding might have caused snickering and raised eyebrows over the authenticity of the Dominican men's emotional commitment to their English wives, but Sosúans also acknowledged that these men were "very lucky." With their marriage certificates to English citizens, they were steps closer to migrating—legally—to Europe.

THE SEX TRADE

4. SOSÚA'S SEX WORKERS: THEIR FAMILIES AND WORKING LIVES

I come from a poor family, with little skills, what else could I do? My husband left and gives me no money for the children. I have to make money for my children.—Response I often heard in interviews to my question "Why did you choose sex work in Sosúa?"

Why do some poor, Afro-Dominican single mothers choose to work selling sex? Nanci explains why she chose to sell sex in Sosúa over other work options available to poor women like her: "Prostitution is much easier than working in the *zonas francas* [factories in export-processing zones]. It is worse there. They work eight hours or more a day for less money." In contrast, in Sosúa's sex trade, "you work three or four hours a week, and get to go to restaurants and out dancing." Even if "you are with a man you don't like," she states, "it's over in a short while." For Nanci, the possibility of earning more money in less time attracted her to Sosúa's sex trade. The past jobs these women held—in factories, farms, hair salons, restaurants, and private homes—generally yielded around 1,000 pesos (U.S.$83) a month and only rarely held the possibility of making more money than their families' living expenses. With some foreign clients paying 500 pesos (U.S.$42) and Dominican clients paying 200–300 pesos (U.S.$17–U.S.$25) for a single sexual encounter, which can last from under an hour to an entire night, the sex trade pays more for less work. However, in this chapter we also hear from many women who complain that sex workers in Sosúa just barely "get by."

While the sex trade, in theory at least, pays more money than the requirements of daily survival, in practice Sosúa is a costly place to live. Rooms in boardinghouses rent for 30–50 pesos (U.S.$2.50–$4.00) a day, while renting an apartment ranges from 1,500 to 3,000 pesos (U.S.$125–$250) a month. Moving into an apartment also includes start-up costs that most women cannot afford, such as outlays for a bed, kitchen wares, and household supplies. And since none of the boardinghouses have kitchens, women who live in them must spend more to eat in restaurants and for takeout foods. On top of these costs, sex workers (who work in the tourist bars) are usually arrested two to ten times over the course of a few months. It costs around 500 pesos (U.S.$42) every time a sex worker is arrested; the police will not release her without first being paid a bribe. To make matters worse, the competition for clients is so steep, particularly during the low tourist seasons, when the tourist bars are crowded with sex workers, that days can go by before women find a client. Thus, even though the sex trade appears to yield savings above and beyond the remittances they send back home and their daily living expenses in Sosúa, most women earn just enough to stay afloat in Sosúa and to send modest remittances to their children. Eventually realizing there is no windfall in Sosúa, and missing their children, women usually return to their home communities in less than a year, just as poor as when they first arrived.

Women migrate to Sosúa's sex trade after an individual calculus in which they weigh the potential risks and the financial benefits— benefits unavailable in other forms of work open to poor women. Put simply, the sex trade is one of the few avenues available to poor, uneducated women who strive for economic advancement. Other factors inform their decisions: the Dominican economy, the local economy in their home communities, and their education and skill base. Moreover, even though they might have heard through their female-based social networks about the obstacles to making a lot of money in Sosúa's sex trade, it is difficult to understand the daily stresses and dangers without actually undergoing them. It is different from communications about other forms of labor in that it might not be possible to grasp what it is like to work in the sex trade until actually selling sex.

In this chapter and the next, I explore these women's responsibilities as single mothers, their families' poverty, and the lack of profitable work opportunities in their home communities. They see sex work in their late teens to late thirties both as a short-term survival strategy as well as a long-term advancement strategy to meet their obligations as single mothers, which stem, in large part, from the instability of consensual unions. In the first section of this chapter, "Overview of the Dominican Economy," I provide a brief overview of the larger Dominican economy in which these women weigh one paid labor choice over another. I then explore, in the second section, "Family Responsibilities and Work Histories," women's responsibilities in their households that have informed their work choices.[1] Their limited wage-labor opportunities combined with their familial responsibilities demonstrate the need for, and lure of, opportunity myths about sex work in Sosúa. They reveal how the material reality of Dominican women's lives blends with the myths of economic—and romantic—opportunities in tourist areas. Then, in the third and fourth sections of this chapter, I turn to the daily rhythms of life in Sosúa's sex trade. In order to understand why women's time in Sosúa meets, falls short of, or exceeds their expectations, I detail what living and working as a sex worker is all about. The choices sex workers make once they arrive, most important the type of clients they work with, determine the range of risks—and rewards—they assume. "Living and Working Conditions in Sosúa's Sex Trade: The Dependents," the third section, explores life selling sex with Dominican clients; while "Living and Working Conditions in Sosúa's Sex Trade: The Independents," the fourth section, looks at selling sex with foreign clients.

Overview of the Dominican Economy

The Dominican Republic since the 1960s has turned away from an agricultural economy based on sugar exports and import substitution toward an economy dependent on tourism, export manufacturing, and agribusiness (Safa 1999b; Itzigsohn 2000).[2] The Dominican Republic was dependent on sugar exports until the United States significantly cut sugar quotas in the 1980s to protect its own sugar industry in Florida (Safa 1999b). Since then, tourism has surpassed sugar exports as the leading revenue earner. Revenues from tourism represented 8.6 percent of exports of goods and services in 1977, 30.4 percent in 1986, and 40 percent in 1990. Sugar, in contrast, provided only 8 percent of export revenues in 1990 (Itzigsohn 2000).

FEMINIZATION OF THE DOMINICAN LABOR FORCE
Accompanying these changes has been a "feminization of the labor force." The economic conditions created through structural adjustment—such as cuts in government programs, declining real wages, and growing inflation—have pushed women into the paid labor market (Safa 1999a: 291). From 1981 to 1991, the average annual rate

of growth of the female labor force was 4.2 percent, compared with 2.8 percent for men (Safa 1999a:291).[3] This influx of women who seek a cushion from the jarring effects of structural adjustment, combined with lowered trade tariffs in the United States, created a low-skill employment "boom" in free-trade zones. This boom in export manufacturing also occurred after structural adjustment programs mandated currency devaluations, which lowered the cost of labor in the Dominican Republic to U.S.$.56 an hour in 1990 from U.S.$1.33 in 1984 (Safa 1999a: 292). The number of Dominicans working in free-trade zones jumped from 20,000 in 1982, to 182,000 in 1987 (Safa 1999a: 292). The majority of these workers were women, who Helen Safa estimates make up 60–80 percent of the workforce in export manufacturing (1999b: 1).

Despite the job creation through export manufacturing, the low wages offered cannot keep pace with the cost of living. In 1992 it was estimated that a family of five required 7,580 pesos a month (U.S.$632) for basic necessities, but free-trade zone workers were earning a monthly minimum wage of only 1,269 pesos (U.S.$106) (Safa 1999a: 296–97). Nor have minimum wage increases in free-trade zones kept pace with rises in cost of living, with the real hourly minimum wage in the Dominican Republic declining 62.3 percent between 1984 and 1990.[4] This clear gap between factory wages and family's monthly expenses helps explain (as Nanci did in the beginning of this chapter) why women might choose the sex trade— especially since they have control over how many hours they work.

Women's choices about work options also intersect with changing gender relations in the household. With men losing their agricultural jobs, and development strategies favoring female workers, particularly in export-processing zones, many households have substituted women's earnings for men's (Safa 1995a).[5] Dominican women's wages have become central to households, as financial strains on poor families have increased in the past two decades. Unemployment has risen among men who previously worked in the sugar industry, while the limited social services supplied by the Dominican government have eroded.[6] Consequently, women have picked up where men's earnings and the state's help have dried up. Moreover, since Dominican women generally contribute a larger proportion of their wages to the household than men,[7] their earnings clearly contradict notions of women's paid labor as supplementary or secondary vis-à-vis men's labor and income (Safa 1995). However, Safa fears that women's central role in export-led industrialization "may re-inforce their subordination through poorly paid, dead-end jobs" (1995a: 123).

Family Responsibilities and Work Histories

To support my argument that the global sex trade relies on and perpetuates inequalities, here I analyze some of the inequalities that begin at "home," meaning conditions within the Dominican econ-omy (both nationally and in their local communities) that push poor single women into the sex trade, as well as conditions within poor Dominican households (both when women are growing up in their parents' households and later when they are raising their own chil-dren). Constrained by poverty, little or no education, and virtually no social networks to help land secure, well-paying jobs, these adult women's work trajectories were almost predetermined—much like the Mexican girls about which Lourdes Benería and Martha Roldán write: "All the decisions for [their] future[s] were adopted during [their] childhoods and almost always were beyond [their] control" (1987: 84).[8] The sex workers I met who were using their earnings from the sex trade to send their children—sons *and* daughters—to private elementary schools, and in a few exceptional cases to college, were trying to ensure that the next generation had more opportuni-ties to get ahead (progresar) than they did. Ani, who sent her oldest daughter to college with the financial help of her parents-in-law, explained, "My kids are going to be professionals, not work at the kind of jobs I have had. I want them to be somebody, not like me."[9]

Women—poor women—who take care of families experience a variety of burdens. Women such as Elena, who are the sole breadwin-ners for their dependents, shoulder many financial responsibilities, and it consequently becomes difficult for them to quit the sex trade. A web of individuals, usually children and older parents, depend on them. They have been taking care of themselves and others for a long time. Sadly, some of these women's mothers died when they (the sex workers) were young, at which time these young girls often left their fathers' households to live in—and to work in—wealthier house-holds. Or once they became pregnant and/or moved in with their boyfriends/fathers of their children, their parents considered them adults and thus financially independent. Few jobs appear to these women to pay as well as the sex trade, especially since their previous wage-labor experiences have been in insecure, low-paying jobs, such as domestic or restaurant work or hair styling. Moreover, nearly everyone they know works in similar types of jobs. Thus, women such as Elena typically have a mountain of obligations (financial and emotional), while the family and friends that comprise their safety net are similarly strapped. And even though (as I explore below) poor Dominican women regularly come to the aid of friends, what they can offer one another—a meal, babysitting, bus fare—does not permanently catapult them out of poverty but rather helps them through the day or week.

GROWING UP IN HOUSEHOLDS WITHOUT MOTHERS

The absence of mothers can have serious effects in women's lives. Sex workers raised in households without mothers, or other female kin, often assumed considerable responsibilities and challenges early on in their lives. I met a number of sex workers who had left their families' homes soon after the deaths of their mothers. Similarly, Mercedes González de la Rocha found among the working poor in Mexico that while men who are widowed or separated usually re-marry or "incorporate a woman through other means" into their household (such as having a sister come to live with them), children of widowed fathers move out to live with grandparents or aunts, from either side of the family (1994: 162).[10] Nanci, for example, left school at age eight, after her mother died. Sent home from school for having lice, she never returned. "I did not like school very much. I wanted to fish and to harvest rice. And my father did not make me go to school." Soon after she left school, her father sent her to live with a well-off family. "After my mother died we moved to different places. And then I worked for a family as a maid for food and clothing only. Not for money. I was ten." Nanci wonders what her life would be like if her mother had not died: "Who knows, if my mother were living, I might never have had a child, I might never have been in the street [meaning in the sex trade], or any of this. Who knows, maybe I would not have married." Following her mother's death, Nanci was expected to take over her mother's household responsibilities, and once she had a child of her own (at age eighteen) she was completely on her own.

Teresa, another sex worker, explained how being a mother delin-eates between *señoritas* and *señoras* (girls and women): "Once girls have children, they are no longer señoritas," and therefore they are no longer their fathers' responsibility. She elaborated: "Look, fathers by law are supposed to take care of their kids. Young girls whose fathers look after them don't need to be in the street. Some have kids, that's different." Once Elena had her daughter, for example, she was on her own. She moved out of her parents' home to work in a cousin's roadside café, where she and her baby daughter slept in a room in the back. We went to visit the café, and she proudly showed me where she had made a home for the two of them and was financially independent for the first time.

When parents do help, their aid can substitute for an absent husband's negligence. This help takes different forms, such as money, food, housing, and child care. Following the breakup of their marriages, many sex workers report that they returned to their parents' homes with their children. Single mothers without family to rely on—especially their mothers—are at an obvious disadvantage. One sex worker, who worked in a bar that caters to Dominican clients, cited the death of her parents and thus the end of any financial help to her household, as the turning point in her life that pushed her to decide on sex work: "I have been married three times and have five children. My first husband gave me 300 pesos [U.S.$25] a month for one year and then stopped." With the fathers of her children out of the picture, her parents helped out financially. But once both of her parents died (within a short time of one another), she felt she had no place to turn. "With papa dead, I had to come here"; "I have to take care of my children—I have a five-year-old. I'm here so I can buy a house. I already have a stove and a few other things. I have to make sacrifices." Her parents had not owned a house, so she had no family house into which to move, nor other household members with whom to pool resources. And without a close female family member to watch her children, she used a large portion of her earnings to pay a baby-sitter. For this woman, sex work's high wages (relative to other jobs open to poor women) offered the kind of financial safety net her family once provided.

Maribel and Her Sisters. The far-reaching effects of a mother's death are poignantly apparent in the experiences of three sex workers, sisters all under the age of eighteen (seventeen, sixteen, and fourteen) when I first met them in 1995. They left their father's home, following the death of their mother, to work in homes of middle-class families in Santo Domingo. They spoke of physical and emotional abuse in their father's home by a succession of women with whom he was romantically involved, as well as by the families who employed them. The father sent Maribel, the youngest of the girls, to work for a family when she was only seven years old in exchange for food and housing (much like Nanci). She tried to make sense of her father's decision: "When my mother died I was small, so my father thought this was best." When her father remarried, she moved back in with him and his new wife. But Maribel had a terrible time with her father's new "wife" (in a consensual union). "She was very bad and hit us all a lot; we were all very small. So because of this we [her sisters and she] decided to leave the house." At eleven years old, she went to work as a domestic for a middle-class family in Santo Domingo, a job she liked because "it was taking care of children." "I lived in their house, and they paid me 400 pesos [U.S.$33.30] a month, and I took care of two kids, cleaned the house, and cooked." Eventually all three sisters left domestic work. The oldest sister worked in a disco in Santo Domingo as a waitress, the second oldest married and had a baby, and Maribel migrated to Sosúa to find work in the tourist industry. She worked briefly as a domestic for a Swiss couple, but this job was cut short when they were arrested (for a crime they allegedly committed back in Switzerland) and deported (yet another example of foreigners using Sosúa as a refuge from the law). At this juncture, at fourteen years old, she turned to sex work.

I must emphasize that I did not realize that Maribel was only fourteen years old until I had interviewed her multiple times and then rechecked my tapes and field notes. She not only looked eighteen or older but carried herself as if older than she was. She lied about her age to everyone in town, and her sisters also covered for her. I was not the only one fooled; for example, when I spoke with the peer educators from CEPROSH about her age, at first they did not believe me. Once convinced, however, they were alarmed and advised Maribel to quit the sex trade. Short of having the police forcibly remove her from the tourist bars when she was looking for clients, there was not much—besides counseling her—they could do to get her out of the sex trade.[11] Eventually, she started to work as a waitress at a restaurant on the beach and went to the tourist bars (to look for clients) less frequently. She also attended German language classes paid for by a foreign-resident friend—a former client.

Only months after Maribel had first arrived in Sosúa, her two older sisters also migrated to Sosúa's sex trade. The middle sister's marriage had broken up, so she left her baby in Santo Domingo with a paid baby-sitter, while the oldest sister alternated between working in the sex trade in Sosúa a couple of nights every other week and waitressing in Santo Domingo. She used sex work in Sosúa as a second source of income to supplement her wages as a nightclub waitress. While in Sosúa, she stayed with her youngest sister before returning to Santo Domingo. Maribel's, her sisters', and Nanci's early departures from their parents' homes are more common in rural areas, especially in poor households without what I call "mother stand-ins" (female kin who take over responsibilities traditionally understood to belong to mothers). In the case of Maribel and her two sisters, their father, stepmother, or other family members failed to act as mother stand-ins.

In the following subsection, I explore the various child-care arrangements sex workers put into place for their children while they work in Sosúa's sex trade. It had only been since the early 1990s that Dominican women began to migrate to Sosúa in significant numbers; thus the consequences of mothers' migration and the resulting reconfiguration of the household are not yet clear for this generation of children who have been living with their grandmothers, other female family members, or paid female caregivers.[12]

SEX WORKERS' CHILD-CARE ARRANGEMENTS

Because very few sex workers decide to bring their children with them to Sosúa as Elena did, they must make alternative mothering arrangements. That Dominican constructions of "womanhood" are tied up with motherhood means rearing children is generally regarded as a woman's role. In most cases mothers or sisters take the sex workers' children, but other female kin also help out; these kin include aunts, mothers-in-law, and close friends or neighbors. Without female kin to help care for their children, paid arrangements can prove stressful. Rosa, a nineteen-year-old sex worker, for example, was worried about leaving her son with a paid female caregiver in Santo Domingo: "You know, when a child is with someone other than his mother, it is not the same. I think the baby-sitter is tired of him. So I am going home." After working for six months in sex work, and saving some money, Rosa left Sosúa because she did not trust her son with a nonfamily member. Yet leaving children with family members also has its disappointments and difficulties. Patricia, a resort waitress, was left as a girl with her aunt while her mother went to work in French Guiana. "She treated me badly, not equally. She did not treat me as she treated her own children."

The linkages between household economics and the social disruptions from migration for sex work are clear within sex workers' conceptions of mothering. Living away from their children while they are in the care of other women diverges from traditional notions in which mothers provide daily care to their children. But mothering from a distance—Pierrette Hondagneu-Sotelo and Ernestine Avila use the term *transnational mothering* for this arrangement when women migrate overseas—means that some mothers and their children live apart for long periods of time, thus "radically rearrang[ing] mother-child interactions," a situation that "requires a concomitant radical reshaping of the meanings and definitions of appropriate mothering" (1997: 557). Even though their children are far away, sex workers in Sosúa talk constantly about being mothers. Justina explained the hierarchy of her obligations: "I'm a mother first and a daughter second—men come last."

Dominican women act as "mother stand-ins" throughout their life cycle, especially because they migrate internally and internationally to support their children. Caring for small children is a lifelong role for poor women, even years after their own children are grown. Yet young women also act as mother stand-ins, as Elena did for her two teenage sisters. Their biological father had abandoned their mother when they were toddlers, and their mother had died when Elena was young. Following their mother's death, they lived with their mother's second "husband," whom the girls thought of as their father. Yet despite the close relationship between the girls and their stepfather, Elena volunteered to take care of her younger sisters in Sosúa: "My father is poor, he works only a few days a week on a farm. He has very little money for food and other things. So I told him I would take my sisters, since I make more money." She also was financially responsible, on occasion, for her stepfather's second "wife's" daughter. This teenage girl spent part of her time with Elena and part of her time back in the *campo* (countryside) with her mother and stepfather. The sex trade having placed Elena in the position to outearn her stepfather, she inherited financial responsibilities for her extended family—responsibilities traditionally left to male breadwinners. A few years later, Elena was no longer responsible for her younger sisters (they both married), but she still acted as a "mother stand-in"—this time for a good friend's eight-year-old daughter while her friend, Mari, lived in Germany for a year and a half with her German husband. (I recount Mari's story in chapters 3 and 6 and in the Conclusion.)

WHEN MEN LEAVE

Since all but two of the sex workers (Nora, who said she was infertile, and fourteen-year-old Maribel) I interviewed are mothers, and most of these mothers did not receive any financial assistance from the father(s) of their children, I cannot ignore the role of men's abandonment of their financial responsibilities to their children in setting the stage for poor mothers' participation in paid sex. Even when men did help out, not one of the sex workers I met received financial help on a consistent basis. The prevalence of female-headed households in the Dominican Republic, where mothers as young as fourteen and fifteen are the sole financial providers for their children, produces economic insecurity among women and leads them to seek jobs, such as sex work, which promise immediate infusions of cash into the household.[13] Although Dominican law 24-97 requires fathers (and mothers) to fulfill their "moral and material responsibilities" and penalizes them for abandoning their children or failing to provide child support, its enforcement has been inconsistent. Many women are reluctant to use the law, as Mercedes, a sex worker, spelled out, "Sure I can use the law to get the father of my children to pay. But even if he pays once, I have to report him to the police every month to get him to pay up." But the police proved unhelpful, and Mercedes feared her ex-"husband's" (their "marriage" was a consensual union) violent reprisals. "What do the police do? They put him in the jailhouse for an afternoon, and afterward he comes to find me and beat me." Eventually Mercedes concluded, "It isn't worth it."

A partner's departure usually signals the end of his financial contribution to the household, and poor women know they cannot count on him ever again. Women's decision to migrate to Sosúa to sell sex might occur soon after separating from their consensual union "husbands," sometimes within days or weeks of men's departure. "My 'husband' and I have been separated for nine days," explained Felicia, who had just arrived in Sosúa. "He does not give me money, and I have two kids." With only a third-grade education, she, like so many of the other women in Sosúa's sex trade, does not have any marketable skills. "We are all here out of necessity. I have nothing. I have to do this. I don't know anything. If I had help from my husband, I would not be here." Felicia did know, however, women in Sosúa's sex trade and put these female-based social networks into action. "A friend of mine knew I needed money. She is a friend of the bar owner. And my sister works in a bar across the street." Felicia began working (and living) in a bar that caters to Dominican clients.

Felicia also brought a friend with her, Margarita, from her home community. Margarita's husband had left her for another woman— "his first family." Margarita had been his mistress. He has four children with his "first wife" and only one child with Margarita. She believes the number of children he has with this other woman makes a difference in his level of financial commitment, asserting that only if "you have five or six kids with one man" will he "give you money" even after he has left the household. Margarita has little confidence that she could ever rely on a man again. "This is why I am here. . . . Men are not faithful. I can't imagine being with one man my whole life." Why did Felicia and Margarita migrate to Sosúa's sex trade upon their husbands' departure from the household, rather than migrate to Santo Domingo, for example, to work in factories in export-processing zones or as domestics (two jobs commonly occupied by poor women and neither of which pays over 1,000 pesos [U.S.$83.33] a month)? Once these women began supplying the only income stream into the household, they felt the most likely way that they could replace their "husbands' " lost income was through the sex trade.

JOBS PRIOR TO SEX WORK

Jobs available to poor Dominican women with little formal education pay wages that make it impossible to escape poverty. Within this context, sex work appears as a potentially profitable alternative. Poor women, such as Felicia and Margarita, only can find jobs within the insecure and low-paying informal sector. Working part time as domestics (as Felicia did) or as hair stylists in salons (as Margarita did) are typical ways sex workers earned money prior to migrating to Sosúa. Certain jobs are understood—such as hair styling—to not supply enough money to keep a household running unless the low wages are pooled with those of husbands, mothers, sisters, or other family members. Felicia's reasons for landing in Sosúa are not unusual: even though she had a job as a domestic, she did not earn enough money to support the family. "I only made 500 pesos [U.S.$42] a month. I did the laundry, ironing, everything—for only 500 pesos! But this is not enough to live on." Felicia and Margarita summed up the dilemma for single mothers like themselves who leave school in their early teens, receive no formal job training, and thus have few well-paying job options open to them: "If you have a husband who pays for food and the house, then you can work in jobs like hair styling. Otherwise it's not possible to work in jobs like this." While they were "married," Margarita and Felicia conceived of their wages as secondary or supplementary to their husbands'.[14] Patricia Pessar found a similar ideology which held that women's earnings in New York merely "helped" their husbands. As a result, Pessar writes, these women only "nibbled at the edges of patriarchy" (1995a: 62). I too did not find among the sex workers in Sosúa challenges to gender relations that grew out of a feminist consciousness. Rather, even as sex workers become their families' main breadwinners—and outearn male migrants there—they still cling to traditional understandings of gender relations. Traditional gender ideologies are most clear, for example, in women's pursuit of marriage to men—either Dominican or foreign—as a solution to their financial problems.

Living and Working Conditions in Sosúa's Sex Trade: The Dependents

Not every woman who arrives in Sosúa to work in the sex trade is in search of building transnational ties. They migrate to Sosúa because they have heard of Sosúa's tourists and money, and they plan, usually without a specific strategy in mind, to benefit—somehow—from the tourist economy. Even if they have friends from their home communities in Sosúa's sex trade, they generally know little about its daily goings-on. For example, they might have heard of the police roundups but have no idea how frequent, frightening, and expensive they are. Fewer still know that they must vie with countless other women just like themselves to catch the attention of potential clients.

Women new to Sosúa soon realize that working with tourists pays more than working with Dominican clients. Elena, for example, first worked and lived in a bar that catered to Dominican clients, then switched to tourist bars once she saw that she might make more money with foreign clients. Women also learn that the real prospect of significant earnings, enough to have a savings account on top of sending money home to one's children, lies in developing ongoing relationships with more than one foreign client at a time. However, when women first arrive they might not have decided which client base they will work with. This decision—whether to sell sex to Dominican men or to foreign men—determines the amount of money they make, the number of hours they work, their degree of independence, and even where they live. In fact it is easy to identify sex workers' client base by their living arrangements. If women live at a bar, they work with Dominican clients. If they live on their own, and either pay for a room in a boardinghouse or rent a house or an apartment, they work with foreign tourists. These two dimensions of the sex trade in Sosúa—client base and housing— profoundly shape the experiences of sex workers. There are benefits and drawbacks to the different arrangements, yet much depends on the personality and comfort level of individual women. Working with Dominicans might pay less, but living at a bar is rent free and entails fewer responsibilities than living alone. The downside of living in Dominican bars, however, is significant: isolation from the communities around them and vulnerability to the whims of the bar owner. But going to the bars where the tourists hang out presents its own problems, such as tangling with the police and competing with scores of other Dominican and Haitian women. Successfully work- ing these bars requires assertiveness and an ability to communicate, any way they can, with non Spanish speakers. For some women, the tourist bar scene involves too many demands and dangers.

Because the differences in client base and housing arrangements ultimately result in different degrees of independence and depen- dence for the women, I use the terms *dependents* to talk about women who work with Dominican men and *independents* to de- scribe women who work with foreign men. As one of my aims is to demonstrate women's creative use of the sex trade in Sosúa, I have chosen terms that call attention to women's struggles to get ahead (progresar) through the sex trade. While the dependents must abide by the rules and schedules set by bar owners and administrators, the independents essentially are freelance sex workers.[15]

Women who work with Dominican clients live and work in the same space. Typically, dependents work six days a week. The work-day begins around three or four o'clock in the afternoon, as the dependents start primping for the men, who start arriving from around four o'clock on to drink beer and to talk with the women, the bar owner, and one another. As the evening goes on, more customers arrive, the noise level increases, and women dance with customers and try to get them to buy more drinks. Everyone who is drinking gets progressively more drunk. Meanwhile, women wait and hope that some of the customers will pay to go with them to their bedrooms. Women in these Dominican bars say that they spend anywhere from five minutes to an hour with their Dominican clients. Afterward they go back to the bar and resume drinking and dancing with customers—and hope for more clients.

The women's small rooms are either inside the same building as the bar or out back, behind the bar, usually a "long house" structure of rooms. The construction of the bars vary, with combinations of cement or wood or palm frond walls, topped by cement, corrugated tin, or palm frond roofs. If the rooms are not adjacent to the bar, but are located at back behind it, they usually are made of the cheapest materials available, such as wood with palm roofs (instead of ce-ment). Most of these bars are located off the main paved road, within the labyrinth of dirt paths that make up Los Charamicos. During my first research trip to Sosúa in 1993, I got lost—even after making maps—trying to find my way to these bars without help. I also dreaded doing interviews in the bars' backrooms that were the women's bedrooms. Windowless, dark, and dank, they all seemed to blur together. Later, when I returned in 1994, I learned how to find even the most out-of-the-way bars without help, and I became less claustrophobic spending hours in cramped spaces. I even became accustomed to the constant stench of the bathrooms or outhouses (since there was virtually no circulation of fresh air through these living quarters). Eventually, each bar and each room began to take on its own unique characteristics.

Between one and twenty women might live and work in a bar at a given time. Although the rooms are small, it is not unusual for two women to share a room, even a bed. During the weeks before Christmas and Easter, however, when sex workers return home to their families to celebrate the holidays, women who remain behind usually have their own rooms. If both women who share a room have clients at the same time, one of them borrows another sex worker's room. Since clients rarely spend the entire night, women do not have problems finding a place to sleep. Besides a double bed, the rooms have a small table that holds women's makeup and bathroom necessities, perhaps a straw chair, and some kind of rod or string on which to hang clothes. Typically with no windows and no natural light, the bedrooms are so dark that day and night are virtually indistinguishable. In most women's rooms a makeshift electrical outlet powers a single light bulb, when there is not a blackout. With the power going on and off throughout the day, candles are in every bedroom. A suitcase sits off to one corner, a reminder not only of the women's mobility but also of the fact that their few possessions can fit into one piece of luggage. Plastic bins are an essential part of all rooms; without running water, women use one bin for washing and one as a toilet in the middle of the night.

At the bars there typically is some kind of outhouse, and, occasionally, one showerhead shared by all. Yet as water shortages in Sosúa can be worse than the power outages, women usually end up bathing with a bucket of water. The bars also have at least one communal spigot where the women can wash their clothes. Some women have a few cooking pans and eating utensils, and in some instances where there is outdoor space available, bar owners permit women to start fires out back to cook breakfast or dinner. Others let women use the bar's cooking facilities, the most common being a small charcoal pit over which pots are placed. A few of the sex workers own expensive items such as a mosquito net, or even more rare, an electric fan or a walkman.

Although these conditions sound uncomfortable and sparse, and not particularly private, they are similar to women's living conditions in their home communities. In fact, women from rural areas might never have lived with electrical power or running water. Women personalize their rooms in different ways, despite few material possessions. They bring family photographs, for example, and place them on their makeup tables or tack them to the walls. These photos, almost always of their children, are windows into the women's lives—and responsibilities—back in their home communities, glimpses of why they are in Sosúa. Because poor families generally do not own cameras, photographing one's children involves going to a studio. These photos show children standing in front of studio backdrops of a winding river or of a New England fall countryside. The children's new outfits reveal their mothers' care. Little girls wear party dresses with layers of lace, frill, and crinoline; matching lace socks and headpieces complete the outfits. Little boys grin from under baseball caps and toddler baseball uniforms, or they are decked out, like miniature grooms, in tuxedos and suits. Although poverty generally forces these mothers to buy one disposable diaper at a time (usually just for nighttime), these women clearly spend a considerable portion of their household budget on their children's formal outfits, which they wear every Sunday for visits with family and neighbors.

In addition to photos, other items, such as religious objects, also speak of their private lives outside of sex work. Some women display pictures of their favorite saints and light candles. Few of these women have any kind of music in their room or a television. Those who can read often have Dominican comic book versions of Harlequin Romances strewn about their rooms. These small books, made out of cheap paper, cost only a few pesos each and can be traded in for others at the newspaper and school supplies store in Los Charamicos. Aside from newspapers from time to time (usually bought by the bar owner), these romances are the only form of reading the women undertake.

Since sex workers move around a lot—back and forth between home and Sosúa, or between bars—many rooms remain undecorated. Yet rooms of women who have been living at the same bar for a while (over six months), have more of a "lived-in" feeling about them. One room in particular stands out: its occupant took great care to decorate the room for her own comfort, not to romance or seduce clients. Her room was unusual precisely because the women's rooms were strikingly unromantic.[16] By putting up curtainlike billows of pink fabric on her walls, including around the perimeter of a sealed-up window, she transformed an otherwise dark and depressing room into a colorful, cozy den. She also hung a curtain on a string across her room to partition off her bed from the rest of the room, separating her work life from her personal life. She spent a lot of time, and some money, sewing these curtains. It is the most effort I have seen a sex worker put into fixing up a room, suggesting that she had no plans to leave the bar in the near future.

Besides decorating their rooms, the dependents can control little else. They depend on the bar owners for housing, for their main (midday) meal, and for clients. They also must depend on them for protection from violent customers or from those who refuse to pay. In return for their housing and lunch, sex workers must work exclusively at these bars. In other words, bar owners or administrators / managers demand that the women living there work only for them. On a slow night, they are not allowed to look for clients at another bar. Nor are they permitted to alternate between working in tourist bars and the Dominican bars in which they live, even though the tourist bars are open after the Dominican bars close. Rather, women must be on site, in the event that clients request them. If it were discovered that a woman had snuck off after the bar owner or administrator had gone to sleep, she would be "fired"— kicked out of the bar. Although I know of one woman who secretly worked at tourist bars after hours, this is highly unusual.

The type of women who choose to work with Dominican clients over foreign clients usually lack the daring either to defy the bar owner or to try and pick up clients in the unfamiliar tourist bar scene. It is because they are uncomfortable with foreign men that they find refuge in the Dominican bars. For this group of women, Sosúa brings many firsts: their first time living outside of their home communities; their first time living apart from family and support networks; their first time selling sex; and for some who previously might have worked out of their home (sewing, hair styling), their first time having to negotiate with an employer. Generally, they are a quiet, unassuming, honest, and trusting group of women. Whereas the groups of women who work in the tourist bars walk around town loudly talking and laughing, shouting to one another across the street, and taunting and teasing male motoconcho taxi drivers waiting for passengers at intersections of the paved (and semipaved) sections of Los Charamicos, the dependents rarely leave the confines of the bar, even during their time off. As the independents cajole motoconcho drivers into free rides, and demand the best produce at the marketplace, making themselves an extraordinarily visible and vibrant part of Los Charamicos, dependents remain virtually hidden behind the walls of the bars. Even within the bar, these women try to go unnoticed and not make waves. Nearly every time I visited Dominican bars, the women working there spoke to me in hushed and conspiratorial tones, unless the bar owner or administrator was out.

Carlos, the owner of the Seabreeze, a bar located on the main road outside Los Charamicos, had perfected the use of scare tactics to maintain considerable control over the women working for him. Even though the police almost never make arrests inside Dominican bars (and instead focus on the streets around the tourist bars), bar owners such as Carlos seize on dependents' fears of working the tourist bars. Women living at the Seabreeze recounted to me how Carlos had told them that if they left the bar, even in the mornings, they could be arrested (which was not impossible, given the police's indiscriminate arrests of Dominican women living in Los Chara-micos). But he also went so far as to manufacture a tall tale of jealous wives / girlfriends. Women working for him explained: "Carlos told us that the neighbors living nearby snitch on the men they see entering this bar. He said that we might get hurt—stabbed—by the men's wives or by jealous clients." My research assistants who have lived in Los Charamicos for years assured me that not only had this drama never happened to any women at the Seabreeze; it had not happened in any other Dominican bar that they knew of. Yet Carlos exploited these women's economic marginality and fanned their fears of living in an unfamiliar and fast-paced place by spinning a story of danger at every turn. He deliberately played on these rural women's fears of the "city" and the risks of sex work. When I asked him about his exaggerations, he justified the stories with "I know that in *other bars* women have gotten hurt." Moreover, in his instru-mental fictions he portrayed the women as the sources of danger. "There are problems because the women pick fights."

THE POWER OF OWNERS:

NONPAYMENT, EXPLOITATION, AND ABUSE

Although Carlos exaggerated external physical dangers facing the women working at his bar, it is clear that sex workers—whether they work with Dominican or foreign men—risk rape and abuse every time they are behind closed doors. Sex workers working at Dominican bars arguably enjoy greater protections: the bar owner and the other women who might be within shouting distance. Yet this protection can fail when owners ignore or facilitate abuse and exploitation. Juana's story illustrates the women's vulnerability to the whims of the bar owners and the clients. One evening, after Carlos already had gone to bed, a client went with Juana back to her bedroom. The next day, the owner demanded that Juana pay *la salida* (a fee owners charges a client each time he enters a sex worker's bedroom) because he had not been around to collect it. She had no choice but to pay the fee out of her own pocket and was furious: "All he cares about is that he gets la salida. He does not care if we are paid, how we are treated, or if we go to hell." Although Carlos called my attention to his small profit margin, women such as Juana saw him as "making a lot of money off of us. If we drink with the men, they drink more. Sometimes eight or nine drinks!"

During the same period of time when Carlos took advantage of Juana, I interviewed five other women who had sexual relations with clients who refused to pay afterward and about whom Carlos had done nothing when the women complained to him. Since this happened to nearly half a dozen women in such a short period of time, it is likely, as the women suspected, that the clients were telling their friends to go to the Seabreeze for free sex. One woman believed that Carlos—who had nothing to lose, as long as he was paid for the bar bill and la salida—was in on it: "If I tell the owner what is he going to do? Nothing. The men who come here are his friends." Another sex worker spoke up: "I have had only two men in eight days. But only one paid. I was afraid if I said anything to the client he [the client] would beat me up. My kids need me. We all have sex— we do it, but sometimes we don't get paid." As she was speaking, her coworkers were shaking their heads in agreement and encouraging her, so she started to get very angry. She spoke forcefully and began to wave her hands. "Look, the client pays 50 pesos [U.S.$4.17] for the bed to the bar owner up front. Why can't he also pay the woman up front?" When she told Carlos that a client walked out without paying, he "acted surprised" but did nothing. "Who lost out? Me!" she screamed. Despite their receptiveness to her candor, the women had been careful to shut the door to the bedroom where we were talking. Although they willingly talked openly with one another, and with CEPROSH's peer educators about their mistreatment, they were afraid to take their concerns directly to the owner. Carlos, meanwhile, bragged about his concern for the women working for him: "I leave my bed to see what is going on when the women have problems." The women assured me, however, that he was of little help.

Although the women at the Seabreeze expressed an awareness that the bar owner treated them unfairly, their discussion of their working conditions did not reflect a larger sense of class, race, or gender consciousness. Rather than connect their individual experiences with other poor Afro-Dominican women's exploitation in the sex trade, they poignantly narrated their sense of powerlessness by focusing on their own specific incidences of maltreatment. One complaint I heard repeatedly at Dominican bars, for example, was how unfair the owners were for not providing a meal on Sundays. Lacking extra cash (especially with decreasing numbers of clients), often sex workers, as one at the Seabreeze explained, "don't eat on Sundays."

Sex workers' experiences working for women suggest that the female administrators are not necessarily more fair or more concerned about their workers than the male owners and administrators.[17] Supervision by a woman does not translate into greater solidarity; in fact, since some women administrators have ongoing relationships with regular clients, they can represent "competition" and actually take business away from sex workers. They, like men involved in the bar business, generally view sex workers as irresponsible, self-absorbed, and unpredictable. While trying to find a woman who had moved from one bar to another, I asked the female administrator if she knew where she had gone. She sighed in exasperation and threw up her arms. "You know these kinds of girls. They come and go. They tell me nothing. They move, and I never hear from them again." However, some female administrators appeared to take safety issues—especially AIDS—more seriously than their male counterparts. One female administrator, for example, never missed a safe-sex presentation by the peer educators from CEPROSH (CEPROSH requires that male administrators and owners leave the bar during presentations). During the sessions, she also asked the most questions. Her enthusiasm set the tone for the meetings, which often spurred other, less vocal, women to join in.

DOLORES: AN EXCEPTION

Of course some women thrive in the Dominican bar system. Dolores's experiences at the Seabreeze do not resemble those of her coworkers. Even her bedroom was remarkably different from other women's rooms; she owned considerably more material possessions than the other women I met in any of the Dominican bars (and in many of the boardinghouses for that matter). The relative comfort in which she lived, and her financial success in the sex trade, have been due to two factors: the amount of time she has spent in the sex trade and her experience in the sex trade overseas in Curaçao and Panama. Dolores proudly took me on a tour of her room, boasting that she had the largest room at the bar "because I've been here the longest." While admiring Dolores' room, my research assistant noticed that Dolores had two electrical fans. Impressed, she asked Dolores how this was possible. "I took one from the other rooms," she replied. "And Carlos allowed this?" the assistant asked incredulously. "Yes," Dolores beamed. "I bring him a lot of business." Her nightstand displayed a cosmetic and perfume collection unrivaled by other women living in the Dominican bar system in Los Charamicos. She had several expensive European products (such as by Lancôme) and perfumes she had bought while overseas or had received as gifts from clients while there. Quite unusual was her sit-down, salon-style hair dryer, and Dolores herself was covered in jewelry. She wore at least ten gold chains around her neck and a gold ring on every finger (except her thumbs). Although clients in Curaçao and Panama bought her a few of the pieces, she had purchased the rest. Jewelry doubles as an investment, a kind of savings account, so her collection was a sizable asset. In a pinch, she could sell a piece in a pawn shop. Most impressive, however, was a house in her home community she had purchased with her earnings in the sex trade. With 3,050 pesos (U.S.$254) in the bank, and a house in her name, she was one of a small number of sex workers I met—either dependents or independents—who have made long-term gains in sex work beyond day-to-day, hand-to-mouth living.

Her time overseas, however brief, was critical to her being in a position to purchase a house. At twenty-six years old, Dolores already had been married three times (in consensual unions) when I met her during her second stint at the Seabreeze. She first had worked at the Seabreeze after she had left her third husband because, as she explained, "he became a policeman, and he started to scare me. I did not trust him anymore." She stayed at the bar for one year—a considerable amount of time given that most women left the Seabreeze after a few weeks—and then went to work in the sex trade in Curaçao for a year. She returned to her home community for a short while and then was off to Panama to work in the sex trade there. She traveled to both places through an agency in Santo Domingo that advertised in a newspaper that it supplied the papers necessary to work overseas. She explained that the agency advanced her 6,800 pesos (U.S.$567) for the papers and airfare. While in Curaçao she saved U.S.$750 in addition to paying off her debt to the agency. She was not as successful in Panama, however. She was deported after the police raided the bar where she was living and working (she showed me her passport with her deportation stamp). It was at this point, following her deportation, that she came back to the Seabreeze for the second time.

Dolores's coworkers at the Seabreeze, in contrast, often did not have enough money for breakfast. Their rooms were sparsely decorated and contained few personal possessions. They too wore all the jewelry they owned, maybe one or two rings and one necklace at the most. Their cosmetics were of cheaper quality, mostly made in the Dominican Republic. Perhaps most striking was that whereas they resented the bar owner, hated their time working in the sex trade, and emphasized that their responsibilities as mothers led them to sex work out of "necessity," Dolores, in contrast, admitted, "I like sex work. It's a good job. You can make good money that you can't in other jobs."

Her coworkers also resented Dolores, in part, because she had a good working relationship with the bar owner, as well as a roster of regular clients—whom she and other sex workers in Sosúa referred to as *amigos* (friends). She claimed that her amigos pay her 350 pesos (U.S.$29) every few days, the highest fee I had ever heard of Dominicans paying (the usual fee is between 200 and 300 pesos, or U.S.$17–25). She was clearly successful at keeping regulars coming back to the bar to buy drinks and to pay la salida, and the bar owner depended on her experience and ease with clients. She also brought two women with her from her home community to work at the Seabreeze. Dolores's experiences with living overseas and a long history with a range of clients help explain why she was not pushed around by the owner or clients at the Seabreeze. As a veteran in the sex trade and an experienced international traveler, she intimidated—and bossed around—the other sex workers at the bar. Most nights Dolores was the only woman at the bar who made any money. This cash came at a price, however. She was chilled out of the other women's gatherings in their rooms, and they spoke in whispers whenever she was around. They felt Dolores was too nosy about their private lives, while at the same time secretive about her own. They were also scared of her. After hearing Dolores alert the bar owner and the peer educators from CEPROSH about a coworker she alleged was HIV positive, Dolores's coworkers feared that she could just as easily spread rumors about them.

STAYING A DEPENDENT

It is the unusual woman such as Dolores who can make a career in the Dominican bars—let alone a successful one—by developing strategies to circumvent the many obstacles to accumulating assets. Befriending the bar owner by bringing him new sex workers, building a regular client base, charging a high price, and spreading rumors about other women's HIV status (and possibly scaring clients away from them) are all ways women can do more than just stay afloat. Yet most of the dependents could only dream of Dolores's success. The vast majority barely eked out a living. So why do they stay, especially if they have so many troubles with the owners, administrators, and clients? Many of them arriving just days after men in their lives abandoned them, their aim often was simply to stay afloat in Sosúa. After all, their previous jobs never paid more than subsistence wages, and the obstacles to making money in Sosúa are in keeping with their past experiences. Once the reality of few clients becomes apparent, some women settle into sex work as a job for the moment, while others go home. But going home has its problems too. Some women did not have the bus fare, while others refused to leave Sosúa until they had some money saved to bring to their families. They felt caught in their own cover stories they told to their families and neighbors. By returning home early and empty handed, they could expose their own deceptions.

Another option, of course, is to try one's hand at working with foreign clients. Foreign clients can mean having greater control over working conditions and more money but also involve more risk-taking. When I asked women why they did not move out, find a room in a boardinghouse, and work in the tourist bars, the women expressed a sharp fear of the police. Many also emphasized that they did not like or feel comfortable with the women who worked in the tourist bars. Yet when pressed, few personally knew any women working in the tourist bars, but they had seen the bars at night in full swing and observed women jockeying for clients. They were extremely put off by having to pursue clients aggressively. A few women acted out for me how independents grab a man's arm, groin, or even his wallet as he strolls by the tourist bars in the center of El Batey. Without physically grabbing men, they worried, how could they possibly attract attention in bars crowded with so many other women?[18]

Ramona's experience in the Dominican bar system (also at the Seabreeze) helps sheds light on why women stay. She had traveled to Sosúa after her husband took over their business, a bar they had started together. She cried as she told me how she ended up in Sosúa: "I had a bar like this one, but my husband just took it. The lease is in his name. We were together for seven years." As they were not legally married, she believed she had no legal recourse to prove the bar was also hers. Even more traumatic, her husband forced her and their son out of their home. Ramona felt she had no choice but to send her son to live with her mother and to try sex work, at least for a while. "I cannot make much money elsewhere, so I said, OK, I'll give this a try." Her social networks led her to the Seabreeze (the bar owner's wife is a friend of her sister) and by default to working with Dominicans. Once in Sosúa, she of course learned more about the potentially lucrative sex-tourist trade, but she decided to stay at the Seabreeze. Too scared of the police who circle the tourist bars, and intimidated by the thought of working with men who do not speak Spanish, she explained that working with tourists was not for her.

Ramona had co-managed and worked in a bar, so I had expected her to be more savvy than the other newly arrived women. After all she had been around plenty of drunk men. Yet her shy behavior revealed her not only as inexperienced in her new role as sex worker but also painfully uncomfortable. Like many other wives of male bar owners, including the wife of the Seabreeze's owner, Ramona had cleaned the bar during the day and had overseen its drink supplies. However, even though she helped serve drinks, it was her husband who tended bar into the late hours of the night, thus keeping her apart from the male world of drinking and pool playing.[19] In many ways Ramona was unprepared for work in the sex trade.

Fashion is one way, in addition to housing arrangements, to discern quickly who works with Dominicans and who works with tourists. In her late thirties, Ramona was older than most sex workers. Her wardrobe did not help her blend in either, instead calling attention to the fact that she just had arrived from the campo. She tried to transform her rural housewife's wardrobe into what she believed would make her fit in at a bar in a cosmopolitan town such as Sosúa. Using heavy black eyeliner and styling her hair into a side ponytail, she tried to look the part. But unlike some of the women working the tourist bars who make enough money to buy a few new clothes and accessories, Ramona did not have enough disposable income to help stretch her wardrobe. Rather, she was forced to make do with what she already owned. One day, for example, she wore black, cutoff jeans with a long green-and-black print polyester shirt that she belted. She paired these with dangling white plastic earrings, thick translucent pantyhose, and white plastic sandals. Put together, her outfits—like this one—screamed, "newcomer to Sosúa." Women working with tourists also wear makeup but generally not nearly as heavy as Ramona's. Their hair is styled in salons, rather than self-styled as Ramona had done. They buy jean-shorts, instead of cutting old jeans themselves. They wear tight Lycra shirts (that resemble sports bras) and stay away from loose body-concealing clothing such as Ramona's long shirt. They wear a lot of jewelry but never pantyhose with shorts, although black hose are considered stylish at night—but only with skirts and dresses. And finally, the independents wear sporty sandals or flip-flops by day, while high heels are de rigueur for evening. While women who work in tourist bars try to outdo one another with a succession of new outfits and accessories, Ramona could scarcely keep up with her *campesina* (peasant) wardrobe.

The fashion differences between the two groups are also clear during the day and reflect how they spend their leisure time. Women who live at Dominican bars wear big housedresses or oversized T-shirts over shorts during the day while they clean their rooms or the bar, or do their laundry. The women, in general, are not out and about town and thus have little reason to dress up. The bar owners supply their lunches, the women are often fearful of leaving the bar, and their meager earnings are already earmarked for their families and not available for discretionary spending. As a result, nearly all of their downtime is spent hanging out at the bar—even for women who work for bar owners who are not as controlling as Carlos at the Seabreeze. The independents, on the other hand, obligated to go out to Los Charamicos's cafés at lunchtime (since none of the boardinghouses have cooking facilities) usually dress well.

In fact, because the dependents are nearly always at their place of work, it was much easier for me to schedule interviews with them than with the very mobile independents. They also were up early in the morning, in part because their clients do not stay the entire night. Elena, though from the campo herself, offered a different explanation for the dependents' early rising that suggests a perceived class difference (based on sophistication, street smarts, and fashion, though not necessarily socioeconomic background) between the two groups: "They are campesinas and are used to rising like the chickens, like back in the campo. They keep the same schedule here that they did back home." Always dressed in the latest styles, renting her own apartment (after a brief stint in a Dominican bar when she first migrated to Sosúa)—Elena no longer considered herself a campesina: she had adapted her rural life's rhythms to those of late-night, tourist-oriented, urbanized Sosúa.

Living and Working Conditions in Sosúa's Sex Trade: The Independents

Whereas women who sell sex to Dominican men try to minimize the risks they encounter, risk taking characterizes the sex trade with foreign clients. The first big endeavor fraught with risks that these women undertake is making enough money to pay their rent. They must tangle with the police, which means risking arrest and paying bribes. They also must negotiate price and condom use with foreign clients (who might not speak any Spanish) and risk rape and beatings once they leave the safety of the bars. At the same time, however, they make their own hours and are indebted to no one.[20] And unlike women who live in Dominican bars, women who rent houses or apartments live among Sosúa's residents (as do women who rent rooms in boardinghouses, though to a lesser degree). Their neighbors, for the most part, are not sex workers. Thus these women are not socially isolated from the larger community, and they have the option of participating in Sosúa's daily rhythms.

FOREIGN CLIENTS CONFRONT CONDITIONS
OF WORKER POVERTY

Like the accommodations for women working with Dominicans, those for the independents can be quite stark. Since some women bring foreign clients back to their rooms, these men see the women's living conditions. Even if the rooms are well lit and furnished, there is no concealing the conditions of poverty in Los Charamicos. In my conversations with sex tourists, they kept returning to the theme of sex workers' poverty. Some women intentionally bring clients back to their boardinghouse rooms or apartments to show

how little they have and thus evoke sympathy and—possibly—big tips. Bringing tourists back to their rooms, thus, can work in the women's favor. Such was the case when Jürgen initially saw where Elena lived and cared for her daughter and sisters. He called her one-room shack surrounded by mud, trash, and sewage a "toilet" and wired Elena money to improve her living arrangements immediately after his first vacation in Sosúa. Although clients such as Jürgen often gave sex workers money and presents once they saw how few material possessions the women owned, sex workers' practice of bringing men to their rooms was not always an explicit strategy to obtain more money or material goods from foreign clients. Rather, because the all-inclusive hotels prohibited the entrance of any nonpaying guests into the hotels, clients often wound up at the women's boardinghouse rooms. One sex worker, who lived in a particularly dank boardinghouse, proudly held up a knapsack that an Italian client had left with her. "They [the foreign men] don't like where we live. One gave me this before he left." She also tacked pictures to her walls of white, European models from a German woman's fashion magazine that a German client had bought for her. Sometimes clients return the next day to take women out to lunch or dinner or to drop off presents such as perfume, clothes, or jewelry. If women have photographs of their children, clients might bring gifts for them too. As indicators of the women's responsibilities, family photos in this setting thus assume a role beyond personal mementos.

Independents' rooms also contain other signs of their work with foreign men, including those of ongoing transnational connections. Some have a folder of papers necessary for travel, such as a passport and other documents, along with a collection of addresses and fax numbers and photos of their foreign clients. Many display photos of themselves out on the town with white, European men. Almost every one of the sex workers who works with tourists has a piece of a foreign client's clothing, most commonly T-shirts with sayings emblazoned on them in various languages. All of these items function as status markers of the women's prestigious ties to fuera.

Once European tourists walk behind the quaint facades and into the buildings in Los Charamicos to buy sex, they enter a different world. These are the same buildings they pass by during the day with their cameras, snapping pictures to show their friends back home how "locals" live. But inside the boardinghouses, clients see the unfinished walls and ceilings and smell the communal toilet. The women's reality of coping with the daily demands of poverty clashes with idealized fantasies of having uncomplicated sexual relations with fiery Afro-Caribbean women. As soon as tourists step out of the tourist zone of First World bars, hotel rooms, restaurants, and shops, and into the private world of an "authentic Dominican," they confront—even if only for an hour—the reality of how the poorest class within a developing country lives. Tourists' fascination with the "real lives" of "authentic" others transports them from their everyday lives (see MacCannell 1976 in Urry 1990). The act of seeing— what Urry calls the "tourist gaze"—or doing something that tourists normally would not see or do at home is central to the tourist experience (Urry 1990). This group of men "see" much more closely than the average tourist how local Dominicans live, which, in turn, might shape some of their actions. For example, it is possible that their increased awareness of the financial demands on these women persuades them to wire money when they return to their home countries (as Jürgen did). It also may play a role in how they justify (to themselves) paying for sex. Julia O'Connell Davidson (1996) found in Cuba, for example, that the practice whereby male tourists move out of their hotels during their vacation to stay with sex workers may help the men to see themselves as helping the women, not just using them.

LIVING ARRANGEMENTS: BOARDINGHOUSES
The majority of women who sell sex to tourists live in boardinghouses that rent rooms on a daily and weekly basis. Boardinghouses that rent to sex workers become known as such, and usually other Dominicans do not try to rent rooms there. In fact, in an effort to discourage chulos—and, for that matter, any men who might try to make money off sex workers—many boardinghouse owners who rent to sex workers refuse to rent rooms to men. Nor are women's boyfriends allowed to live with them in the same room. Single-sex housing also keeps down the noise and reduces the likelihood of fights, explained the owner of a boardinghouse across the street from my apartment. Essentially small hotels, boardinghouses contain between five and fifteen rooms, with one woman to each room. The rooms generally are nicer than the rooms in which the dependents work and live, but there is a wide range of housing opportunities, and, surprisingly, the cost does not vary as dramatically

8. A boardinghouse in Los Charamicos

as the living conditions (the daily rent is 30–50 pesos (U.S.$2.50–4.17)).

Women who arrive in Sosúa do not necessarily shop around for the nicest boardinghouse. Rather, they settle into places based on their social networks, where, for example, they might know one of the other sex workers or have heard good things about the owner. Otherwise, if they do not have any connections, women are likely to choose the first boardinghouse they walk into, rather than hunt for the nicest accommodations. Often they are unaware that better accommodations might exist. Since the rooms in the first boardinghouse they survey might appear nicer than their living conditions back home, women are disinclined to continue looking. Impressed by the sturdy cement structure and a few pieces of wooden furniture, they do not look further to find rooms with furniture sets (carved wooden bed backboards, dressers or armoires, and nightstands), windows, and, as in the case of one boardinghouse with just three rooms, private bathrooms. Women frequently are seduced by the appeal of living alone, most never having had their own rooms. Living away from one's family not only offers freedom from the daily chores involved in taking care of other household members but also from sharing space—including a bed—with them.

Most accommodations in boardinghouses fall into a middle category of comfort, between the cheaply constructed, sparse, window-less rooms at bars with Dominican clients and the more comfortable boardinghouse rooms furnished with complete bedroom furniture sets. A typical room in this middle category is in a cement building with either a cement or corrugated tin roof. Like the rooms in Dominican bars, they are small and contain the same articles: a double bed, chair, and small table for accessories. One important difference is that women do not receive any meals at boarding-houses, nor have access to any cooking facilities; therefore they must earn enough money not only to pay the 30–50 pesos (U.S.$2.50–4.17) rent every day but also to eat out in nearby restaurants. Although no one dictates their schedules, and they consequently do not have to work every night, these women feel intense pressure to earn enough money to keep pace with their daily living expenses.

PRIVATE DWELLINGS

I use the term *private dwelling* to indicate any other kind of rental ar-rangement that is not a boardinghouse, in other words, a private house or an apartment. Even more self-sufficiency is needed to rent a private dwelling than to rent a boardinghouse room, and to do so women also need start-up capital. "Renting a house means having a lot of money to buy things, and life in the Dominican Republic is very expensive," said Tomasa, who lived in a boardinghouse. "You need a bed, a stove, and things for the kitchen. Women who work in the tourist bars are very intelligent; they know how to do all this." Tomasa took pride in characterizing her coworkers at the Anchor as "intelligent." Whereas the dependents might describe the indepen-dents as aggressive, the independents see themselves as skilled nego-tiators with tourists and astute money managers. But setting up a household in Sosúa, no matter how modest, is not always possible for even the most savvy women. Without money on hand to pay one month's rent up front, as well as to furnish an apartment, boarding-houses are the only alternative. In Tomasa's case, she chose a boar-dinghouse because she did not have enough money saved to buy needed household goods, and she had already spent money to buy those household items back in her home community. Since she, like so many of the sex workers in Sosúa, did not plan on staying longer than six or eight months, she did not see the point of spending money on making a home in Sosúa. Despite her intentions, however, To-masa was still in Sosúa at least a year longer than she had planned.

Even though it requires significant resources, renting a house or an apartment is the only arrangement available to sex workers such as Elena who bring their children to Sosúa. Although bringing children along is uncommon, women who do not have family members to care for their children—and who do not want to pay nonfamily members—have little choice. A paid baby-sitter in one's home community also can be much more costly than renting a house in Los Charamicos. Obviously, while in Sosúa sex workers still need to pay for child care when they work at the tourist bars, but their late hours mean it is neither difficult nor expensive to find someone to watch over their children while they sleep. Former sex workers (dependents) who are married to Dominican men (usually ex-clients) and who live in Los Charamicos with children of their own, for example, make money by watching their friends' children. Or, if a sex worker has a daughter (at least approximately ten years old or older), then the daughter watches her younger siblings.

During the day, sex workers and former sex workers trade off watching one another's children, thus saving money and freeing one another to run errands and to tend to other household responsibilities. For example, when Elena's teenage sisters are not in high school, they watch Elena's children. Otherwise, one of Elena's friends watches them or one of her three older married sisters (all married in consensual unions to Dominican men). Moving her daughter to Sosúa made sense for Elena since she has a wide child-care circle from which to draw.

THE WORK ROUTINE

The independents' daily schedule is quite different from the dependents' routine. They wake up around noon or 1:00 p.m., then go to lunch with their friends at one of the small restaurants or cafés in Los Charamicos. They spend the rest of the afternoon either napping or running errands, which usually includes a visit to the Codetel office to see if they received any faxes from clients in Europe. Since the independents make at least 500 pesos (U.S.$42) a client and set their own hours, many decide not to go to the tourist bars every night. This reduces the risk of arrest and creates personal time for themselves. Limiting the number of hours they work during the low tourist seasons is far more difficult, however. Many find that fewer available clients means that they must spend longer hours in the bars.

The independents do not begin primping for the evening until much later than the dependents, around 9:00 or 10:00 p.m. Some get their hair done in salons during the day, help one another with their makeup, and share clothes. The independents own two sets of clothes: day clothes, such as the latest jeans and tops sold in the stores in Los Charamicos, and work clothes. Spandex tops and pants, miniskirts, midriffs, and low-cut minidresses are just some of the outfits they wear to the tourist bars. The stores in Los Charamicos, consequently, stock clothes a mother might buy for her school-age daughters along with these flashier outfits, some of which resemble costumes worn by dancers or other performers. Not every independent, however, cultivates this stereotypical sex worker "look," typically a fashion of makeup, high heels, and tight clothes. Instead, Nora, for example, preferred dresses and skirts that fall below the knee because she was uncomfortable wearing tighter and shorter outfits. She laughed, pointing to her sister Irene, with whom she rented a one-room house and who loved to get dressed up in "sexy clothes." But Nora liked to wear clothes that are "decent." "I don't wear things where my body is falling out of them like my sister." Nor did Nora wear as much makeup as her sister. "I take my time getting dressed, I try to make my makeup look really good, not too much." Nora believed that the way she dressed affected the way she was treated in the bars: "It's important to dress decently because men treat you the way you carry yourself."

Once dressed, the women share motoconchos to El Batey. Before it burned down, the Anchor was the liveliest tourist nightclub in El Batey. It drew all kinds of tourists—ranging from male-female couples out for a night on the town to single men looking for sex workers. Within a few blocks of where the Anchor was located are other night spots in El Batey: bars, restaurants, and several dance clubs. A casino is also just on the outskirts of Sosúa. But sex workers often find it difficult to enter these venues without clients as escorts, and unlike the Anchor (and other open-air bars and nightclubs) the indoor dance clubs usually have cover charges. Some women also hang out at the bars on the beach where the men drink, but again they risk arrest if they are not accompanied by a tourist.[21] Sex workers, however, criticize women who work the bars by day and

9. Clothing store in Los Charamicos

generally are very protective of their time away from clients during the day. For this reason, if a client wants to make another "date," sex workers try to make them for the next evening rather than for the beach—or some other activity—the next day.

Sosúa's sex workers have wildly diverging opinions on the best clients: young or old, Dominican or foreign, and then many hierarchies according to nationality. No single stereotype seems to dominate. Some women declared that German men, for example, pay the worst, while others were adamant that German men paid the best. I also have heard different women characterize different men (according to nationality) as the most unpredictable and, thus, potentially violent. While some sex workers complain, for example, that Dominican men treat women roughly, Ani (who has worked both with tourists and Dominicans) thinks sex with Dominican men is more gentle: "With a tourist, if he pays you 500 pesos (U.S.$42), he wants everything. You have to spend three hours with him; he has to smoke; you have to touch his chest." But she prefers a Dominican client because "he does his things fast." No one consistent portrait of women's experiences with clients emerged; once they leave the bars with men—whether Italian, German, or Austrian—they have varying experiences that are, largely, unforeseeable. They, of course, try to select clients who appear to present the least trouble—men who agree to pay their asking price and to use condoms and who seem sober and clean. They hope the men keep their promises, do not turn violent, do not take a long time, and do not ask for anal sex. Aside from these general concerns, however, each sex worker has her own view of the qualities she looks for in a client.

Conclusion

Women land in Sosúa's sex trade for many reasons, most notably because of their familial obligations as heads of household, combined with limited job skills and limited social networks. Their caretaker responsibilities for their children, and in some cases for other family members, greatly influence their decision to choose sex work. As the next chapter examines, these women rely on a variety of strategies to minimize the risks of sex work, while maximizing its payoffs. In the midst of countless dangers and uncertainties, they try to control their working conditions. And though the independents pursue multiple channels of income simultaneously—quite visibly at times as they crisscross the town on motoconcho taxis, between their boardinghouses, Codetel, and the tourist bars—the dependents also develop long-term saving strategies within the less glamorous and less visible confines of their bars.

5. ADVANCEMENT STRATEGIES IN SOSÚA'S SEX TRADE

After considering why women end up in Sosúa's sex trade in the previous two chapters, I now turn to how they make the most of their time while in Sosúa. Having argued up to this point that women who work with foreign clients have a greater degree of control over their working conditions than women who work with Dominican clients in Sosúa (as well as in other Dominican towns), I feel it is important to consider the role Sosúa-as-sexscape plays in determining this agency. In other words, what does it mean to sell sex on a "global stage"—in a transnational town with an international sex-tourist trade, in which Afro-Dominican local women sell sex to white foreign men—as opposed to selling sex on a "local stage" (in Dominican bars in the backstreets of Los Charamicos, far from tourist establishments, as well as in Dominican towns where local women sell to local men). Two features of Sosúa's sex trade with foreign men make sex-for-sale in this sexscape different from the sex trade in Dominican towns with Dominican men: the absence of pimps and the opportunities that accompany meeting foreign men. The context in which sex is exchanged for money—on a global or local stage—cuts to the heart of the politics of agency, which is why I suggest that in Sosúa's sex-tourist trade, women, in Anne McClintock's (1993a: 2) words, "exchange sexual service on *their* terms and on *their* conditions."

Even though women who work with foreign tourists in Sosúa's sexscape might have a greater degree of agency than women in most other sites, we must always keep in mind that they are working in a very dangerous business. Once the doors shut to clients' hotel rooms, or the women's boardinghouse rooms, anything can happen. The fear of violent clients forces Sosúa's sex workers to remain vigilant at all times. Although there are no pimps to collect the women's money, police bribes and fear of arrest nonetheless compromise women's control over their working conditions and their earnings. In this chapter, I relay techniques women—both the pendents and independents—have developed to limit men's po¹ over them as they struggle to keep control over their sexual encot ters. This chapter reads more as a story of ongoing challenges and erosion of women's agency than as a romanticized account ʋ women agents who control the levers of globalization. It does recount, nevertheless, these women's resourcefulness, collaboration on safety issues, long-term planning, and persistence. This chapter documents Sosúa's sex workers' attempts to control their conditions of work by avoiding, or at least reducing, the dangers of sex work while, at the same time, fashioning ways to get ahead financially. In the first section of this chapter I examine the ways women—nearly all first-time sex workers—learn how to protect themselves and, in the second section, how they learn to achieve their financial goals. In the final section I consider the central themes in their narratives as well as in their gossip about other sex workers.

Learning How To Protect Themselves

Every woman who arrives in Sosúa defines success differently and has different goals in sex work. While some women have long-term strategies, such as saving enough money to start a business back home, others have more modest goals and use sex work only to attain immediate aims. Knowing their personal boundaries—what they are willing and not willing to endure to earn money—helps Sosúa's sex workers achieve their goals with the least stress and disappointment possible. Even if they hate the work, women who alter their working conditions to better suit their comfort level are more likely to have better experiences. Working within their comfort level not only helps them feel as if they have some control in a job where they regularly encounter risks and uncertainty, but, in turn, it also increases their safety and, possibly, their financial success. When women first arrive in Sosúa, they are unfamiliar with all the ways bar owners, clients, coworkers, and the police try to take advantage of them. Since most have never worked in the sex trade before, they must learn, on the job, how to choose the best working environment and how to protect themselves. Only after they gain their bearings can women devise strategies for making sex work profitable. The following subsections detail how workers confront the different violent situations they encounter.

VIOLENT CLIENTS IN DOMINICAN BARS

Despite attempts on the part of these women to control their working conditions, violence is an inevitable risk they undertake in the sex trade. Women who work with Dominicans generally experience less violence with clients than women working with tourists. The atmosphere in Dominican bars can be more controlled and secure than in the tourist bars. The bar owner personally knows many of his customers, and new faces stand out among the regulars. Men who travel from other towns to buy sex do not go unnoticed. Consequently, if a client is violent with a sex worker, the bar owner, sex workers, and regular customers might recognize him the next time he tries to enter the bar. If the bar owner wants to avoid problems and to protect the women working for him, he can kick the offender out of the bar. Or at the very least, he will prohibit him from buying sex. If a bar owner does not notice that a previously violent customer has returned (or if he does not care), the women themselves often refuse to sell sex to him. However, as was the case with Carlos, the owner of the Seabreeze (from the previous chapter), some bar owners do not care what happens to the women working for them. Women are safer if at least some of the bar's sex workers have been living and working at the bar for a while. Seasoned sex workers can warn newcomers about the bar's customers. Without this kind of advice and experience, sex workers have no way to avoid clients with a history of abuse. Women working at bars where there is a high turnover of sex workers—such as the Seabreeze—are at a disadvantage.

VIOLENT CLIENTS IN TOURIST BARS

The tourist bars in Sosúa present more dangers: new faces appear in these bars after every international flight lands in Puerto Plata. Although foreign residents frequent these bars, the majority of customers in tourist bars are in Sosúa only for a few weeks of vacation at most. The women cannot know, just by looking at a man, how he will act once they leave the bar together. Nanci's experience with three German men who, as she described, "did not look dangerous" illustrates the gamble women take when they leave the bars with strangers. She was abused as soon as she left the safety of the bar. She left the Anchor with a German man and was soon joined by two of his friends in a rented van. The plan was to continue drinking at the men's hotel, but as soon as they got into the van, the men began beating Nanci. A few minutes down the road, at the treacherously steep entrance to Los Charamicos, they pushed Nanci out of the van while it was moving. She continued to roll down the steep hill, injuring her legs and face quite badly. To Nanci, these men had not appeared different from the countless other men with whom she had left bars before. Despite sex workers' attempts to screen clients, women cannot reliably predict clients' behavior. A man who is sober, clean, polite, and agreeable to a women's asking price as well as to protected sex can still be violent or HIV positive. Nor do women have any assurances that clients will keep their promises regarding payment or condom use.

As part of their strategy to keep safe and to work within their personal boundaries, some sex workers actively avoid the tourists' hotels and instead try to persuade their clients to go back to their boardinghouse rooms. Julia, who lived in a boardinghouse on the main street in Los Charamicos, was convinced that the houses create the safest conditions for sex work. When I first met Julia, she only had been in Sosúa for six months and had previously sold sex to tourists in Boca Chica. She was twenty-four years old, with two children, and she received no support from their fathers. She was a leader, very self-assured, and mature. Consequently, the other sex workers she lived with in the boardinghouse looked up to her. They imitated her elegant hair, makeup, and clothing style and followed her around in the tourist bars like an entourage. They watched—and learned—as she appeared to talk and dance with clients with ease. Strong willed and self-directed, Julia set firm boundaries in her work. She was clear about the conditions under which she would go with a client—and she even spoke for two of her coworkers who were in her room while we were talking: "We don't go with Dominicans; we go with ricos [that is, tourists]. If I can't communicate with them, I look for others. And I won't go with drunks." She had also set boundaries on how long she would stay in Sosúa. "I'm leaving here in a couple of months," she assured me.

While there, she had managed to start a savings account, even though most of her earnings were spent on her children. She did not like the work, however: "The work here is bad: you go to bed late, it's dangerous, and you are apart from your family." She was most afraid, she said, "of a condom breaking." She carefully tried to limit her risk by devising ways to enforce limits with clients: "If men don't want to use condoms, I kick them out. If a man does not want to pay, I threaten him with my fists until he gets scared." Even though she found that "sometimes men hit back," she insisted she was "never hurt" and claimed that living in a boardinghouse protected her because she could "start screaming until . . . friends or the owner [would] come running." Julia took pride in her ability to look out for herself, but not all women, unfortunately, have avoided serious injury, as Nanci's beating indicates. Nevertheless, Julia used the boardinghouse system and her network of friends to protect herself.

THE POLICE

Dangers for women working with tourists begin when they travel by motoconcho taxis from their boardinghouses and rented apartments in Los Charamicos to the tourist bars and nightclubs in El Batey. Sex workers such as Nanci and Julia—and their motoconcho drivers—gamble every time they travel to the bars. Unless word has gotten back to Los Charamicos through the network of motoconcho drivers that the police are arresting sex workers, they have no idea what is waiting for them on the other side of the beach. The police do not arrest every driver who delivers a sex worker; they arrest those who try to elude the police with women onboard. This brief three-minute motorcycle ride can end a woman's night out even before it begins. Simply hanging out in front of the bars, any time of day or night, can also result in arrest—or worse. Nora, a twenty-nine-year-old sex worker in Sosúa, told of a night the police beat her when she resisted arrest. At the Anchor all night until the early hours of the morning, she still had not found a client. At around 7:00 a.m. the police came by and tried to arrest her. She cried as she recounted what happened: "The life here is very dangerous— because of the police. They mistreat us. The police beat me the other morning because I did not want to go to jail. I was drinking and talking with some Spanish men. A policeman saw me and tried to take my hand and I wanted to get away, but I couldn't because he started to hit me. I wanted to get onto a motoconcho taxi, but I couldn't because he kept on hitting me. I started yelling." Nora spent two days in the Puerto Plata jail. A photographer for the then-new Dominican weekly newspaper *Vocero* happened to witness the event and captured the beating on film. The story ran in the newspaper and confirmed a widespread belief among sex workers and other residents that the police are virtually unrestrained.

Violence against sex workers has not been limited to beatings or rape by clients or to abusive run-ins with the police. In 1995 two brutal murders of sex workers, allegedly committed by German men, rocked the sex-work community as well as the Sosúa community at large. No one I spoke with could recall there ever having been a murder of a sex worker. Yet over the previous few years, Sosúa had become increasingly violent for sex workers at the hands of foreign clients. In nearly every issue of *Vocero*, there was a story of foreigners' involvement in criminal activities. The story on the front page of the 26 July 1995 issue, for example, was a typical one. The paper ran a police photo of three young German men and three young Haitian women lined up against a wall at the police station. The headline read: "Gang of Foreigners Caught." The story described how the police arrested this "gang" for changing counterfeit U.S. dollars. But it was the last line in the story that fueled fears and played up newly circulating images of German criminality: "In past months, various foreigners, mostly German, have been involved in a number of crimes such as rapes, robberies, the transport and possession of illegal firearms, and other crimes." Even though Sosúans had been reading and talking about the rise in crimes involving foreigners, the two murders deepened Sosúans' fear and—since neither murder was solved—feelings of powerlessness.

The Murder of a Teen Transvestite. The first murder involved a thirteen-year-old boy who dressed as a young female sex worker and hung out at the tourist bars in El Batey.[1] He was last seen leaving the Anchor with a German man and, reported some sex workers, a female sex worker. His body was found the next day on farmland owned by an original Jewish settler on the outskirts of Sosúa. His genitals had been mutilated and his body was wrapped in barbed wire. Within the rumor mill—extremely efficient both within the Dominican and foreign-resident communities—several versions of what happened circulated. The perception that foreigners in Sosúa are above the law dominated the accounts of the murder within the Dominican community. In these stories Dominicans recounted that the alleged murderer paid U.S.$20,000 to the Sosúa police to secure his release. This theme of buying freedom also suffused the rumors within the foreign-resident community, which had been increasingly alarmed by the type of foreigner that Sosúa was attracting—both as tourists and residents. As one U.S. citizen and small-business owner joked, "I would not be surprised if the guys who committed the Oklahoma bombing show up here in Sosúa" (this was before Timothy Mc-Veigh's arrest). She and others in the foreign-resident community felt their quiet town had become a haven for thugs fleeing the law in their home countries. To make matters worse, since neither community had confidence in the ability or honesty of Sosúa's police force, both Dominicans and foreign residents felt increasingly unsafe and besieged. Another version of the story circulated within the Dominican community; this one centered on the boy's enemies among female sex workers because his popularity with male customers made him fierce competition. Some sex workers believed that one or two female sex workers either participated in, or watched, the murder. Trading even further in myths, Dominicans in Los Chara-micos suggested that the boy knew he was going to die: they claimed that only weeks before his murder, he had been thrown out of a window by a client. Because of this previous brush with death, and because his family allegedly called him *el diablo* (the devil) on account of his transgressive lifestyle, people spoke of him as if he had been marked to die. In these stories, his family (who lived in Puerto Plata) was portrayed as awaiting their son's inevitable death.

The Murder of a Sex Worker. In another murder, a German man was implicated in the death of a female sex worker. Her body was found in a hotel located on the main street in El Batey. The *Vocero* reported that the alleged murderer had registered in the hotel with a German passport, reserving a room for one week and paying for three days in advance. The hotel's domestic staff explained to the police that the man had asked that his room not be cleaned. It appears that the man strangled the woman, stuffed her body under the bed in his room, and then fled the country before her body was discovered. In the same week, another violent incident involving a sex worker, this time a Haitian citizen, occurred. According to a *Vocero* reporter, the woman was found naked on a deserted road, her hands tied behind her back, and her breasts burned. A German man was taken into custody and charged with abusing the woman, who survived the ordeal. These violent events sent shock waves throughout the sex-work community. Sex worker after sex worker expressed disbelief, noting that nothing like this had ever happened before. Women who were veterans at working in the tourist bars were horrified. Many told me, "Sosúa used to be safe for sex workers, but now it is different than before." A number of women decided that they were going to leave Sosúa earlier than planned; it was getting too dangerous. Others focused their fears and anger on German men. "We are all very afraid," explained Nora, who had endured her own violent encounter with local police. "Some women are saying that they do not want anything to do with the Germans. Even though they pay more money than the Spanish, I'm not going to look for my death also. I'm going to make money so I can leave here." Just like the foreign and Dominican residents of Sosúa who were nostalgic for a lost, more idyllic pretourism Sosúa, Nora missed the sex trade of her early years (in the mid and late 1980s)—before Sosúa had become an international sex destination. "It used to be better than now," she said. "The tourists gave you more money than now. And there weren't as many problems. There were not as many criminals as now. Now there's a lot of drugs, violence, and even murder." As frightening as these three violent events were, there was no noticeable exodus of sex workers or even a temporary lull in their nightly appearance at the tourist bars. Only hours after we spoke, Nora was back in the bars, and she even left with a German client. Without savings, and with both of her parents deceased, she felt she could not afford to leave the sex trade. While other women were eager to leave Sosúa and its sex trade, after thirteen years there, Nora had made Sosúa her home. She had learned to coexist with Sosúa's increasing dangers.

Achieving Financial Goals:
Transnational versus Local Relationships

Although I have argued that Sosúa's transnational connections through marriage to foreign tourists and migration off the island distinguish working in Sosúa's sexscape from other Dominican towns, it is also possible for sex workers (both independents and dependents) to make financial gains in Sosúa without establishing transnational connections. The reverse is also true: not all women (the independents only) who establish transnational connections necessarily leave Sosúa with any signs of greater financial security. In fact, some dependents make more long-term gains (such as starting a small business or building a house in their home communities) than the independents. Women in both groups—dependents and independents—have had widely varying financial success in the sex trade. While some have savings accounts or build houses with their earnings, others do not have enough money to pay the motorcycle taxi fare from their boardinghouses in Los Charamicos to the tourist bars in El Batey. Some sex workers save, despite the obstacles, while others just get by day to day. As women's stories reveal, financial success in sex work depends more on whether sex workers save money, not with whom they earn it. Ties closer to home with amigos (Dominican men who are quasi-boyfriends, quasi–regular clients) often turn out to be more durable than those resting on relationships with foreign men. We have seen how Elena's long-term security proved illusory when she depended solely on Jürgen. Moreover, amigos not only provide extra money but are also potential husbands.

RITA AND CARMEN:
FINANCIAL GOALS WITHIN REACH

Despite an array of forces beyond their control, sex workers attempt to shape their experiences in Sosúa. Rita's and Carmen's stories, for example, demonstrate how women use Sosúa's sex trade to meet clearly defined financial goals: for Rita, paying hospital bills and for Carmen, building a house. Both of these women set reasonable, attainable goals in the sex trade, and, unlike Nora, who stayed in Sosúa indefinitely with no plans to leave, their earning strategies had strict deadlines.

Rita: Saving for Her Daughter's Surgery. Rita arrived in Sosúa already knowing what she would do—and not do—to earn money in sex work. Above all, she told herself, she would leave Sosúa as soon as she could pay for her daughter's operation. She stuck to this promise. But she also set other personal boundaries that limited more than just the length of her stay in Sosúa. She refused to work with clients who, she explained, were "dirty, drunk, rude" or who "refused to use condoms, or to pay my price." Her maturity (she was in her late twenties) and confident demeanor (she is exceptionally beautiful, bright, charming, and articulate) helped her communicate with foreign clients, a stumbling block for many of the younger, less confident women. If, after spending hours at the Anchor, she still had not met a client who passed her standards, she would leave alone and get a good night's sleep. Most nights, in fact, Rita did not rush to leave with just any man.

Unlike her coworkers, Rita had a "husband" in her life, but his job as a taxi driver in Santo Domingo did not pay enough to cover their medical bills.[2] Rita told her husband and children that she was working as a bartender in a resort. She claims that her husband believed her, especially since prior to traveling to Sosúa she had been a bartender in Santo Domingo. While she was away, her mother took care of their children. Because her husband covered their children's daily living expenses, Rita was able to save all of her earnings in the sex trade (other than her boardinghouse rent and food). His contributions to the household help explain Rita's ability to save considerable sums quickly. In addition, Rita worked in Sosúa from the end of November through January, the high tourist season. It is possible that she might have had a more difficult time meeting clients on a consistent basis—and thus saving as much money as she did—during the low tourist season.

Despite her financial success in Sosúa, Rita hated her time in sex work: "This job is shit. It's the worst job you could have. There are diseases, rape, and then the police." Nevertheless, she stayed in Sosúa until she met her monetary goal, convinced no other legal job would pay as much money in a short period of time. Some clients helped her, such as a Swiss man who gave her an extra 700 pesos (U.S.$58) on top of the 500 peso (U.S.$42) fee when she told him she was in Sosúa to make money for her daughter. She and her husband did not own a house but had been living in a friend's house, so she also was trying to save enough to buy a house. Sticking to her plan, Rita left Sosúa after a few months there. It is possible she will return periodically to Sosúa, as other women have, when she and her family need money to solve short-term crises. As much as sex workers such as Rita hate the work, leaving Sosúa is not easy, especially if they have not achieved even their short-term goals. Nearly every woman I met told me that she would be gone in a couple of weeks or months, but many were still there months later. Rita could leave not only because she had achieved her financial objective but also because she had a job as a bartender waiting for her at home in Santo Domingo. In contrast, most sex workers have no such post-Sosúa job prospects.

Carmen: Saving for a House. Like Rita, Carmen managed to save more money than most sex workers in Sosúa. With her earnings she built a house in Santo Domingo, where she planned to move and to support herself by waitressing or cooking in a small restaurant. Impressively, over four years in sex work Carmen saved 25,000 pesos (U.S.$2,083), even though she primarily had been working with Dominican clients. When Carmen first came to Sosúa, she worked in a Dominican bar, but she switched to working with foreign clients after the bar closed (and she stayed living at the bar, paying rent, similar to an arrangement with a boardinghouse). An astute money manager, she diligently saved money every week, no matter how little she earned. She was the only sex worker I interviewed who could recount, off the top of her head, her weekly and monthly household expenses—not only her living expenses but those of her children living with her mother. Just as Rita would not leave the bar with men she thought unacceptable, Carmen, too, was emphatic about only working under conditions she was comfortable with. Getting arrested was Carmen's worst fear, and she avoided it at all costs. When she heard the police were arresting women for congregating outside the tourist bars in El Batey (as women often did to talk, smoke, or greet customers), she stayed in Los Charamicos.[3] Rather than sacrifice all earnings during these periods of heightened police activity, however, Carmen put alternate earning plans in place. She would take a bus to a small town about thirty miles away to work in a bar that catered to Dominican clients. She went to such efforts not only out of fear but also for practical financial reasons: though she only made 150 pesos (U.S.$12.50) with a client there, she believed it to be better than giving her money to the police. She did not like this bar in the countryside, however, and complained that the men there were campesinos: "They are dirty and smell. The man I went with last night did not even know how to do it—so it really hurt. He was so stupid. But it was over in minutes. He also tried to kiss me—I really hate that, when they want to get all close and hug you, especially when they have bad breathe like this one did. He stunk of rum."

Despite Carmen's self-reliance, an amigo, Jorge, figured prominently in her savings strategy. Carmen saw her relationship with Jorge differently than he did. He claimed to love her and called her his girlfriend. She, on the other hand, had feelings for him, but was "in love" with another man, a Dominican with whom she had had an affair (before she came to Sosúa). He ended their affair and went back with his wife. Carmen thought about him all the time, however, so much so that her "heart hurt." She suspected that this unrequited love had extinguished any sense of sexual pleasure with other men. "I used to enjoy sex with Jorge, and even with some clients, but no more. I feel nothing."

Jorge is the nephew of the owner of the boardinghouse where she lived, and he visited her once a week from Santiago, where he lived with his mother, about two hours from Sosúa. Carmen described Jorge as "very young"—she scrunched up her nose in disapproval of this point because he was twenty-one, while she was in her early thirties. Since Jorge only had one daughter and she and her mother were fuera, in New York, Jorge spent much of his income from a job at a zona franca on Carmen. With no rent to pay and no dependents (on the island), Jorge was a reliable source of financial support—certainly more than a Belgian client who had sent her a few money wires and then dropped out of communication (to whom she wrote the love letter transcribed in chapter 3). Even though Jorge did not "make a lot of money," Carmen beamed when describing that he had bought her furniture for her house in Santo Domingo. Her relationship with Jorge was an economic safety net. But as her travels to nearby bars indicate, Carmen did not rely solely on his money. Rather, she diversified her "risk" in the sex trade by working with both foreign and Dominican men. She built her house with many small sums from different sources saved over time: money and gifts from Jorge, money wires from the Belgian client, earnings with Dominican clients, and earnings with foreign clients.

After finishing the foundation to her house, Carmen announced that she was staying in Sosúa until the whole house was completed, "with windows, doors, and furniture—everything." Having one's own house is one way the poor secure against times of economic crises. When I asked Carmen what she would do if she ever won the lottery, her dream centered on making modest improvements to her house: "I would do many things. I would make my house two floors. And I would have a colmado to take care of my kids."[4] She also dreamt of meeting an hombre serio—much like Jorge, "but older." "My dream is to live in my house with my kids and with a man that helps me. With un hombre de la casa, no de la calle [a man of the house, not of the street—meaning a reliable man, not one that is always out drinking, going with sex workers, or having affairs]."

Rather than fantasizing about moving to Europe and an idealized life she might have there, Carmen's dreams were within reach. Expanding her house was certainly more attainable than marrying a rich European. Ironically, as one of a minority of sex workers who focused on building local ties, Carmen met and married an Austrian man in Sosúa a couple of years later, and they are now living in Europe together.

Guarding her money from men in her life was a key component of Carmen's savings strategy. Believing that men, including foreign men, "take care of themselves first," she had learned not to expect anything from them but instead to depend only on herself. She was careful not to reveal how much money she had to any men in her life (Dominican or foreign) and laughed at sex workers who were "foolish" enough to let men siphon—and even live off—their girl-friends' earnings and money wires. She never told Jorge about her money wires from the Belgian client. She feared that if she told him, she risked leaving Sosúa with nothing, like so many of her friends. "These women give their money to their men." she said, throwing up her arms. "Their boyfriends wait at home and drink while the women work. If I'm in the street with all the risks of disease and the police, I'm keeping the money or giving it to my kids. I'm not giving it to a man, no way." She also acknowledged, however, that it is not always easy for women to keep their money out of reach from their boyfriends: "Part of the problem is if women do not give their money to their men, they beat the women." Carmen not only kept her financial status a secret from her Jorge, but she also did not tell her Belgian client about her partially constructed house in Santo Domingo. "I did not tell him I am building a house. I do not have money, and it would seem like I do." She was cautious with foreign men, aware that she could not count on them for long. She was proven right when she stopped receiving any faxes or money wires from her Belgian client (years before she eventually married the Austrian man). She mocked her coworkers, whom she believed were naive to fall for tourists' promises, mimicking them by using a high-pitched ultrafeminized voice: "I'm going to meet a tourist, and he is going to take care of me."

Yet even though women like Carmen challenge dominant gender ideologies by crafting earning and savings strategies that rely on their hard work, they often reproduce traditional understandings of gender roles when they seek to marry as a way to solve financial burdens that stem from being single mothers. In sex workers' narratives, men are both the cause of—and can be the cure for—the women's problems. Like other sex workers in Sosúa, Carmen blamed men's financial irresponsibility and sexual infidelity for leading her to the sex trade, and yet she also turned to men and to marriage as possible routes out of sex work and financial distress.[5] Carmen had migrated to Sosúa after her Dominican husband abandoned her and their children. She might not count on men to fulfill their promises—or even their familial financial responsibilities—but she nonetheless makes the best of whatever they offer her, at least for as long as it lasts. Poor Dominican women, as Carmen's story suggests, move between periods of fierce financial independence, when there are no men or family members to help, and periods of dependence, when they turn to men—such as Jorge—or family members (if parents are alive) for financial contributions to the household.

MULTIPLE EARNING STRATEGIES AND FEMALE-BASED SOCIAL NETWORKS

In this subsection I closely examine the strategies that savvy, experienced sex workers such as Carmen enact both to solve crises and to move closer to their financial goals. The theme of social networks runs through the various strategies. While some sex workers seek out Dominican amigos to secure a steady source of income and gifts close to home, others strategically choose sex work with foreign tourists to transnationalize their economic support networks. Moreover, once in Sosúa, these women create female-based social networks to replace their family and kin networks back in their home communities.

Help from Dominican Men. Developing ties with Dominican men can create a more durable safety net than ties with foreign men. These amigos, such as Jorge, can help solve immediate problems by supplementing unpredictable income in sex work. Amigos also can turn into husbands. I met a number of sex workers who have "married" (in consensual unions) Dominican clients, including two of Elena's older sisters who left sex work and now live in Sosúa with their children and Dominican husbands (not the children's fathers). Ani, a thirty-four-year-old sex worker who has had a five-year career in and out of sex work (first in Curaçao, followed by Santo Domingo, Boca

Chica, and finally Sosúa), explained that since she does not always have clients, amigos have helped her make ends meet: "You need amigos. If you have a problem, like something breaks in your house, or your child is sick and you need money for the doctor or medicine, they can help." These amigos share similarities with the "sugar daddies" Mark Hunter writes about as pushing the discussion "beyond prostitution" to one about "transactional sex" (2002: 100). As school girls and older women in South Africa seek men to help either with subsistence or to increase their consumption possibilities, Hunter analyzes links between gifts, sex, and the spread of HIV.

At any given time, Ani receives money from several Dominican men with whom she has ongoing sexual relationships, which has allowed her to improve her standard of living. When I met her, she had stopped working in the sex trade and was working part time in the office of a taxi company. She paid a large part of her household expenses, however, with money her Dominican amigos gave her. She was living much more comfortably than any of her neighbors. She rented an apartment in a concrete house in which she had a refrigerator and a living-room furniture set. She also had accomplished another goal of many sex workers: bringing her two youngest daughters—who had been living with their paternal grandparents—to live with her. It is unlikely Ani would be living in this apartment without one particular amigo's help. Although she called him her esposo, he was legally married to another Dominican woman, indicating that he was probably from a higher social class than Ani. He spent as much time as he could with her and paid for most of her rent and other expenses. He also helped her get her job as a taxi dispatcher, which she explained she would not have been offered without his help. Her social networks did not extend far enough to find jobs other than waitressing, cleaning houses, or working in the zonas francas. She also would not have been able to pay her bills on her part-time salary at the taxi company without his financial help. She was careful to set aside some of the money he gave her, along with money two other Dominican amigos also gave her on occasion, saving what she could in a bank account. She knew that the money her main amigo gave her would never be enough to start her own business, and she recognized that since he was not the father of her children, they were not his first responsibility. It was up to her, she knew, to secure their future, especially because she could not be certain how long he would remain in their lives. She also worried that not only was her age pushing her out of sex work but also that soon she would be too old to be his—or any other man's—"mistress."

In short, there is no easy fix for these poor mothers. There is no guarantee that one relationship or another will pay off in the long term. Although Ani raised her family's standard of living through an economic support network of Dominican men, her family's long-term financial forecast ultimately depended on her capacity to earn a livable wage without men's help. Also as women age, the "help" of amigos is less and less likely. Consequently, Ani decided to get a visa to go to another Caribbean island where a friend's husband's brother owned a restaurant and nightclub. She was preparing to move there for ten to twelve months to work in the sex trade, one last time, to save enough money to start her own small café. Because of her age, she knew that this probably would be her last opportunity to make a lot of money in sex work. While waiting for her visa, however, she met a Spanish tourist. They spent his vacation together, and she later moved to Spain to live with him. Ani's life history—much like Carmen's and her unforeseen move to Austria—is full of sudden changes of fortune such as this quick turn of events. They, like many poor women, must be prepared to seize any available opportunity, no matter how unexpected, inconvenient, or imperfect, to try to pull their families out of poverty. Ani explained that she did not "love" her Spanish boyfriend but saw her romantic needs as secondary to her family's financial needs. She simply could not let the opportunity to live fuera in Spain slip by.

Help from Foreign Men. Whereas relationships with Dominican men can yield small but steady payments, building ties with foreign men can translate into substantial income. For example, over the years, Ani's various Dominican amigos each gave her on average 300–500 pesos (U.S.$25–42) a month to help her get by. But when foreign men wire money to women in Sosúa, it is usually at least U.S.$100 at a time. Although the money wires can be relatively generous, they also can be less reliable than the smaller flows of money local Dominican men offer. A woman might receive faxes and money wires every two weeks from a client in Europe and then not hear from him for three months. He might disappear from her life, or he might send a fax saying he is on his way to the Dominican Republic the next week to spend his vacation with her.

Luisa had transnational connections other sex workers envied, but her transnational ties were short lived. She, quite remarkably, received U.S.$500 every two weeks over a six-month period from a German client who had wanted her to leave sex work to start her own clothing store. She told him she had stopped working the tourist bars and that she used the money he was sending her to buy clothes for the store. Months later, when he found out that she was still working in the sex trade, had not opened a store, and was living with a Dominican boyfriend, he stopped wiring money. The way he found out testifies to the increasing efficiency of the transnational networks linking Sosúa and Germany, as well as the critical role of fax machines in the building and maintenance of these social networks. Carla, another sex worker and a friend of Luisa's, also had an ongoing fax and money wire relationship with a German man, who knew Luisa's German boyfriend. This is not uncommon; the men in the tourist bars often are on vacation with other male friends from Europe and go out to the sex bars together. Luisa believes Carla faxed her (Carla's) boyfriend in Germany, who then told Luisa's boyfriend, essentially "blowing the whistle" on Luisa's infidelity and her phantom clothing store. After this revelation, the money wires dried up, and Luisa's German boyfriend stopped returning to Sosúa to visit Luisa.

At this juncture, Luisa's expenses soon outpaced her dwindling resources. She had not saved any money, and she was renting a two-bedroom apartment, twice the size and double the rent of her friends' apartments. Without the money wires she could not make the rent, because she also sent money home to her mother in Santo Domingo, who cared for her twelve-year-old son (who, tragically, later died in Hurricane Georges in 1998, when his grandmother's house collapsed). In addition, she supported her Dominican boyfriend, who lived with her and did not have a steady job. Other sex workers called him a chulo living off of Luisa's earnings and money wires, and they gossiped that Luisa was foolish for bankrolling him, especially because he was not the father of her son. With the money wires ended, Luisa was forced to hock some of her necklaces and rings in a pawn shop, some of which she had bought with the wired money.

Women's luck can change overnight. Luisa was incredibly lucky to meet this German client at the Anchor; most of the women working there night after night never receive a single money wire transfer. Those who do generally receive significantly smaller sums than Luisa and on a much more infrequent basis. Sex workers cannot bank on tourists' promises that they will stay in touch by fax, send money wires, and return on future vacations. Nor can they be sure that money wires will continue once they begin. In most cases a woman's luck runs out, and she never hears from the man again. Luisa knew the end would eventually come, but she did not know when; nor could she be certain that she would ever find another tourist to replace him. Women such as Luisa who do not save money from their earnings in the sex trade, or from money wires from foreign clients, leave Sosúa just as poor as when they first arrived. Unlike Rita, who systematically saved her sex-work earnings, and Carmen and Ani, who ploddingly saved both earnings from the sex trade and the money their Dominican amigos gave them, Luisa did not plan for the day when her German liaison might end his relationship with her.

Social Networks: Reducing the Effects of Poverty, Dangers, and Stress. Experiencing financial roller coasters—sometimes one day to the next—poor Dominican sex workers turn to one another for help. They use female-based social networks to fill in the extensive gaps in the Dominican governments' spending on social programs. The help women give one another, moreover, can be as predictable and steady as foreign men's support can be unpredictable and inconsistent. Women I met in Sosúa (sex workers and nonsex workers) help one another find jobs, share child care, and loan one another small amounts of cash in times of crises such as for children's medical emergencies. This sharing of resources, both material and otherwise, with extended family and kin helps single mothers keep a household running. Social networks of female family members, neighbors, and friends are one way poor women can "patchwork" together their families' survival (Kibria 1993). The construction and maintenance of these local social networks, like the building of transnational ties, highlight how poor women in Sosúa actively attempt to counter poverty. Without them, sex workers expose themselves not only to financial insecurity but also to loneliness and danger. However, these networks and relationships are not created overnight, and their maintenance requires a great deal of work. As Mercedes González de la Rocha writes, "Poverty does not turn a neighbor into a baby-sitter, nor a mother-in-law into a gift-maker.

Relationships and their meaning and nature cannot be taken for granted as natural elements. They are instrumented, built, and cultivated" (1994: 13). For example, Elena's three older sisters alternate taking care of one another's children as well as their neighbors' children. Other single mothers in town help out neighbors by cleaning each other's houses or doing laundry, in exchange for receiving help with the same household tasks. Also, it seems that friends never stop by empty handed. Whether carrying a ripe mango or cold bottles of Coke, these women constantly and actively maintain their social networks.[6]

For sex workers who live in boardinghouses, friendships not only offer companionship but also protection. When friends share a motorcycle taxi from Los Charamicos to the tourist bars in El Batey, it not only reduces the cost, but it allows them to keep track of one another. Elena was lucky that she was with her friend Andrea, for example, when she was arrested during the episode I recount in the Introduction. Otherwise, Elena's family would not have known what had happened to her. Once in the bars and nightclubs, friends keep an eye out for one another and let one another know whom to stay away from. They point out which men are very drunk, known to be violent (in the case of men who have been reappearing night after night during their vacation, or are return sex tourists), refuse to use condoms, or want only to pay cut-rate prices. They also notice with whom their friends leave, sometimes telling one another where they are going. Or, if they take clients back to their boardinghouse rooms, sex workers remain vigilant for any unusual noises behind their friends' doors.[7] If a woman goes to a tourist's room and does not return home by the next afternoon, her friends inquire about her at the cafés and the other boardinghouses to try to find out if anyone has seen her.

Since sex workers (independents) frequently switch boardinghouses or move into apartments, and then possibly back again to a boardinghouse, over time they get to know a wide circle of sex workers. Critical information passes through this network: which returning sex tourists are verbally or physically abusive, whom the police arrested the night before, and which sex workers might be involved in selling or using drugs, or in petty thievery from clients. This information network can quickly degenerate from a source of helpful, factual information (who was arrested, where, and when), to a fount of speculative gossip (how much a woman charges, whether or not she uses condoms or steals men's wallets, and so on). Nevertheless, these networks help women physically and emotionally to survive sex work. For some migrants, the emotional strain of living apart from one's family, as well as from one's social and economic support networks back home, can have serious psychological and social effects.[8] Moving to Sosúa and participating in sex work can be a particularly "stressing" event. Being separated from their children greatly stresses and saddens many of the women, and living in constant fear—of the police, clients' violence, and AIDS—creates even more stress. By building new social networks, mainly of sex workers, these women help one another cope with living and working in Sosúa. Although there are countless instances of sex workers helping one another—with bail money or by sharing housework, food, and clothes—competition and the rumors it spawns are also a prominent part of the sex workers' community. I examine such rumors in the next section on gossip.

Sex Workers' Gossip

If networks among sex workers in Sosúa can provide material resources and friendships, networks also provide social pressure about norms and behavior, norms that are revealed in sex workers' descriptions of their own lives and activities and their gossip about others. Examination of the themes in sex workers' self-descriptions and gossip about one another unveils a kind of "code of behavior" or "script" sex workers learn and usually adopt as their own within days of arriving in Sosúa. Newcomers quickly catch on to the major themes their coworkers expect them to stress: motherhood and the suffering and sacrifice it demands, safe sex, and frustration with Dominican men's infidelity. This script sustains their idealized construct of themselves as self-sacrificing mothers who are not *really* sex workers. By setting up a kind of code of behavior, sex workers pit themselves against other sex workers. In so doing, they attempt to preserve their self-esteem in the face of constant public scrutiny and stigma as they also try to avoid being the object of gossip themselves. In this section, I examine the central images in sex workers' self-descriptions and in their gossip about one another. I continue this discussion in the next chapter, in a section "Capitalizing on Stereotypes," and consider how they incorporate foreign men's stereotypes about them in their descriptions of themselves.

Although my field notes are bursting with sex workers' gossip about one another, the material—necessarily part fact, part fiction, and part tall tale—is ethnographically more problematic. Here, I use sex workers' gossip as a guide to their perceptions of both their social obligations to their families and their daily experiences in sex work. Gossip and slander are rich soil for anthropologists: they challenge us to understand why informants choose to tell or make up certain stories about themselves or others and what these stories reveal about the values and beliefs of those who tell them. Since "different narrative strategies may be authorized at specific moments in history by complex negotiations of community, identity, and accountability," the politics of representation renders the anthropologist's task all the more difficult (Visweswaran 1994: 15). At different times, sex workers spin tall tales about other women and get caught in contradictions about their own lives. In order to unravel the contradictions, omissions, and exaggerations in sex workers' stories, it is useful to explore the images that they seize upon and to question why these particular images are more acceptable than others to them.

The central image sex workers overwhelmingly use in their self-desciptions and in gossip is that of the "good mother." Within a matrix of maternal responsibility and morality, sex workers depict themselves as, above all, selfless, responsible, and caring mothers. By using the themes of family obligation and sacrifice, sex workers liken themselves and their concerns to those of other poor mothers in Sosúa. "We poor women suffer a lot" is a phrase Dominican women in Los Charamicos frequently employ in daily conversation. In fact some women adamantly do not identify themselves as sex workers. One woman, Helena, explained: "In my head I don't see myself as a prostitute." In sex workers' self-descriptions prostitutas or putas are set in opposition to good mothers. These dichotomies (selfless mothers as Madonnas and selfish mothers as putas) engage notions of honor and shame that have been extensively analyzed in studies on the Mediterranean (Davis 1977; Herzfeld 1985) and on Latin America (Melhuus and Stolen 1996). These writings explore how a woman's (and, by extension, her family's) reputation rests on her chastity, whereas a man's status is derived from his success in business and with women. In his book on manhood, for example, David

Gilmore examines what makes a man "good at being a man" (Gilmore 1990). Similarly, Dominican sex workers rely on dominant gender ideologies—especially about motherhood—to determine not only what makes a woman good at being a woman but also what makes a sex worker good at not really being a sex worker.

Such insistence that they are not like "other" sex workers pervades Sosúan sex workers' self-descriptions. Simultaneously their gossip about other women mirrors the criticism and rumors that Sosúan residents circulate about them. Sex workers often describe "other" sex workers as dangerous (transmitters of AIDS and petty thieves that prey on unsuspecting, or drunk, tourists), untrustworthy (liars about their HIV status), and manipulative (opportunists when it comes to men and money). Ani, for example, singles out sex workers who steal from tourists, and she imagines that their plunder has made them wealthy and enables them to live well in "two-story houses surrounded by lots of land." Although sex workers help and support their coworkers, they also actively castigate one another by appropriating the dominant discourse of women's sexuality as dangerous and uncontrollable. (However, as I explore in chapter 6, for Sosúa's sex workers being a "good mother" is not incompatible with having a sexualized identity). The sex workers' criticisms of one another contrasts with Nici Nelson's findings among female beer brewers (and part-time sex workers) in Kenya, who, marginalized by the larger society, "feel that they must stand together or fall separately" (Nelson 1978: 88). Nelson contends that their stigma as "bad women," "helps to heighten a sense of sisterhood, mutual responsibility, and solidarity" (1978: 89). Although Dominican sex workers share the sentiments that, in Nelson's words, "women must help each other" (Nelson 1978), divisive discourse allows them to position themselves as different from—in a way, superior to—their coworkers.

Rita (who paid for her daughter's operation with income from her sex trade) carefully distanced herself, for example, from other sex workers by elaborating on what characterized other women as putas while emphasizing that she was "not of the street." She explained, "I'm different from other prostitutes. I'm not used to this life. I don't like the Anchor, and I am embarrassed with tourists. I don't approach them—that's shameful. I sit and wait and order a beer myself. And I'm afraid of AIDS so I always use condoms unlike other women." She continued, "I stay with one man a night, while some women go with four or five"[9] and remarked that she was a discriminating seller and unwilling to have sex for money with anyone willing to pay. "I make sure they are clean—their hair and teeth." She also refused to go out with clients during the day; that was *her* time. Rita saw herself as worlds apart from the other, more aggressive women in the tourist bars, so much so that she did not consider herself a *prostituta* at all. Rather, she was a *señora,* a lady, and took a nonaggressive approach with tourists, "My style is different—I always dress like a *señora.* I sit and wait to be invited for a drink. I would rather go home alone than throw myself at a man like some of the other girls." Her "style" meant she did not "make as much as some of the other women," who were more confrontational in their attempts to get clients. Rita's approach reflected not only her desire to distinguish herself from "real" *prostitutas* but also her own comfort level which, as I discussed earlier in the chapter, is inextricably linked to safety. By gossiping about "other" sex workers as behaving in a way they claim they do not, "good mothers" such as Rita set themselves apart from "other" women—the "real" *prostitutas.*

MULTIPLE SCRIPTS

The women I spoke with not only adhere to accepted themes but also diverge from them. Beyond the scripted, obligatory themes, sex workers' narratives display a diversity of motivations, experiences, and values. They are not, as Abu-Lughod describes, automatons "programmed according to 'cultural' rules or acting out social roles," but "people going through life wondering what they should do, making mistakes, being opinionated, vacillating, trying to make themselves look good, enduring tragic personal losses, enjoying others, and finding moments of laughter" (Abu-Lughod 1993: 27). As they struggle to make themselves appear in the best possible light, the sex workers I interviewed presented deeply ambivalent—and at times contradictory—accounts of their experiences in Sosúa. This ambivalence reflects the trade-off between the potential material rewards of sex work and the risk-filled work itself, along with its rejection within Dominican society. Although most sex workers do not like the work, it affords them much leisure time, frees them from daily household responsibilities, and, depending on how much of their earnings they decide to send home, provides them with disposable income—often for the first time in their lives.[10] They entertain themselves by eating out in restaurants, buying clothes, and consuming items that either were not available back home (especially if home is very rural), or were unaffordable.[11] Sosúan migrants soon find, however, that the more they engage in these new leisure activities and consumption opportunities, the less likely they are to return home with any economic security. As she worked to build and to furnish her house, Carmen, for example, never bought new clothes or jewelry for herself. In turn, she derided coworkers who allowed themselves these indulgences and gossiped that they were spoiled, selfish, and irresponsible mothers.

Sosúa's sex workers also are careful in their conversations with one another and other residents in Los Charamicos not to dwell on the material rewards of sex work. To do so would be tantamount to an admission that they spend their earnings on nonessential items for themselves rather than remit them to their children back home. Sex workers' stories often alternate between complaints about the suffering they endure in sex work, and praise for the money it procures. In the same breath they describe how much they hate the work and extol its high earnings and flexible hours. Francisca's opinion of sex work captures the contradictions running through sex workers' narratives: "On one side tourism is good, on the other not. Tourists don't care what we are, who we are, if we are sick or whatever. You know when they drink they care about nothing. Tourists come here for vacation with putas. This makes me ashamed. But I make money in this work for my children that I can't make in other jobs. And I work fewer hours. So in this way tourism is good for our country; without it we would have no work." Despite their best efforts to stick to the accepted scripts of motherhood and frugality, they diverge by drawing on multiple—and contradictory—scripts simultaneously. In so doing they reveal themselves as real women, not idealized visions of martyred mothers.

If, however, sex workers deviate too flagrantly from the accepted roles, they bring on harsh criticism and possible isolation. Ana did just that. Her boasts of enjoying sex work and pursuing it for personal fulfillment rather than for family obligations made her the object of her coworkers' gossip. Rather than dwell on the accepted tropes of motherhood and suffering, she bragged instead about how she lived it up on what she earned: "I like to buy new clothes when the vendors come around. I always have snacks and nice meals." She showed me her latest clothing purchases and also bragged about her gambling trips to Santo Domingo: "Once a month I go to the big casinos because I love them." Further diverging from the role of the good mother, Ana did not send money to her children—which helps explain why she had far more disposable income than most sex workers—and did not express any desire to be reunited with them. In fact her children lived permanently with Ana's mother, and she and her mother did not speak. Ana clearly broke with several expected roles of Dominican women: she rejected motherhood and its obligations; she did not get along with her mother; and she bragged of living well rather than underscoring the hardships of her life. Not surprisingly, Ana was not well respected or liked by the women with whom she worked and lived. Her open gloating of her financial success only added to her coworkers' resentment, while they were disdainful, perplexed, and saddened by her neglect of her children. She in fact had so alienated her coworkers that after a disagreement, her roommate dumped water on her while she was sleeping.

Perhaps more egregious than openly spending money on oneself is spending it on men. "Luisa is crazy," her friends gossiped; "She spends all her money on her *chulo* [pimp] who does not even work." Women such as Luisa, whose story of her large money wires and phantom clothing store is told earlier in this chapter, who receive money from men overseas are enviable, but how they spend that income determines their reputation. Even though many depend on money from regular clients, and look forward to marrying so that their husbands can take care of them financially, sex workers nevertheless are proud of their ability to earn money to raise their children without the help of their children's fathers. Moreover, women certainly did not want to be seen as irresponsible as the men who left them. "At thirty-two years old," complained Carmen, "Luisa should have known to live less extravagantly and to save money." Especially for someone like Carmen, who cautiously "guarded" her earnings from the men in her life, Luisa's spending on her boyfriend was synonymous with wasted income. Luisa's stigmatization by other sex workers contrasts sharply with the uncritical admiration her Dominican boyfriend enjoyed among his friends for sponging off of her. This group, composed of men who, like him, had migrated to Sosúa to work in the tourist trade, seemed to affirm his machismo the less he appeared to work and the more he appeared to live off of Luisa. An inversion of gender roles in Sosúa's tourist economy allows men like Luisa's Dominican boyfriend to openly—even flamboyantly—rely on their girlfriends' participation in the sex trade. While Sosúa's migrant men brag to one another about how little work they do and how comfortably they live (courtesy of their girlfriends' earnings), Sosúa's migrant women working in the sex trade scold one another for working too little and living too comfortably. As they temper their displays of monetary gains so as to not compromise their reputations as mothers sacrificing for their children, men such as Luisa's boyfriend, openly enjoy freedom from gender ideologies that make demands on them as the main breadwinners.

GOSSIP AND COMPETITION

Gossip can bring people together as well as pull them apart. When it takes the form of what Patricia Meyer Spacks calls "serious" gossip "in private, at leisure, in a context of trust, usually among no more than two or three people," it functions as a sign of "intimacy" and it "provides a resource for the subordinated . . . a crucial means of self-expression, a crucial form of solidarity" (Spacks 1985: 5). Although "intimate" discussions are essential to the friendships sex workers forge in the bars and boarding houses, the distinctions that sex workers draw among themselves divide them. Spacks's description of two kinds and purposes of gossip helps bring gossip's function within the community of sex workers into focus: "At one extreme, gossip," she writes, "manifests itself as distilled malice. It plays with reputations, circulating truths and half-truths and falsehoods about the activities, sometimes about the motives and feelings of others. Often it serves serious (possibly unconscious) purposes for the gossipers, whose manipulations of reputation can further political or social ambitions by damaging competitors or enemies, gratify envy and rage by diminishing another, generate an immediate sense of power" (Spacks 1985: 4).

As sex workers compete with one another for clients, especially sober, clean, and generous customers, the atmosphere in the bars and boarding houses is ripe for gossip and back-biting. But Sosúa's sex workers use gossip to protect not only their client base but also their health. Rumor-spreading acts to discipline fellow sex workers into practicing safe sex and at the same time vents fears and worries. Fears over the transmission of AIDS and sex workers' desire to protect themselves from infection led to the following incident, to which I alluded briefly in chapter 4. Dolores reported to one of the peer educators from CEPROSH that there was a woman working with her at the Seabreeze who had AIDS.[12] Dolores proudly exclaimed that she was HIV-negative, always used condoms, and regularly went to the Tuesday clinic in Los Charamicos for STD testing, as well as for HIV testing in Puerto Plata. What led Dolores to believe her coworker had AIDS, and why did she relay her impressions to the peer educator? Dolores might have been spreading gossip with the intention of stigmatizing a colleague (and thus driving her clients away), but she might have had other motives as well. Anyone who is very thin is rumored to have AIDS, and Dolores observed that this woman was indeed quite thin. She also shuttled between her home and the bar to avoid the days the peer educators scheduled their *charlas* (talks / presentations). Dolores saw this pattern emerging and concluded that it was not coincidental. Since they worked together in a small Dominican bar, where the same clients came back week after week and the women shared clients, Dolores could have been looking out for her own health. Because of the ever-present risk of condoms breaking, sex workers are always nervous about AIDS.

Dominican women's gossip about Haitian women incorporates these themes of unsafe sex and AIDS. The stereotypes Dominican sex workers trade in reflect larger prejudices and discrimination that Haitians confront throughout Dominican society. The most common criticism of Haitian sex workers is that they "charge less than Dominican women" and "go with anybody." Price-cutting suggests that women are not discriminating or are even desperate. Desperation implies that a sex worker, willing to work for low wages, might also work without using condoms. By depicting Haitian women as less discriminating, Dominican women also position themselves within a higher class which affords them greater choice. These accusations have particular racial / ethnic, national, and class significance, since Dominican sex workers rarely accuse other Dominicans of price-cutting; rather, it is a charge they reserve for Haitian women. Over and over I heard Dominican sex workers criticize Haitian sex workers for charging tourists less (100–300 pesos [U.S.$8.30–25.00]) than what Dominican sex workers charged (500–800 pesos [U.S.$42.00–66.70]) for sex. When I asked Haitian women, however, how much they charged with tourists, they told me the same range Dominican women charged, between 500 and 800 pesos.

Sex workers also judge the care their fellow sex workers provide to their children. Within these judgments lies a tension between the importance of caring for one's children and the need to migrate to find work and, subsequently, live apart from one's children. Despite Latina women's valuing of "solo-mothering in the home as an ideal," sex workers who migrate internally to Sosúa face the same problems of mothering from a distance as "transnational mothers" (Hondagneu-Sotelo and Avila 1997).[13] Mothering from a distance challenges traditional Dominican ideals of what constitutes "good mothers" and "bad mothers."[14] Yet Sosúa's sex workers almost always explain their decision to keep their children apart from them and the sex trade as a way to protect them. Tomasa, for example, lived in a boarding house where children are not allowed, while her daughter lived with Tomasa's mother in Santo Domingo. She wanted her daughter far from Sosúa's sex trade: "My daughter is six and I don't want her here to hear all of these bad words and to see the street life. She is smart and would understand too much." For Tomasa, being a "good mother" meant she must disrupt the idealized notions of caring for one's children every day.

Within the social code of sex workers, some women have abused the practice of delegated care and have lived apart from their children for too long. This is a particularly vague and indeterminate line. Although sex workers usually opt to find a safe and caring environment for their children instead of subjecting them to Sosúa, leaving children in someone else's care, even a grandmother's, has limits. Ani castigated Justina, for example, who has not lived with her children in ten years. Ani, proud she had saved enough money to bring her two daughters to live with her, thought ten years was too long to live away from children. She saw Justina as putting herself first: "When Justina says that being a mother is the most important thing to her, it's not true. She is the first in her life. She does not want to leave the sex trade and go home and make sacrifices." Rather, Ani believed that while Justina was away from her family she was "free to do what she wants. She is obligated to no one. She does not have to clean or cook for anyone other than herself. She is the queen." For Ani, sex work not only required "fewer hours than other jobs," but it also was an easier job than taking care of children, a husband, and other relatives.

Conclusion: Women's Work and Agency in Sexscapes

Scholars have written much about what Saskia Sassen (1999: 84) calls the "feminization of the proletariat" and what Guy Standing (1989) refers to as the "global feminization of labor" in export manufacturing. The past three chapters have built on that work, giving us a glance at women's labor choices, working conditions, and agency in another global industry that is overwhelmingly dominated by women. In Sosúa's sexscape, we see some of the themes that have appeared in this broad feminist scholarship on women, work, and globalization, such as women's family obligations and their education and work histories. These personal factors shape decisions to enter the sex trade and affect women's power and agency both while in sex work and after they leave it. Much of the feminist scholarship on globalization attends to questions of women's agency—not just women's "responses" to globalization but also their attempts (like those of Sosúa's sex workers) to make globalization work for them.[15] The daily struggles of women in Sosúa's sex trade that I have documented in chapters 3–5 provide a nuanced picture of women who confront the inequities of globalization. Their strategies are constantly met with challenges, while their financial successes are often short lived. Nonetheless, their narratives are critical for gendering analyses of global capitalism, particularly since they suggest that transnationalism "from above" does not go unchallenged—even by the poorest and the most marginalized women. These women's stories add to feminist scholarship on women-as-agents who resist global capitalism from above. But they also contribute to a more detailed rendering of globalization, focusing our view on the global sex trade in this particular sexscape. The sex trade *in Sosúa*, with its own idiosyncrasies, offers an important variation on familiar themes in this feminist scholarship: What does it mean for women's power / agency in the global sex trade when they work in a pimp-free environment? What kind of obstacles stop sex workers from achieving their financial goals, especially since we see that similar advancement strategies, undertaken by a variety of women, nonetheless result in uneven outcomes. And what are the challenges to traditional gender relations and ideologies when women outearn men? The particular characteristics of Sosúa's sex-tourist trade allow us to see whether poor women in "local" places can "leave the worst excesses of patriarchal oppression behind" and find new and beneficial opportunities within globalization (Basu et al. 2001: 943). In the next chapter I examine another characteristic of Sosúa's sex-tourist trade: the increasing association in Europe of Afro-Dominican women with sex-for-sale. I also consider what this association means for these women if they visit or migrate to Europe.

IV

PLAN ACCOMPLISHED: GETTING BEYOND DOMINICAN BORDERS

Throughout the book I have stressed the role of imagination and fantasy among Sosúan sex workers, particularly how some women have idealized foreign men over Dominican men and have romanticized what life would be like in Europe for them and their families. What happens when Dominican women's dreams of marriage to European men and migration to Europe actually come true? How does the fantasy of living in Europe with foreign husbands compare to the reality? In this chapter I present women's stories of what life is like in Europe for Dominican sex workers and resort workers. This chapter also examines tourists' perceptions of the Dominican Republic and Dominican women. What prompts a European man to take a flight to the Dominican Republic for his vacation? What are some of the tourists looking for when they start relationships with Dominican women (both sex workers and resort workers)?

In order to get at how foreign tourists imagine Dominican women before the men even arrive on the island, as well as how Dominican women imagine foreign men, I examine some of the cultural representations and gossip each group consumes and produces about one another. These depictions fuel their imaginations and, in some cases, play a role in initiating their migration to one another's countries. I focus on the forms of communication through which they find out about one another as well as their respective "home" countries: communication that ranges from word of mouth (gossip), to print media, and the Internet (in the case of the men only). On the Internet, whether advertising for a Dominican girlfriend in an on-line classified advertisement, joining an e-mail pen-pal service that supplies e-mail addresses of Dominican women, or swapping information about Dominican women with other sex tourists through membership-only "travel services" for sex tourists, men trade in and perpetuate sexualized—and often racialized—images of Dominican women. These assumptions—based on race, gender, class, and nationality—are present in both sex tourists' and sex workers' descriptions of one another.

One of my aims in chapter 1 was to expand the concept of "transnational"—especially what qualifies as part of a transnational social field—and to explore the ways that gender, race, and nationality are mutually constituted within transnational contexts. Here, to further that aim, I examine the various media images of sex worker and sex tourist and their respective countries of origin, as well as descriptions of their experiences with one another and of living in one another's countries. These images and media depictions connect Sosúa to cities in Europe as part of a transnational social field. Each group imagines the other as the opposite of the racialized sexual, romantic, or economic partners they meet in their home countries. They also imagine one another's countries as offering opportunities out of their reach in their home countries. These images are sustained not only by the brief encounters of sexual liaisons but also by the fact that a small sector of sex workers and resort workers are able to maintain relationships with European tourists over time and space.

Dominican Women in Europe

The new cultural and economic loops between the Dominican Republic and Europe raise important research questions, such as how gender relations will be configured in these new households and how Dominican women will navigate racism and anti-immigrant sentiment they might confront in Europe.[1] Underlying Elena's experience with Jürgen (depicted in the Introduction) is another important question: To what degree are the sex workers' fantasies about foreign men shaped by the fact that the women are themselves migrants, having left their homes to seek their future in Sosúa? The mobility strategy these women pursue changes their life, not only by bringing them into a new transnational social world but also by exposing them to new experiences of migration and wage work. Both migration and wage work can have an impact on gender relations and on the expectations women place on men. Scholars of migration have asked whether it reaffirms or reconfigures "traditional" gender roles, while research on women and work questions whether wage labor increases women's authority in the household.

These studies reveal that the experience of living in a new country, when combined with wage labor, often gives women greater social and economic independence and status.[2]

The lives of Dominican sex workers in Sosúa highlight the complexities of these questions since these women often begin migration (internally) already burdened with weighty responsibilities as heads of households. This chapter considers how women's experiences and responsibilities as heads of households inform the way they seek authority in their future relationships—with foreign or Dominican men. Dominican women's internal migration for the sex trade, and external migration with European boyfriends / husbands, is a complex social terrain in which gender roles are both reaffirmed and reconfigured. Although the sex trade allows women to outearn Dominican male migrants in Sosúa, they have little similar potential source of authority or independence in their relationships with foreign men. In fact, they become dependent on these men not only for money but often for much more if they move to Europe as did Nanci, María, and Tati.

NANCI

Whereas most sex workers explained their transnational relationships in terms of strategic economic imperatives, Nanci recounted a love story. "This is completely for love," she gushed. Her story of romance and migration was well known among the sex workers in Sosúa and many dreamed of being in Nanci's position. In chapter 3 I wrote about Nanci's extensive photo, letter, and fax collection from at least fifteen different European men. She also had been receiving money wires from five or six European men at the same time. And over time, she received three marriage proposals. She eventually chose Frank, a German man close to her age (she was twenty-three and he twenty-eight), over her other suitors. Nanci chose him, she explained, for love. She beamed when she spoke of him: "He is a wonderful man." He spoke Spanish and got along well with her three-year-old son who was living with her in Sosúa. From his pictures, Frank was clean cut, good looking, and, according to Nanci, loving and protective of her and her son. He bought her a plane ticket and helped her get a tourist visa so she could visit him in Germany for a month.

After this first visit, Nanci had all the markers of overseas travel: running shoes, designer jeans, a fashionable spaghetti-strap tank top, and a black leather belt with a large silver buckle in the shape of a flower. All of these items were obviously new, expensive, and bought outside of the country. Her son was wearing a tie-dyed Mickey Mouse T-shirt with "As Cute as Ever" written on it. She pulled out a photo album and showed me pictures of her visit to Germany, including pictures of Frank's parents and their middle-class home where Frank also lived. Nanci had a very positive experience with Frank's parents, who had gone of their way to make her feel a part of the family. Frank's mother, who had been learning how to cook Dominican food, surprised Nanci with a *sancocho* on the night of her arrival.[3] She also had cried at the end of the visit when they took Nanci to the airport. Nanci's relationship with Frank was off to a good start, and her adjustment to living in Europe seemed promising.

Not all Dominican women recount being welcomed as warmly, however. One woman explained that her German boyfriend's family was shocked that she was black. They avoided getting together, and when they did, they ignored her. Others described families' unwillingness to make themselves understood, let alone attempt to speak Spanish. These women described feeling shut out and lonely. Nanci is aware of Dominican women's run-ins with racism in Europe but explained that during her first visit to Germany she did not have any firsthand experiences with racism. She was concerned, however, that Frank's family and friends would find out that she had been a sex worker in Sosúa. "When Frank first vacationed in Sosúa, he was here with his cousin and two friends" (who knew Nanci was in the sex trade). "We hope they don't say anything. Frank's parents would die if they knew." A former coworker of Nanci's, Rosa, lives thirty miles away from Frank's family with a German man she also had met in Sosúa's sex trade. Nanci worried: "Rosa's mother-in-law knows what Rosa did in Sosúa. And she knows I'm a friend of Rosa's. What if she ever said anything to Frank's parents?" Nanci's ties to Sosúa through Rosa put a new twist on the importance of social networks in the migration process. The nascent networks linking Sosúan sex workers to towns in Europe act as both sources of support and concern for former sex workers. The emotional and economic support immigrants derive from networks linking sending and receiving countries is well documented (Fong 1994; Rouse 1992). Dominican sex workers, however, are a group of migrants who might prefer to "start over." These women often believe that struggling in isolation in their new European settings is preferable to being found out.[4]

After her visit to Germany, Nanci soon married Frank and moved, with her son, to Germany. Nanci's and Frank's relationship did not last. After marrying and living in Germany for a year, the two of them moved back to Sosúa, where they had a little girl together. But soon after moving to Sosúa, Frank ran off with another Dominican sex worker and stopped all financial support to Nanci and the children. Even though Nanci went to a lawyer and got Frank to pay child support for one month, there is little Nanci can do, because Frank and his new girlfriend have moved to Germany. Nanci simply does not have the resources to pursue legal action for child support from the Dominican Republic while Frank remains in Germany. I was saddened to see that the one relationship I knew of that seemed to grow out of what Nanci described as amor rather then residencia had crumbled and that Nanci had experienced such a dramatic reversal of fortune. She was back living, with her two children, in a two-room shack in worse poverty than before she had met Frank. (Before Germany, she had been renting a room in a freshly painted, middle-class Dominican house.) The strain on Nanci was visible, and even Elena and some of Nanci's other friends remarked about it. Nanci, who always had taken great care to keep her house clean and to dress stylishly, was living in clutter and filth. She and the children wore stained clothes. Her lively sense of humor and optimism, in the days when a number of European men where faxing her and sending her money, had been replaced by indifference. The absence of the extra money from transnational money wires clearly was hard felt. Nanci was back in sex work, and Elena and she, who had been best friends, had grown apart. Nanci, lamented Elena, "only thinks of discos." "She thinks like a prostituta." By invoking the image of a "prostituta," Elena suggested her friend was acting like the newest—and youngest—group of sex workers who Elena gossiped used sex work for the moment rather than to get ahead (progresar). Elena was deeply worried about her friend but was at a loss as to what she could do for her. "Did you see the house and the old clothes she was wearing? She is not doing well." She thought Nanci needed to regain control of her life but was adamant that sex work was not the way: "She should not be back in the bars." Rather, Elena tried to persuade her to work in a restaurant like she was.

MARIA

Unlike Nanci's story of love—at least initially—Maria's relationship as she described it with a German man (whom she had met as a sex worker) was only for money and visas. Even though the German man wanted to marry Maria, the goal of many Sosúan sex workers, she was clearly reluctant. Pushed into this transnational relationship by her Dominican boyfriend, Juan, who physically abused her, Maria was not in love with this German man and dreaded going to Germany to visit him. He had been quite generous with Maria and had sent enough money on a regular basis that she was able to quit the sex trade and bring her children to Sosúa to live with her. It is at this point, when Maria rented a house, that Juan, whom she had met when she migrated to Los Charamicos, moved in with her. Juan greatly enjoyed the material benefits of Maria's ongoing transnational liaison and pressured her to continue the relationship. In a way, this was Juan's transnational "fantasy," not hers. Extremely shy, Maria replied to her German boyfriend's faxes only at Juan's urging. He knew her transnational ties could prove to be a gold mine, and he was right. From the money wires the German boyfriend sent, Juan bought an impressive stereo system, a large color television, and a stove. They moved from a one-room wooden shack into a concrete house.[5] Juan had worked only sporadically before the money wires but gave up looking for jobs altogether once the wires started.

When Maria finally moved to Germany, she returned only weeks later. She had not liked it there: it was too cold, she missed her children, and, most of all, she was not in love. As it turned out, residencia was not enough for her. When she returned without the windfall of money Juan had hoped for, his beatings escalated. She eventually left him, however, and moved into her mother's home with her children. Afraid to bring along the things bought with the money wires, she left them behind with Juan. While Juan benefited from Maria's transnational relationship, Maria, like Nanci, ended up back where she had started off before she had ever been involved with a foreign man. In Maria's case, her greater earning power over Juan's translated into exploitation and abuse.

TATI

Few women actually make it to Germany as Nanci or Maria did. So when Tati, like Maria, chose to return to the Dominican Republic, her Dominican friends and neighbors saw her as crazy. As she explained, "This is what all the women want. . . . They think that these men will have money and will solve all your problems." Yet Tati was desperately lonely in Germany and felt that her German boyfriend (they were not married yet), though able to supply her with material comfort, did not really understand her. "I did not like not being understood. I missed being near my family. I missed Dominican food and seemed to always have the flu. And I stayed in the house all the time. You need some kind of work."[6] Without speaking German, and no social networks through which to meet friends, Tati was dependent on her husband for money and a social life. She said that he treated her well, by giving her presents and remaining faithful, "not running around with other women." But he drank often and did not want her to telephone her family. Afraid she might leave him, he gave her only small amounts of money at a time for specific purchases, in an attempt to make sure she never had enough money to buy an airplane ticket to fly home. Even though she was a good seamstress, he forbade her to work outside the home and refused to buy her a sewing machine. She became increasingly fearful that if she let him know she was planning to leave him, he would kill her. "You know many of these men kill their wives." Unable to remain a day longer, Tati boldly went to the police. A few days later, she flew home to the Dominican Republic, courtesy of the German government. She waited at least another week before she called her husband to let him know where she was. At first he did not believe her. Even though the police had interviewed him about abuse (while Tati was in a safe house waiting for her flight to the Dominican Republic), and decided that he in fact had not physically abused his wife, he never thought that she would find a way back to the Dominican Republic.

LIVING WITH GERMAN MEN:
FANTASIES VERSUS REALITY

Even after relationships end and women return to Sosúa broke, the community of sex workers still idealizes these failed migration stories. The facts that Jürgen was an alcoholic and that he and Elena always fought were never mentioned in gossip. Similarly, Maria's and Tati's social and economic isolation in Germany—their inability to find work outside the home due to not speaking German and their consequent dependence on their husbands for friends and spending money—was left out of their friends' depictions of their time in Germany. These aspects of living in Germany are passed over, when sex workers gossip, in favor of foregrounding perceived material benefits.

Sylvia Chant and Cathy McIlwaine (1995) found that Filipina women who use the sex trade to marry and migrate also hold unrealistic perceptions of life in other countries. They write about a masseuse who left her English soon-to-be-husband after living in London for two years with her children because he "was little more than an acquaintance" and she "found it increasingly difficult to hide her growing disquiet and unhappiness, especially away from the emotional support of her family" (1995: 248). Thus, despite women's economic strategies and aspirations to migrate overseas, marriages not based on romantic love are not "good enough" for some women. When Maria and Tati chose to leave their German "husbands" and Germany because their newfound material and economic security could not mitigate their feelings of not being in love, their more realistic depictions of life in Germany were cast in neighborhood gossip as the exception, not the rule. In fact, even Tati's frightening story of being held against her will became a story of craziness and lost opportunity—not courage.

The social isolation in Germany can be acute. Unlike New York, Germany lacks the Dominican-run or frequented social clubs, associations, restaurants, or stores to help women such as Nanci, Maria, and Tati feel at home. In fact, because of language and other cultural barriers, sex workers who have returned to the Dominican Republic after living in Europe explain that they rarely left their European boyfriends' or husbands' houses other than to go food shopping. Andrea, for example, told me that during her first "trial" visit to live with her boyfriend in Germany, she "stayed in and watched Spanish TV" (I wrote about Andrea's plans to divorce her German husband to marry a wealthier German man in chapter 3). She only left the apartment "to go to the supermarket," but she did not like going out alone. "I don't think it is a good idea for a woman to go out alone in the street. People can see that I am Latina." But when I specifically asked if she experienced any racism, Andrea, like most other sex workers from Sosúa who have lived in Europe, dismissed my suggestion. "Many people think I am Spanish, they don't know I am from the Dominican Republic." Andrea's lack of racist run-ins in Europe was passed along in sex workers' stories about life in Europe, even though they acknowledged that both Andrea and Nanci were light skinned and had pelo bueno (good—that is, straight—hair). "Andrea does not have difficulties in Germany, because she is white," Elena explained.[7]

In terms of gender roles in these women's households in Europe, Dominican women, by default, step into a traditional role for women as homemaker. Since these women do not work outside of the home, and they are migrating as the wives / girlfriends of men who are legal citizens with established lives and social networks, they do not experience any of the increased decision-making authority in the household as might other women migrants who engage in wage labor (or who are married to coethnics who also are migrants and therefore along with their husbands are on the margins of their new culture). Nanci is the only Dominican woman I interviewed who had a formal activity outside of the home: English lessons. At the language school, she met her only friend in Germany—outside of her husband's social circle—a woman from Turkey. Some of the isolation is self-imposed, such as Nanci's fear of "discovery" that kept her from socializing with Rosa, her friend from Sosúa who was also a former sex worker. In other cases, such as Tati's, her husband built a relationship of dependency by tightly controlling her contact with anyone outside the home, including forbidding her to work. In many ways, former sex workers living in Europe experience a significant rollback in independence and household decision-making authority from their days in Sosúa, where they lived on their own terms, not doing daily household chores for a family, earning more money than most Dominican men, and enjoying a support network of friends and coworkers.

In sum, in sex workers' depictions of life in Europe, problems of speaking another language and living in another culture, questions I raised about potential racism, and issues in domestic life with less-than-loving husbands who have traditional expectations for household roles were all waved away. Women such as Andrea (who is dumping one German man for another with more money) became symbols of all that is possible in Germany, while Nanci's friends blamed her (Nanci) for the breakup of her marriage. In Elena's words, "Nanci never should have moved to Sosúa with her German husband with all these sex workers here. No man would stick around." And by portraying Maria and Tati as foolish, the sex workers who were "waiting" in Sosúa (for their chance to get fuera) asserted that they would never choose to leave Germany as these two women did. With so many perceived economic benefits of living in Europe, the women who gossiped about Maria's and Tati's return assumed that they could stick it out and feign love. Life allá in Europe is, for now, imagined as better than aquí (here on the island)—at least until more women cycle through these new transnational social fields.

European Men Imagine Dominican Women

Because of the proliferation of discussions and pictures of Dominican women on the Internet—on "travel services" for sex tourists, pen-pal services, and on-line classified advertisements in which foreign men "advertise" for Dominican girlfriends or brides—as well as in the European media, Dominican women increasingly have been associated with sexual availability. When I first conducted fieldwork in Sosúa in 1993, male sex tourists could not find much information on Sosúa or on Dominican women through the Internet; now they can. Since the mid-1990s, Dominican women have been increasingly featured on Internet sites that cater to men looking for "mail-order brides" or for sex workers on the men's vacations. Dominican women, for example, are now regularly featured on sex-tourist Internet sites such as the World Sex Guide, and Travel and the Single Male, and there are pen-pal sites entirely dedicated to Dominican women.[8] I have watched as sex tourists first started posting Internet messages about their experiences in one town, Boca Chica, then expanded into postings about other destinations in the Dominican Republic (including Santo Domingo and Sosúa). I also have watched as various Internet sites have developed extensive photo collections of Dominican women that foreign men have met or can meet.

Yet since nearly all of the sex tourists I interviewed in Sosúa traveled there based on the recommendation of friends, word of mouth plays a decisive role in these sex tourists' decisions on where to vacation. Most of the sex tourists I met in Sosúa had been to other sex-tourist destinations. As seasoned sex tourists many told me they were "bored" with other destinations and decided to "try" Sosúa and Dominican women. Just as Dominican women look to European men to be everything they imagine Dominican men never will be, European men, too, compare Dominican women to European women. They imagine Dominican women as more sexual, more compliant, and having fewer financial demands than European women. European men also often expect Dominican women to adhere to very traditional—and regressive—understandings of gender roles.[9] And race plays a central role in how the white European sex tourists imagine Afro-Dominican sex workers. Women's skin color was mentioned again and again in my interviews with sex tourists, as well as on the Internet. Typical Internet postings about Dominican women focus on race, such as the following posting to the World Sex Guide: "Most of the girls in the Dominican Republic are very dark Spanish to deep black. So, if you like white girls only do not go there." And a group of friends who had traveled together from Germany told me in English that "Dominican women are beautiful, there is a range of skin color." One of the men piped up, "I like them in the middle. Mocha. And they are not short like other Latin women."

German sex tourists who were drinking at a bar on the beach (during the day) also explained their interest in Dominican women in terms of race. They nodded along when the German bar owner described for me why he thought German men like dark-skinned Dominican women. For him, sexual proficiency was tied to skin color: "Dominican girls like to fuck." He compared German women's sexual skills with those of Dominican women. "With German women it's over quickly [the men at the bar roared at this]. But Dominican women have fiery blood." As if letting me in on a secret, he leaned in closer to me and waved his cigarette: "German women don't know how to fuck." He and his bar patrons attributed part of Dominicans' "natural" skill at love-making to the climate. "When the sun is shining, it gives you more hormones." Then, ribbing me, the North American, he teased, "I bet people from Florida are better lovers than those from Vermont." Adriana Piscitelli has written about similar associations European sex tourists in Fortaleza, Brazil, make about Afro-Brazilian sex workers' skin color and their sexual proficiency. One English sex tourist told her "I have been to bed with some of them. Dark, medium, light. In the first two days I went crazy" (2001: 12). These male sex tourists in Fortaleza, like foreign men in Sosúa, also compared Brazilian women with women from their home countries. "The accessibility and 'warmth' of the temperament of the Brazilians are, in this way, contrasted to the arrogance of the Germans, and the 'closed' nature of the Portuguese women and the . . . calculating nature and the haughtiness of the Italian women" (2001: 12).

Sosúan sex workers take great pride that European men have told them that they are more sexually appealing than European women. They often draw on and perpetuate sexualized stereotypes of Afro-Caribbean and Latina women, bragging that Dominican women dance more sensually than European women and are better lovers. Elena boasted, "These men are here because European women are cold. Not Dominican women—we are *caliente* (hot)." In fact, when describing themselves Sosúan sex workers often employ the same sexual images that European male sex tourists use. Elena's German "husband," Jürgen, for example, characterized Dominican women as sexy, generalizing that "everyone in Germany knows about the Dominican Republic, you know, like Thailand. And they know about Dominican women and how sexy they are." At the same time, Elena, too, plays on the stereotype of the "hot Dominicana." The relish with which she recounted the following story reveals that she and her friends value—and accrue certain advantages—from Dominicanas being perceived as both sexy and sex experts.

The story emerged one afternoon in Los Charamicos while I was talking with a group of women who were all friends. We were sitting in the shade of one of the few trees left in Los Charamicos. Some were sex workers, and some had left sex work to marry Dominican men. I brought up the topic of foreign tourists and asked how they thought these men saw them. Not one of the women could contain herself; at once, between howls of laughter, they shouted out "hot," "sexy," and "Dominicana." For these women, being Dominican means being sexual. Elena quieted the crowd, explaining she had a good story to tell: "I was at the Anchor one night and a Spanish couple approached me. They said that in Spain Dominican women have a reputation for being good lovers. So they wanted me to go to bed with the wife, not the husband, so that she could learn what it is that Dominican women know." This story set off the already rambunctious crowd. "What did you do?" "Did you do it, did you do it?" Elena's older sisters who were there protested protectively: "She would never do that, never." After letting her friends carry on for a few minutes, Elena piped up, "Of course I didn't go with them." She and the crowd reacted within an accepted cultural script to the two revelations: first, they expressed revulsion at the mention of sex with a woman; and second, they cheered Dominican women's international fame as excellent lovers. Their dramatics highlighted Sosúa's sex workers' code of behavior that both viewed homosexuality as transgressive behavior and endorsed the European couple's explicit acknowledgment of *Dominicanas* as sexually desirable and proficient.

After being told over and over by European and Canadian men how hot and sexy they are, sex workers use these stereotypes to capture men's attention. As part of their seduction, sex workers play up in their dress, gestures, and dance what they *think* the men desire. For example, Sosúa's sex workers dance alone provocatively, especially early in the evening before the dance floor fills with couples.[10] Their dancing advertises their sexuality and reveals an understanding of themselves and their *Dominicanidad* (Dominicanness) as sexually charged and commercially valuable. Once couples are on the dance floor, however, sex workers no longer dance alone, but compete with one another by brushing up against potential clients. Lenore Manderson observed similar assumptions about male desire in Thai women's dance/strip performances in Bangkok's sex bars that "presumed fantasies of foreign men" (Manderson 1992: 454).[11]

THE MASS MEDIA

The German media has been covering Sosúa's sex trade since the early 1990s. The word is out, at least in Germany, that this is a place for sex tourists to add to their lists of travel destinations. One German newspaper article, part of a seven-day series on Sosúa's sex trade, "Sex, Boozing, and Sunburn," paints Sosúa as a sex tourist's dream: "Just going from the street to the disco—there isn't any way men can take one step alone. Prostitutes bend over, stroke your back and stomach, and blow you kisses in your ear. If you are not quick enough, you get a hand right into the fly of your pants. Every customer is fought for, by using every trick in the book (Heikhaus 1995b)." Back when the Anchor and the other open-air clubs across the street were in full swing, sex tourists did not have to look far to find women: Sex workers seemed to be at every turn. Some nights, especially during the low tourist seasons, sex workers outnumbered the tourists in the bars. Furthermore, the inexpensive prices often help men, especially first-time sex tourists, make up their minds. Generally sex workers do not charge for separate sex acts, and there is no time limit. Plus, as these women work "freelance," there are no additional fees to any middlemen (such as pimps or bar owners). Of course, without a formal system in which men take cuts from women's sexual labor, the clients also know that these freelance sex workers are vulnerable. Clients who rape or batter sex workers have little fear of reprisal. Some men, such as Dieter, a forty-three-year-old bank employee from Frankfurt, return to the Dominican Republic for all of their vacations. Dieter has been there nine times. While sitting in a bar in the "Bermuda Triangle" (a nickname among German sex tourists for the center of sex-tourist bar activity), Dieter commented "It is *better* here than Thailand"[12] (Heikhaus 1995b). His photo accompanied one of the articles in the seven-day series that showed Dieter wearing a T-shirt with the words *sex tourist* on the front (which, he explained, he had purchased in Thailand). The headlines in this series of articles advertise Sosúa as little more than a sex-tourist destination and all Dominican women as sexually available, for example: "No One Remains Single in the Bermuda Triangle" (Heikhaus 1995a) and "Hot Nights in Sosúa: The Most Sinful Mile in the Caribbean" (Heikhaus 1995b).

THE INTERNET

Just as the German media has portrayed Sosúa as a sex tourist's dream, Internet discussions about Dominican sex workers also stress how easy it is to find beautiful, dark-skinned, sexually proficient women in Sosúa's bars, as the following posting from the World Sex Guide reveals (October 1997):

> Subject: Sosúa, DomRep
> . . . The best way to get a girl is to go to the discos at night. . . . When you enter the disco you will feel like you're in heaven! A tremendous number of cute girls and something for everyone's taste (if you like colored girls like me!). I didn't see any girl I would call "ugly." Most of them are ok, but some look really like models. You only have to sit down at the bar or start to dance, everything will happen without any activity of you. Every time I was there and sat down several minutes later 6 or 7, sometimes 10 girls come in my nearness, start dancing in a very stimulating way and stare at me. But there is no need to take a girl directly; you can take a lot of time to make your decision.

While considerable attention has been paid to the role air travel, instant banking, and other "modern" technologies have played in transnational circuits, few connections have been made among globalization, women's work choices in the global economy, women's migration for work, and the role of the Internet in producing and disseminating stereotypes—based on race and sexual prowess— of women in the developing world. On-line travel services make it increasingly easy for potential sex tourists to research sex-tourist destinations and to plan trips. To help travelers, some services provide names of "tour guides" and names of local bars. Recently there have been so many cyber-advertisements and discussions about Sosúa that male sex tourists are beginning to write not just about traveling to Sosúa for their first sex trip but about their second and third visits. As a result, in Europe—particularly Germany—Dominican women increasingly are associated with sex-for-sale and the Dominican Republic with the sex trade.

In examining desire in colonial Southeast Asia, Ann Stoler looks at the myths of the sexualized Other in colonial texts, commenting that "colonialism was that quintessential project in which desire was always about sex, that sex was always about racial power, and that both were contingent upon a particular representation of nonwhite women's bodies" (Stoler 1997b: 43). Just as Stoler observed in these colonial texts, so too desire, sex, race, and power are tied together in these modern-day cyber-texts, where we see the same stereotypes traded in posting after posting where Dominican sex workers are portrayed as "hot," "dark," "cheap," and "easy to find." In sex tourism, we are well familiar with First World travelers / consumers' seeking— and exoticizing—dark-skinned "native" bodies in the developing world for cut-rate prices. These two components—first, race and its associated stereotypes and expectations, and, second, the economic disparities between the developed and developing worlds—characterize sex-tourist destinations and sexscapes throughout the world. Cuba, for example, draws sex tourists who not only want to live out their "'racialized'-sexual fantasies" but also want to do so on a budget (O'Connell Davidson 1996: 42). Julia O'Connell Davidson explains that a European sex tourist can stay in a Cuban woman's flat, and she will do his laundry, cook for him, act as his guide and interpreter, as well as give him "sexual access" for as little as $5.00 a day.[13]

In the case of the Dominican Republic, the availability of "dirt cheap colored girls" (as one sex tourist posted to the World Sex Guide in October 1997) might be one attraction that draws sex tourists. One veteran sex tourist who previously had been to Thailand and to Brazil on sex holidays was so enticed by other sex tourists' postings about Sosúa's dark-skinned beauties and the prices that he decided to "try out" the Dominican Republic and Dominican women. In turn, he posted his experiences in Sosúa to the World Sex Guide: "Through this page and others on the Internet, I heard wonderful things about the women of the Dominican Republic and decided to check it out for myself."

As I mentioned in chapter 1, the inexpensive prices of *everything* in Sosúa is critical to sex tourists experiences there. Sex tourists can be "big men" not just in the bars and nightclubs where Dominican sex workers shower them with a great deal of attention (much like the experience of salarymen in Japanese hostess clubs that Anne Allison describes [1994] and the experience of strip club regulars in the United States that Katherine Frank examines [2002]), but also *everywhere* in town. With their money power, their consumer spending is sought after by an array of businesses—most of whose goods and services they can easily afford. This is why, I argue, some men might choose to travel to sexscapes in the developing world to buy sex rather than to buy sex in their home towns or in nearby European capitals that boast a lively sex trade. With third world women throughout Europe's sex establishments, and in some cases, the prices for sex acts not dramatically more expensive than in Sosúa, the overall experience as tourist / consumer is important.

The association of Dominicanness with sexual availability and proficiency expands on the idea of performance that I introduced in chapter 3. We saw that nearly all relationships that develop between Dominicans and foreigners have been met with suspicion by Sosúans. Dominican Sosúans might build transnational relationships for transactional purposes, but what foreigners seek in these relationships is less clear. Just as I wrote in chapter 3 that I cannot possibly determine which relationships are for romantic "love" on the part of Dominican Sosúans, I cannot possibly determine with certainty what motivates foreigners to seek relationships with Dominicans. What I did find through interviews with foreign tourists, sex tourists, and foreign residents in Sosúa, as well as through monitoring Internet postings, is that some foreigners are "catching on" that their relationships with Dominican resort workers and sex workers might be for visas and not for love. Some of these foreigners try to take advantage of the Dominicans who are trying to take advantage of them.

Some of the male and female tourists in Sosúa are aware of how difficult it is for Dominicans to migrate off the island and are catching on that their Dominican girlfriends and boyfriends might be "performing" at love. At the very least, foreigners are increasingly informed that visas are a form of currency in the Dominican Republic.

A German beach-bar owner witnessed sex workers' performances day after day in his bar. When I asked about one of his customers, who was lifting up the shirt of a sex worker, he said: "She tells him she loves him, and he believes it. How does she see him? For the money. They are all actresses. The men want to believe, so they do, at least as long as they are on holiday. Once he stops paying, she moves on and forgets him." And a well-traveled sex tourist was cynical about Dominican sex workers' interest in long-term relationships, as his Internet posting to the World Sex Guide revealed: "I know a lot of the reports on the Internet describe how incredibly friendly and sweet these women are and that many of them just want to meet a Westerner. This is not the case. Not even close. There are only $$ signs in these women's eyes. They are business women and nothing more. This is not only my observation—but that of some others I met. . . . All of us have spent lots of time traveling around the world to its various fleshpots and placed these women way down on the scale of overall personality and charm" (September 1996). This advice not to believe what Dominican women tell you was echoed in two other postings: "Don't believe the girls when they tell you they love you— 'mi amor'—there are no freebies" and "Some (of the women) were a little too money intensive."

PLAYING THE GREEN CARD

Other Internet postings by sex tourists suggest that clients are now trying to capitalize on sex workers' desire for a literal ticket out of Sosúa. In other words, they try to take advantage of the women's attempts to take advantage of them. One sex tourist coached other sex tourists that a paid encounter could turn into something more: "Don't discount the possibility of a non-monetary relationship with Dominican women. It's not a hard thing to come by and—in my experience—is more rewarding." This sex tourist also advised that even if his fellow sex tourists are not interested in keeping the relationship going after their vacations end, the illusion of their long-term interest "goes a long way." He suggests, "Ask them if they want to go to the beach? Which one? Are they free tomorrow? They think they're practically married at that point. Tell 'em all about yourself. Make friends with them. That goes a long way. Take them out of one club and bring them to another" (October 1997).

Just as sex workers might perform at being romantically interested in their foreign clients, so too their clients are beginning to play at romance. However, it is difficult to know exactly what they men are trying to achieve. Some simply hope to get free sex, which they can construe as an indicator of their attractiveness. A Dutch resident in Sosúa bragged to me that while sex workers charged 500 pesos (U.S.$42) with tourists, that he had offers to "make love for free." His sex appeal was not only implicit in this bragging but so too was a notion of Dominican sex workers' insatiability.

FEMALE TOURISTS: BEING "PLAYED"

A series of Internet postings, on Dominican One's message board, by female tourists who have been sexually and romantically involved with male Dominican resort workers, suggested that they too were aware that they were, what they dubbed, being "played." "Most of these guys at the resorts are players," warned "Julie," "Ladies, if you don't want to get played, stay sober, use your brain, and don't fall for any of the lines" (4 November 2000). "Shauna" responded, reminding "Julie" that resort workers remain behind, while tourists—female and male—might make promises and then leave. "Has anyone considered how the tourist women are perceived by the Dominican men, the so called players? I have a few friends who have been burned by the women. . . . Remember after the week is over the women go home—the guys have to stay and wait for a call or a letter. Lots of times there is no more contact from the women. They go home to their boyfriends or husbands and forget about their Dominican lover" (4 December 2000). And Roberto, a Dominican living in a resort area, was resentful of racialized and sexualized stereotypes of Dominican men: "I am in an area wher[e] I se[e] and listen to all the part[ies] involv[ed] in this matter, most of the wom[en] who come here are married [or] have a boyfriend, and they come with the mentality of getting [to] satisfy the[ir] fantasy of having you know what—with a [C]aribbean boy—between—black and they al(so) make the dis[gust]ing comment . . . like if the men . . . are s— machine" (4 December 2000).[14]

And in an earlier thread of exchanges, one woman specifically warned other women that the men they meet want to leave the island. These "players," "say the same lines and make the same moves on any good-looking woman who might be their chance at getting off the island or their meal ticket" (3 April 2003). One woman wrote that she met a "good guy" at one of the resorts, but when he realized she was not going back to Canada, he "lost interest." She also described a man who had been performing at love, since he had been married before, not for love, but for "business." However, "they divorced when the visa did not go through" (12 April 2000). In response to these postings by North American women, a Dominican man chimed in about the kinds of people he thought resort areas attract. "Unfortunately around resort areas there are many poor, [un]educated people, many [but] not all are out there to get something out of the dollar bearing t[ou]rists, there are many prostitutes, money beggars, pickpockets, and street vendors out to get the best of the t[ou]rist, why shouldn't they, they know you have the cash and they want part of it." He continued, stressing the desire to get off the island, "Most of the local guys who roam the beaches are guys out to pick a 'Gringa' someone who will get him out for a drink or better still out of the country and out of poverty" (4 April 2000). One posting by another Dominican man not only echoed the sentiments expressed in chapter 2 that tourist enclaves are not authentic but also that individuals working in these spaces are not like other Dominicans: "The resorts area cannot be consider[ed] the real dominican republic and those guys to be the real dominican men" (5 April 2000).

After these initial exchanges, female tourists started using the message board as a way to find out if they too had been "played." They posted queries that included men's names, where they worked, and even what they looked like (in case they had given the women false names). "After reading all the posts on this board on how Dominican men are, [I'm] not so sure I really did meet a good guy. So if anyone knows XX, how about giving me the scoop. He works at the XX Hotel in Punta Cana s[ail])ing, fishing, horseback riding etc." (11 April 2000) (it sounds like he is an activity director).[15] The queries continued, "Well, I guess I have to ask seeing how everyone seems to be asking about their guy that they met. If anyone knows anything about XX it would be greatly appreciated. I would love to know if I was played" (11 April 2000).

"DOMINICAN WOMEN MAKE GOOD GIRLFRIENDS": CYBER-ADVERTISEMENTS AND PEN-PAL SERVICES

Not all men in the bars only look to buy sex for the night, but some also hope to find a girlfriend or a wife. For Jürgen, for example, Dominican sex workers offered more than just sex. He asserted that they make good girlfriends because they are easily placated: "They are happy with enough money to eat and to have a place to sleep. Sure, they want money, but not like women in Germany." By describing Dominican sex workers as having a modest range of commodity needs and desires, Jürgen rendered them more compliant, indeed "simple," and thus less demanding than women he meets in Germany. A Canadian sex tourist–turned–resident went so far as to call Dominican women "children." After moving to Sosúa, he learned that "if you are going to have prostitutes as girlfriends you have to get them when they are young and just starting to sell. Then you have a chance of molding them, getting them to flush the toilet or to stop sticking their fingers up their noses."

In some relationships, such as Elena's and Jürgen's, the couple does not speak a common language. Part of the attraction of a relationship with a Dominican woman might be that she cannot make known her opinions or desires, let alone demands. Indeed, I served as interpreter between Jürgen and Elena when they fought. Since Jürgen spoke English, but little Spanish, and Elena spoke no German or English, she asked me to help her understand why Jürgen was mad at her, as well as to communicate her feelings to him. Annette Hamilton has pointed out that the inability for sex workers to communicate with their foreign clients / boyfriends adds to their "allure and mystery." In the case of Thai bar girls, they are not "devoted to the ceaseless round of rational discussion, demand, insistence, requirement, justification, and so on which is taken to characterize relationships with Western women" (1997: 154–55).

Some of the sex tourists I met in Sosúa said they had male friends who had married Dominican women (not all were former sex workers), and they too wanted to meet beautiful, dark-skinned women. This privileged group that travels without visas can use their vacations in Sosúa to shop for girlfriends / brides. This "bride shopping" as a transnational practice grows out of an exploitative and regressive impulse to find women who might not try to negotiate for any kind of authority in the household. The "asymmetries of domination, inequality, racism, sexism, class conflict and uneven development" in which, Michael Smith and Luis Guarnizo (1998: 6) write, "transnational practices are embedded and which they sometimes even perpetuate" are clearly present in tourism, sex tourism, and the "bride shopping" that might develop while on vacation in Sosúa.

ASSOCIATING A NATION'S WOMEN WITH THE SEX TRADE
The association between Dominican women and the sex trade is not limited to just a few individual women. The rise of sex-for-sale (due in part to the Internet, to sex tourists' travels, and to the migration—and, in some cases, trafficking—of Third World women to nightclubs and brothels throughout the world) has linked certain nations' women to sex work in the imagination of many. In turn, women's mobility has been affected. Immigration officials in Hong Kong, for example, have targeted Thai women at the airport as suspected prostitutes (Schloss 1999). Code-named "Operation Hoover," officers were ordered to stop Thai women aged eighteen to forty. Similarly, Israeli officials have systematically deported Russian women at the airport, assuming these women are being funneled into Israel's brothels. The Russian Ambassador to Israel assessed how such profiling stereotypes all Russian women: "Those who suffer are not only the girls who practice prostitution, but all the women who come from Russia, especially those with fair hair, who are treated badly" (Aharanot 1999). Russian women are also associated with prostitution in Northern Cyprus, a resort area, where, as throughout the Black Sea region, they are derogatorily referred to as "Natashas" (Julie Scott 1995).

For Dominican women, the stigmatizing association with the sex trade (selling sex both on the island and overseas) has prompted women who never have been sex workers to worry that the families and friends of their European boyfriends / spouses might wonder if they had been sex workers. Moreover, since Dominican women's participation in the overseas sex trade has received so much press coverage in the Dominican Republic,[16] women's experiences living and working in Europe are suspect. "I know that when I tell people I was really with a folk dance group in Europe, they don't believe me," a former dancer admitted.[17] Often, in casual conversations with shop owners or friends (who were not sex workers), when Sosúans spoke of a woman working overseas as a domestic, waitress, or dancer, they inevitably would raise the possibility of sex work; or they would explicitly rule it out, vouching for the authenticity of a particular woman's version of events abroad. One Dominican café owner cynically explained why working overseas and sex work are virtually synonymous: "Dominican women have become known throughout the world as prostitutes"; "they are one of our biggest exports."

CONCLUSION: CHANGES IN SEX WORKERS' LIVES, SOSÚA, AND ITS SEX TRADE

Y ou won't find as many girls in the bar as before," assured a taxi driver. "Everything has changed. Tourists now go to new resorts on the south coast. So the prostitutes have disappeared. They've gone home to their families," a store clerk remarked. When I returned to Sosúa in January 2003, and then again in July, I wandered in and out of closed hotels and took pictures of empty and crumbling swimming pools, fallen wires, and holes in the walls where air conditioners used to sit. Chickens clucked where tourists once had sunned themselves. The eerie emptiness of Sosúa was not concentrated to the center of the commercial district in El Batey. I walked to one of the residential areas of El Batey and soon stopped taking pictures, seeing the same thing block after block: apartment complexes, private homes, or small hotels that were left half built. How many pictures of half-finished structures could I possibly put in one book? Would not one photo tell the story sufficiently? What I could not capture in pictures, however, is how Sosúa's streets—both in El Batey and Los Charamicos—were noticeably less crowded day and night. Tourists had gone somewhere else, and with them Dominicans too had left Sosúa. I could see what everyone had told me, that tourism was "dead now." Sosúa with its abandoned or unfinished buildings was a ghost town. Even though I tell the anthropology students in my fieldwork seminar that their fieldwork will never be "done," as people's lives continue to undergo changes, I was unprepared for the extent and rapidity of the changes in Sosúa and in Sosúans' lives.

Elena's Life after Sex Work

Because I opened this book with Elena, it seems fitting to end with her as well. I have written this ending many times. Elena's life, like so many poor women's lives, has been full of changes—some as a result of her decisions and actions, others as a result of forces out of her control. Elena had not been working in the sex trade and had not been trying to meet foreign men, so I was surprised when she told me in the spring of 2001, by telephone, that she had married a German man. I should not have been surprised; Elena is extraordinary in every way. Bright, funny, and generous, she stands out wherever she goes and becomes the center of attention. She does not just walk down the street; she calls out to friends and they to her. After working as a waitress in several of Sosúa's restaurants, taking computer classes,[1] and playing—successfully—various illegal "pyramid" schemes and lotteries, Elena calculated that this marriage por residencia was the only way that she could establish an economically secure life for her family. In her nearly ten years of living in Sosúa's sexscape, Elena has seen thousands of foreign men hang out in Sosúa's bars and night-clubs looking to have sex with—and in some cases looking for ro-mance with—Dominican women. She has watched countless Do-minican women (and men) migrate to town from throughout the island to find work or meet foreign lovers. And she has said goodbye to friends as they moved to Europe with foreign men, including her three closest friends, who moved to Germany—Nanci and Mari (who both returned and now live in Sosúa), and Andrea (who is still there). In short, Elena knew as well as any veteran of Sosúa's sex trade that unless she married a foreign man who could sponsor her overseas migration, she would continue to live hand-to-mouth. She busied herself that spring with the details of getting a visa to visit her husband, who lived permanently in Germany, as the first step to moving there with her family.

Yet more changes were to come for Elena. As I recounted in chapter 1, Elena's new German husband is no longer in her life. She is convinced that he is mentally unstable; once he had insisted they marry after only knowing one another a few weeks, he left Sosúa never to return again. They speak on the phone occasionally, but Elena is sensible enough to recognize that it is foolish to wait for him to send money, let alone for his help with a visa. In fact she waits for nobody, instead solving problems on her own when they arise. She worked for a few months at a bar in downtown Sosúa in 2002, for example, but the German bar owner paid so poorly and was so verbally abusive to her and to the other Dominican employees (call-ing them stupid and incompetent) that she quit. Since then, she has been working at a bar on the beach, with her friend Mari (whom I wrote about in chapter 3; she had lived in Germany with a German man she married, left him, and then moved back to Sosúa, where she took up a relationship with a Dutch man). Elena selected this job because the owner, a Dutch citizen, works most of the year in Santo Domingo. In his absence she manages the bar and answers to no one. She continues to be the sole breadwinner for her two children, and she also has been helping out an older sister who lives with her and only has occasional work cleaning hotel rooms.

Elena, now thirty, and Mari, now thirty-one, have not been in the formal sex trade since their early twenties. They do not go to bars to find clients who are looking to pay money in exchange for sex. Yet sex and romance—or the performance of romance—with foreign men is still an earning strategy for them. Quite unexpectedly, Mari's German husband followed her to Sosúa. A remarkably quiet man in his early-to-mid sixties, Claus decided to live half the year in Sosúa because, he explained, referring to Mari and her daughter, his "wife and daughter were here." Although he is not the biological father of his stepdaughter, Elena and others report that Claus is a caring and generous father. Mari is unimpressed, however, and is bored with Claus. She had initially left him in Germany because she "did not love him." But his move to Sosúa has translated into greater material comfort for Mari and her daughter. The three of them live together, renting the second floor of a cement house in Los Charamicos that has the nicest kitchen I have seen in the town (with a refrigerator, a stove, a sink with running water, Formica countertops, and wooden cabinets). Mari explains that she continues to work at the bar on the beach with Elena as a way to "get out of the house," but most afternoons Claus is there anyway. He watches her flirt with male customers, usually younger than he. He sits quietly while Mari bounces from one customer's lap to another, boisterously teasing them, as they lavish attention on her. Although he was almost always silent, largely because Mari was so dismissive of him, when I engaged him in conversation (a mix of English and Spanish, both of which he spoke well), his face lit up and he could become quite lively. In our conversations, he made clear his adoration of Mari and her daughter, as well as his commitment to living together as a family.

During my prior trips to Sosúa, I had not spent much time sitting at bars on the beach—other than as a way to interview male tourists and sex tourists. Because Elena was working at a beach bar this time,

I spent hours just sitting and talking with Claus and his friends, other foreign men who live or have lived for months (or years) at a time in Sosúa. From this vantage point, I met other couples such as Mari and Claus, some of whom had children together. It is a different Sosúa from when I first arrived in 1993; by 2003 babies of Dominican-foreign couples seemed to be everywhere (both Dominican women with foreign men and foreign women with Dominican men). During the course of my visit in January 2003, for example, I watched one family "reunification" unfold, after Mari had handed a German man, Chris, her girlfriend's baby (not hers), exclaiming "Merry Christmas, Dad." Chris had not known he had a son until his return vacation to Sosúa. Like Claus, he too had lived in Sosúa, once owning a bar of his own. After the tourist business began to dry up, however, he moved back to Germany. When I met him, he was vacationing in Sosúa to visit another Dominican woman (not the mother of his son). He was elated over the news of his son. He showed off his boy, proud of their resemblance to one another. There was no doubt about his paternity: the two were mirror images of one another. He claims he wants to "do the right thing" and help out financially. But the mother, Carla, a friend of Mari's and Elena's, does not expect much from him. Rather, she knows she probably will end up raising her son on her own. Nonetheless, she let her ex-boyfriend kiss her from time to time, later explaining that she would be happy if he sent money and took an interest in their son but that she doubted any of this would come to pass.

I too share Carla's hesitancy to predict what Chris will do, particularly because he drinks heavily. As barkeep, Elena has observed that Chris and his friends drink all day, every day, of their vacation. At her bar alone, she has watched some of them drink from eight to fifteen rum and cokes or beers over the course of an afternoon (the bars along the beach close at sunset). Some days Chris's speech was so slurred, I had a hard time following what he was saying. If indeed he has a drinking problem, this is one unpromising predictor of his future reliability as a financial provider.

Relationships with Foreign Men after the "Formal" Sex Trade

In Sosúa, as former sex workers such as Elena and Mari get older, they continue to look for foreign men to help with their economic problems. Like the liaisons that grew out of their participation in the "formal" sex trade that consisted of going to the tourist bars and finding clients who pay for sex, these relationships, they candidly explain, also are for practical reasons. I had set out to write a feminist ethnography of the sex trade to raise questions about poor women's power, control, and opportunities in a globalized economy. Yet the waters are murky when considering women's agency in the sex trade, no matter how determined and creative their efforts to get ahead. Also unclear is a clear definition of transactional sex in Sosúa. One difference separates Sosúa's sex workers who cruise the bars nightly and "former" sex workers who still use sex as a transaction: for the former, selling sex is their only job in Sosúa. We cannot call postformal sex-trade relationships, such as Mari's, sex work in a strict sense of the word, since their boyfriends/husbands, many of whom they met as clients, do not hand them money after each sexual act. But a transaction transpires nonetheless. Mari has sex with Claus, and in exchange he pays the bills for her and her daughter to live well. Her countertops and matching cabinetry—which are not in any of her friends' homes—are symbols of their arrangement. Mari, however, risks not benefiting in the long term from this relationship. It is likely that if she and Claus split up, she will end up empty handed, just as Elena did when Jürgen kicked her out. The living-room furniture set, television, and of course the kitchen would be left behind. Claus has given Mari jewelry, including a sizable gold heart necklace with four small rubies, which she could always pawn. Moreover, because Claus pays all household expenses, Mari could save the money she earns at the bar. But, unlike her girlfriends, nearly every day Mari has on a new outfit, leading Elena and her sister to criticize: "Mari loves money. It is all she cares about. She spends any money she gets." And, they emphasized, she spends it only on herself. Whereas Elena had negotiated with Jürgen for him to pay for her daughter to attend private school, Mari has not tried to work out the same arrangements. In fact, Elena and her sister are worried about Mari's daughter; Mari often has left her in the care of others—a long and rotating list of female family members scattered throughout the island, and friends, including Elena and her sister. Elena took care of Mari's daughter while Mari lived in Germany, and not once, Elena said, did Mari send money to help with her daughter's care.

Mari's obvious impatience with Claus, indicated by the rolling of her eyes when he is around, and the silent treatment she gives him, along with her flagrant flirting with other foreign men, does not bode well for their relationship. Claus is also well aware that Mari is still involved with her Dutch boyfriend, Edgar, also in his early sixties, with whom she had been living in Sosúa after she left Claus in Germany. Like so many other foreigners in Sosúa, Edgar has been living between Sosúa and Holland, where his mother has been ill and he has been overseeing her care. After having spent time with Edgar, during a field trip to Sosúa in 1999, I can begin to understand why Mari is impatient with Claus. Whereas Edgar was a "gentleman" in a traditional sense, pulling out Mari's chair for her to sit down to dinner, and filling her glass before his own, Claus appears less elegant, as he gooses Mari (back in their house, not in public on the beach) and calls to her from their front porch to bring him—and some of Mari's male Dominican friends—more ice and rum. Needless to say, Elena and some of Mari's other girlfriends are anxious to see how Mari will handle having her two foreign lovers in Sosúa at the same time. Considering the value sex workers (and former sex workers) place on self-sacrifice for one's children, Mari's spending habits and her neglect of her daughter have made her untrustworthy. Elena and her sister know they cannot count on Mari and that she will always look out for herself rather than her friends or family. Because of this, they suspect that Mari's selfishness will catch up with her and that one or both of her foreign suitors / bankrollers will leave her.

Writing about Poor Women/Sex Workers

Elena's decision to marry someone she does not love, and to prepare (unsuccessfully as it turned out) to move to a country in which she never really wanted to live, was fraught with uncertainty and doubt. Her decisions—no matter how imperfect—remind us of the painful decisions confronting poor Dominican single mothers as they seek to improve their or their children's futures. While talking—both on the island and in the United States—about women's sexual labor, I am often asked why Dominican women would choose to sell sex. I offer sex workers' own explanations in the cloak of a mother's sacrifice. And I point out that women's opportunities for control in Sosúa's sex trade are unusual compared to most other sex-tourist destinations. However, these overly simplified explanations obscure the various factors that push poor women into sex work in Sosúa's sexscape, as well as obscure just how difficult it is to work in the sex trade—in any context—without experiencing challenges to one's ability to control one's working conditions.

Some observers (Sosúans, people living in other places on the island and in the United States) judge these women's decisions to sell sex along moral lines, pointing out that many poor Dominican women—the majority—choose other ways to make money than selling sex. Others acknowledge how poor many single mothers are. Sosúan men, in particular, often comment that these women earn the kind of money that poor Dominican men cannot. But these women do not earn money to add to their male partners' contributions to the household; they replace it entirely. Yet Sosúan men seem more comfortable describing high levels of male un- or under-employment than admitting that these women had been abandoned by men and actually chose the sex trade as their own preferred strategy for economic advancement.

Others see them as naive. For example, my undergraduate students found it inconceivable that women in Sosúa would hang their hopes on men the students saw as sleazy and unreliable. But lacking family networks to migrate legally to New York, or the right social connections on the island to land "respectable," well-paying office jobs that offer skill-building and professional advancement, sex workers in Sosúa regard these men—reliable or not, sleazy or not—as representing some small opportunity for economic advancement. Meeting an honest European man who keeps his promise of marriage and visa sponsorship—and then treats his Dominican wife well—might be a long shot, but it is perhaps the only shot Dominican women in Sosúa's sex trade have at leaving poverty behind. The sex trade is not these women's last-ditch effort to get ahead; marriage is. And even when women begin to become too old for Sosúa's formal sex trade, marriage or other relationships with foreign men are still income-generating strategies.

Sosúans know this, which explains why Elena's friends overlooked Jürgen's alcoholism and infidelity. Even years later, after Jürgen abandoned his son and disappeared, Elena's friends still excused his irresponsible and cruel behavior. Just as Tati's friends called her crazy for leaving her domineering German husband and Germany (see chapter 6), so too Elena's friends blamed her for "blowing it" with Jürgen. Was I hearing this correctly? How could they be revising history so dramatically? Had they not seen Jürgen's downward spiral of drinking, binges that left him drunk—no matter the time of day—far longer than he was sober? Did they not remember that Jürgen skipped town, leaving behind an infant son? And had they not heard Elena's recounting of Jürgen's brief return visit, when their son was one year old, when Jürgen rejected him and denied paternity because of the boy's "black skin?" When I raised any of these points with Elena's closest friends, I was told that Elena should have treated Jürgen better and should have been thankful—even if the situation with Jürgen was less than perfect. Jürgen's binge drinking and constant infidelity, they pointed out, was "no worse than any Dominican man's."

I cannot predict what is ahead of Elena. She is certain her German husband will only call occasionally and will not return to Sosúa, send money, or help her get a visa to visit him in Germany. She owes several months of rent to the owner of her apartment, a Dominican woman who lives overseas but whose father collects the rent. She has already brought her television to the pawn shop, along with her favorite necklace, one that Jürgen had given her. She is so resourceful, however, that even during Sosúa's economic downturn after September 11, 2001, that has put other Sosúans out of work, she has managed to stay employed. But wages available to her are modest enough that she is likely to continue living day to day. Working on the beach, meeting many foreign men, of course, she could become involved again with a foreign man, which she would be open to. It is also possible—and she is open to—becoming involved with a Dominican man. Either way, another income stream in her household, no matter the amount or the consistency, would relieve her of the daily pressures she currently manages. I worry about Elena, not because she cannot take care of herself—quite the contrary, she is impressively driven, focused, and responsible—but rather because her many responsibilities and limited resources are daunting. I am reminded of Sidney Mintz's description of Taso, his main informant and friend he wrote about in *Worker in the Cane*, someone extraordinarily talented yet not given the same privilege of geography, and therefore, education that Mintz was. He writes:

> There is the unequalness, the asymmetry that most matters in the relationship between anthropologist and informant, as opposed to the unequalness, the asymmetry that matters between metropolis and colony. For I enjoyed the continuing freedom to associate with others for the fun of it—to teach and think and read and write for a living. After Taso's book was done, I could go

on observing, loafing, experiencing vicariously. My friend, every bit my equal—in most important ways, I believe, my clear superior—went on working with his hands, at terribly hard work, for too long hours, at too little pay. (Mintz 1989: 795)

Like Mintz, I too am troubled by the gulf between my relatively easy life of middle-class comfort and university work of reading and writing and Elena's ongoing daily practical concerns—such as how to pay her rent—and her frustration with not being able to find a good paying job she enjoys. Proud of her daughter's accomplishments in junior high, she already is counting on her future successes: "She will not work in jobs that I have had; she is very smart and will go to college. She can do what ever she wants."

Changes in Sosúa and its Sex Trade

I have, as Marjorie Wolf (1992: 129) describes the process of writing an ethnography, laid out my "best guesses" about Sosúa, but much has changed since my first trip there. People have moved away, bars and other businesses have closed, and the gossip and rumors I have recounted in this book might now be remembered and recounted differently in Sosúa. Since I began this project in 1993, the first women I interviewed have aged, left the sex trade, and, in most cases, left Sosúa. As German citizens began investing and moving there permanently in the early 1990s, it became a striking example of a town that was caught in and shaped by forces of a globalized economy. Since then, the island has undergone further transformation: a new era of democratic government arrived with Leonel Fernández's election in 1996, only to languish with continued corruption; Hurricane Georges in 1998 devastated much of the agricultural sector; the Dominican national economy has experienced inflation, devaluation of the peso, and unemployment; all tourist spaces in the Dominican Republic have been adversely affected by the downturn in international air travel since September 11, 2001; and previously undeveloped and inaccessible beach areas, valued by investors as "pristine" and "authentic," have experienced tourism development.

Most notably, new beach resorts on the south coast at Punta Cana have attracted a new kind of high-end tourist to the island (although La Romana has long offered luxurious accommodations). These new resorts offer a four-star experience, and in the process have been changing foreign tourists' perception of the Dominican Republic as a cut-rate travel experience. Tourist developers have jumped on this idea of rehabilitating the image of the north coast as well: an elegant four-star hotel that offers both all-inclusive packages as well as nightly rates recently opened in Sosúa. Old-time Sosúan residents are skeptical, however, that this single four-star hotel will have any kind of "trickle-down" effect on the Sosúan economy. One store owner shook his head. "Other than popping into town and looking around, these new tourists stay up in the hotel." The management boasted that they are flying chefs in from all over the world—Italy, France, and Japan—so the guests can choose from the hotel's three different on-site restaurants rather than venture into town for meals.

Since Sosúa's series of bar closures by the police in the late 1990s, the sex trade does not dominate Sosúa's public spaces as it used to. Even though many Sosúans (Dominican and foreign) had wished that the very public and frenzied nightly activities of Sosúa's sex trade would slow down, no one could have foreseen that empty, decaying nightclubs and bars would dot El Batey's landscape. However, contrary to what one might think when walking around town with the Anchor and other bars in rubble, the sex trade by no means has disappeared; it is still in full swing, just in a different setting.

SOSÚA'S SEX TRADE TODAY
With the forced closure, arson, and bankruptcy of Sosúa's large open-air nightclubs, the sex trade is mainly indoors now, except for small numbers of women who can be seen hanging out at the smaller bars in downtown El Batey. Although everyone I spoke with by day in Sosúa (shopkeepers, tourist hotel workers and managers, restaurant owners, Dominican and foreign residents) assured me the sex trade had virtually dried up, sex-for-sale is as available as it ever was—it has simply moved from the center of town into nightclubs on the outskirts of Sosúa. It also is as young as it ever was; the Dominican and Haitian sex workers appear to be in their late teens to mid-twenties. Everyone is more chic: female sex workers, male "sankies," and foreign tourists. No longer do women appear to stretch campesina wardrobes: this new crop of sex workers has spent considerable money and time to look as stylish as it does. Some sex workers use the dance floor lights to their advantage, wearing shimmering body-hugging dresses or tops that catch the light. Or they wear the latest hip-hugger jeans, high heels, and elegant evening

bags, all of which indicate they are making money. Not only has fashion changed but behavior as well. There is much more dancing, in part because the clubs play merengue and *bachata* only at the beginning of the evening—to which foreigners have a difficult time dancing—and then the DJs switch to "club music" that is popular in the United States and Europe for the rest of the evening. There is also more dancing because the tourists are no longer just middle-aged German men. Rather, they are from the United States, Canada, and throughout Europe; many are groups of friends—families even (with teenagers)—who travel to Sosúa's nightclubs from their all-inclusive hotels near Puerto Plata.

Not only have I never seen this diverse a crowd before, but I also have not seen such a young crowd (besides the female sex workers). For example, there is a new group of young Dominican male teenagers, dressed in the latest hip-hop fashions worn in New York. They move around all together, dress alike, dance together—much like self-conscious, conformist teenagers anywhere—and are talked about (by female sex workers) as if one entity. One night I was with Elena and her sister at a club, and they insisted these young men were sankies. They poked at me, satisfied with their assessment, when we saw some of these young men dancing with foreign women who were over forty. However, we also witnessed a pairing off I have seen before in Sosúa: young (late teens, early twenties), handsome, Dominican (and Dominican-Haitian and Haitian) men dancing with young (late teens, early twenties), beautiful, foreign white women dressed in up-to-the-minute fashions. The spectacle of patrons wearing the latest clothes, singing along to the latest club music, and dancing with coolness and sex appeal is a monumental change in Sosúa's night life. Gone are the days of Dominican women dancing alone and of sedentary middle-aged men comprising most of the patrons. Gone too are clubs that visibly need repairs. An entrance fee, multiple bars framing the dance floor, professional lighting, a quiet "VIP"-type sitting area—these all create a new night-life scene for Sosúa. A scene that used to be seedy is now chic.

Also new were the young foreign men, in their early twenties, in Gucci loafers, Diesel jeans, and European-tailored shirts unbuttoned to reveal slim, tan bodies. These young men flaunted their sexuality in ways foreign sex tourists never did before: they took the lead with their sex worker dance partners, bumping and grinding, reversing the seduction that used to be a necessary part of the women's job. I even saw one twenty-something man, in full nightclub revelry, take off his shirt and shimmy around several sex workers. These young men acted out "big men" fantasies, perhaps not possible at night-clubs—because of higher prices and their lack of celebrity—in their home cities. They occupied centrally located tables, had bottles of rum on the table, and invited woman after woman (sex workers all) to "visit" them. Their visits resembled auditions. The men kissed each of the women, twirled them around to see all of their bodies, and selected different women to join them at the table throughout the evening. Outside of strip clubs or other specialty male entertain-ment clubs in North America or Europe, where men have to pay extra for such attention, such as table dances that Katherine Frank (2002) vividly describes in her ethnography of male strip club regu-lars, it is not likely that they could find so many women in a single nightclub to fawn over them.

GLOBALIZATION AT WORK

Sosúa's history has long involved ties to places off the island. Today, it is linked to locations off the island through foreign investment in its tourism sector; migration by North American and European expatri-ates *to* Sosúa; out-migration—or the attempts to migrate—by Do-minicans to these expatriates' countries of origin; and tourism and sex tourism. While European sex tourists have informally "spread the word" about Sosúa's women to their friends, the European media has extensively covered the sex industry in the Caribbean in general and specifically in Sosúa. New technologies have further linked spaces on and off the island: Internet sites dedicated to por-traying Dominican women as sexually available and proficient have mushroomed. Histories of ties between distant places is an old story; Sosúans' updated version of the story, manifested through today's globalized economy, has brought rapid and intense transformation into a sexscape.

Many other spaces in the developing world have undergone near-overnight reinvention as a tourist site or as a sexscape; in this way an ethnography of Sosúa is just one more "case study" in tourism / sex tourism development. But the stories here of Sosúans' efforts to be "active agents in their own history" (Ortner 1984) humanize the all-too-frequent economistic depictions of the "tourism cycle." These stories of making a living in Sosúa's tourist economy stand as ac-counts of individuals who navigate and attempt to shape the local articulations of a globalized economy. Their strategies—successful or not—to sell touristic commodities, such as T-shirts, fruit drinks, motorcycle taxi rides, or sex, help elucidate how the seemingly monolithic and overwhelming notion of "globalization" plays out in real lives, both in small and large ways, every day.

By recounting the many and rapid changes in Elena's and her children's lives—along with the lives of other Sosúans—this book tells an ethnographic story of what happens to *particular people* in one *particular place* who become caught up in—and try to control and benefit from—the forces of globalization. Elena's story, for example, is a tale of her exploitation of Jürgen and of her new husband, as well as of their exploitation of her. Her relationships with these men, and the material comfort they made possible for her and her family, are examples of how sexscapes can offer new opportunities to strategizing individuals. However, these relationships—particularly Elena's and her son's painful rupture with Jürgen—also point to profound limitations within sexscapes. Jürgen's sudden financial abandonment of Elena and her daughter and her sisters (before their son was born) immediately reversed Elena's family's economic security, while his racist rejection of their son revealed what can lie at the other end of the spectrum of the desire for difference. In the background, too, lies the agency inherent in simply possessing a German passport or visa. These documents' allowance of legal, unfettered travel remind us that locals' agency in a sexscape is often as uneven as the power dynamics in the relationships between the locals and the foreigners who visit them. Although Elena and other women I have written about were steadfast in their strategies and their actions to get ahead in Sosúa, they realized their financial goals only in fits and starts.

I can only guess that in the future Sosúa's tourist economy will continue to suffer as more beach areas (with longer stretches of beach than Sosúa) are made accessible (by paving roads, building airports, and building hotels) throughout the island. And alongside this development and the construction of built environments by powerful global economic entities, there will continue the construction of imagined environments and dreams of transformation in those places where globalization touches down. Within both these imagined and built places, individuals such as Elena, strong and unequal, will seek to make their own future off the pleasure seeking and fortune seeking of others.

NOTES

Introduction

1   I have changed all the names of sex workers, along with the names of other Sosúans and foreign tourists whom I interviewed. I also have changed the name of bars and nightclubs, as well as of the boardinghouses where some of the sex workers live. In some cases, I have altered readily identifiable characteristics of Sosúans. The only names I have not changed are those of the European Jewish settlers who took refuge in Sosúa during World War II. I explain more about this in chapter 2.

2   When Elena was arrested in 1994, the official bank rate was 12 pesos to the U.S.$1. The values cited throughout the book reflect this rate, unless indicated otherwise.

3   Most of the tourist bars, nightclubs, restaurants, and stores in Sosúa are located in El Batey, the "tourist" side of Sosúa. A beach divides Sosúa into two distinct communities: El Batey and Los Charamicos. In general, Dominicans reside, shop, and go out to restaurants and bars in Los Charamicos, whereas foreign tourists spend their time in El Batey. As I discuss in chapter 2, foreigners own much of the real estate in El Batey, and many Dominicans walk across the beach from Los Charamicos (or take a three-minute motorcycle taxi ride on the road connecting the two parts of town) to work in the tourist businesses in El Batey.

4   Jürgen was in his mid-forties.

5   Jürgen had his own construction firm.

6   The young sex worker Elena had been looking after moved into a boardinghouse.

7   Poor Dominicans are more likely to enter consensual unions than legal marriage. In fact, unless I specifically mention otherwise, sex workers are not legally married to their husbands. Yet since the women I interviewed referred to the men in their lives as their *esposos* (husbands), I also use this term.

8   For example, as women in Los Charamicos prepare the noonday meal of *arroz con pollo* (rice and chicken) that is accompanied by red beans in a tomato-based sauce, they bring a teaspoon or a cup to the nearest colmado to buy a spoonful of tomato paste for the sauce. Women also might purchase cilantro (also for the sauce) by the sprig, rice and beans by the cup, and eggs and diapers one at a time.

9   Elena's mother died when she was young, and her father had abandoned her mother years earlier. The man she calls her father was her mother's second "husband" (in a consensual union). Elena thinks of the woman he now lives with as part of the family. Yet although she refers to them both as her "parents," she never calls the woman her "mother."

10 Although Elena and Jürgen used condoms during their first sexual encounters as sex worker and client, once they moved in together they stopped using protection. Often Dominican sex workers do not insist on condoms with their boyfriends or regular clients, even though they might consistently practice safe sex with new clients. Sex workers explain that not using condoms with their boyfriends is a sign of intimacy. The Centro de Orientación e Investigación Integral (Center for Integral Orientation and Research; COIN) found that although condom use rates between bar-based sex workers in Santo Domingo and their new clients had risen from 67 percent in 1990 to 93 percent in 1996, condom use with regular clients lagged behind, increasing from 32 percent in 1990 to 50 percent in 1996 (Moreno and Kerrigan 2000: 9). In response, COIN and Centro de Promoción de Solidaridad Humana (Center for the Promotion of Human Solidarity; CEPROSH), formerly known as the Comité de Vigilancia y Control del SIDA (Committee for Vigilance against and Control of AIDS; COVICOSIDA) developed new condom promotion strategies based on the Thai 100% Condom Use Programme. The Thai program used various approaches such as government regulations mandating condom use in commercial sex acts in commercial establishments, access to condoms, and sex worker attendance at regular STI screenings (Moreno and Kerrigan 2000: 10; see Kerrigan 2000).

1 A Transnational Town

1   Although I include material gathered from interviews with Haitian sex workers, this book focuses on Dominican women in Sosúa's sex trade.

2   Throughout this book I use the terms *sex work* and *sex worker* rather than *prostitution* and *prostitute*. Although sex work is a dangerous job and sex workers assume a great number of risks, they can be agents, not just victims. Scholars, activists, and women in the sex trade are divided over how to conceive of women's sexual labor. On one side of the debate, the abolitionist camp rejects the terms *sex work* and *sex worker*, in favor of the terms *prostitute* and *prostitution*. As one lawyer who opposes sex work explains, "Just as prostitution is not about choice, it's not about work. Or if it is, it is work in the same way that slavery or bonded labor is work—work that violates human dignity and every other human right" (Leidholdt 1993: 133). Sex workers' rights advocates, on the other hand, embrace the term *sex work* because it situates sexual labor as work that, therefore, should be legal, protected, and safe. Rather than seeing sex work solely as exploitative, they emphasize women's right to choose to exchange sexual services for money on their terms. In Sosúa, women who sell

sex for money usually call themselves *prostitutas* (prostitutes). However, some women who have participated in *charlas* (talks / presentations) with peer educators from CEPROSH, an AIDS-education nongovernmental organization (NGO), call themselves *trabajadoras sexuales* (sex workers) when they learn that this is the term the peer educators use. I use the terms *sex work* and *sex workers* when talking about the women in Sosúa, since *these women* are able in *this setting* to control some of the conditions of their work—most notably because of the absence of pimps.

3 Similarly, Constance Clark writes about Shenzen, China, as a space of "re-generation." Potential migrants see the city "as an anonymous space with myriad possibilities for the re-creation of self and for making a 'second start' in life" (2001: 106). As a special economic zone that attracts youth from across China, many likened the migration to a "small going abroad," since the city is populated by people from throughout China (ibid.).

4 The term *globalization* is used in so many contexts, from "the corridors of politics, commerce, industry, scholarship, communication, environmentalism and pop culture," that it is "not clear whether the parties invoking globalization mean the same thing or even if they are addressing the same issue" (Ferguson 1992: 69). This book offers ethnographic examples of how individuals cope with, try to take advantage of, and resist a globalized economy. These examples counter several misguided assumptions that run through much writing on globalization: first, that this process is "new"; second, that it homogenizes everything in its path and relies on this lack of differentiation; and third, that it is so overwhelming that things "local" inevitably are transformed. Far from being a new process, "when we are talking about globalization in the present context," Stuart Hall comments, "we are talking about some of the new forms, some of the new rhythms, some of the new impetuses in the globalizing process . . . located within a much longer history." Yet "we suffer increasingly from a process of historical amnesia in which we think that just because we are thinking about an idea it has only just started" (S. Hall 1997: 19–20). Nor do global processes necessarily rely on or produce homogenization; rather, the global restructuring of capital often profits "through the differentiation of specific resources and markets that permits the exploitation of gendered and racialized labor within regional and national sites" (Lowe 1997: 360).

5 Saskia Sassen refers to the importance of "recover(ing) place" in analyses of the global economy, since it "allows us to recover the concrete, localized processes through which globalization exists" (1998: xix–xx). I find Anthony Giddens's description of globalization as a "whole series of influences of our everyday lives that are altering not just events on the large scale but the very tissue of our everyday lives" particularly helpful in grasping the localization of globalization (1994: 18).

6 By combining transnational theory with ethnography, Nina Glick Schiller,

Linda Basch, and Cristina Szanton-Blanc (1994) highlight lived experiences in the global economy to show what it is like, for example, to have to migrate for work, or to wage political battles in one place while living in another.

7   Mahler and Pessar guest-edited a special volume of *Identities* entitled "Theorizing Gender within Transnational Contexts," in which the papers analyze "transnational actions" that are "clearly grounded" (2001: 444). They draw from and build on Michael Kearney's distinction between "transnational" and "global": "Whereas global processes are largely decentered from specific national territories and take place in a global space, transnational processes are anchored in and transcend one or more nation-states" (1995: 548).

8   Thanks to Marc Edelman for suggesting this phrasing.

9   Analyzing exotic and erotic representations of the Pacific—such as in the movie *South Pacific*—Margaret Jolly examines how difference "stimulate(s) desire" (1997: 100). Writing about Brazilian women, Angela Gilliam finds that part of the appeal of women characterized as exotic "rests within the unequal economic and social exchange between visitors and the places to which they travel as tourists" (2001: 174).

10 Cities with foreign military bases are an exception. For example, see Kathy Moon's book on the sex trade that grew up around the U.S. military bases in South Korea (1997), Cynthia Enloe's analysis of the links between militarization and women's exploitation (1989), and essays in Saundra Sturdevant and Brenda Stoltzfus's (1992) edited volume.

11 Although this book focuses on women sex workers' experiences, see Mark Padilla's (2003) research on Dominican male sex workers and Gisela Fosado's (2002) on Cuban male sex workers, on how racialized male bodies are also sought after in sexscapes.

12 Mahler and Pessar discuss globalized hierarchies as operating "at various levels that affect an individual or group's social location" such that they "shape, discipline, and position people and the ways they think and act" (2001: 446).

13 Within Sosúa's sex-tourist trade, I never met women over forty who went to the tourist bars to find foreign clients.

14 German citizens comprise the largest group of foreign residents living there. The overall population of Sosúa is estimated at 28,303 (Oficina Nacional de Estadística de la República Dominicana). The German embassy in Santo Domingo estimates that 20,000 to 25,000 German citizens live in the Dominican Republic. Since German citizens are not required to register with the embassy, the embassy does not have any exact figures. Embassy officials estimate that only 1,000 Germans live in Santo Domingo and even smaller numbers are scattered throughout the country. Thus, they assert that the vast majority of Germans in the Dominican Republic live on the north coast.

15 Throughout his important scholarship on the Caribbean, Sidney Mintz has documented how "Caribbean people have always been entangled with a wider world" (1985: xv).

16 Commenting on Catherine LeGrand's research on a United Fruit Company banana zone in Columbia, William Roseberry writes about "the ways in which foreign influences are introduced within preexisting social and cultural relations that reconfigure and localize or situate the foreign" (1998: 515). He notes that even an enclave economy "as infamous as a United Fruit Company banana zone is not just a foreign enclave." Rather, the "presence and *weight*" of the foreign company is "uneven" throughout the banana zone, and "local farmers and elites respond to and take advantage of the company's presence in different ways" (1998: 515).

17 In Sosúa we see, as Smadar Lavie and Ted Swedenburg noted about power relations, that not "everyone becomes equally 'different,' despite specific histories of oppressing or being oppressed" (1996: 4). I am greatly indebted to Nina Glick Schiller's and Sarah Mahler's comments on some of the ideas in this chapter on unequal statuses in transnational spaces.

18 In the last scene of the movie the affluent, powerful Richard Gere character, Edward, "saves" the Julia Roberts character, Vivian, a poor—but resilient—sex worker. As Roberts's "white knight," he arrives hanging out of the sunroof of a limousine carrying red roses. Gere then scales Roberts's fire escape to "rescue" her through her bedroom window.

19 Erik Cohen (1971) and Glenn Bowman (1986) have written on a similar phenomenon between Palestinian youths in Israel and tourist women. The possibility of marriage to and emigration with tourist women offered an escape from "the humiliation of always being marked as inferior in interactions with Israelis" (Bowman 1986: 78).

20 For a critique of this idea of sex workers who need "rescuing," see H. R. Greenberg (1991c). And see novelist William Vollman's brash and insensitive depiction of his "rescue" of an underage Thai sex worker as a manly and daring adventure in the music magazine *Spin* (1993).

21 Dominican Sosúans—both sex and other workers—often use the verb *progresar* to refer to improving one's economic status.

22 See sex workers' accounts of their experiences with clients in Delacoste and Alexander (1987), McClintock (1993a, 1993b), Bell (1987), and Nagle (1997).

23 A 1990 and 1992 COIN (a Dominican NGO in Santo Domingo that conducts safe-sex presentations to sex workers) poll of 500 sex workers in the Dominican Republic found that two-thirds were single mothers with an average of two children, and 72 percent indicated that their primary reason for entering the sex trade was economic need (COIN 1998: 69–70).

24 The introduction of affordable fax services has allowed residents of Sosúa to send and receive international faxes on a daily basis. In chapter 3 I write more about sex workers' "transnational courting practices"—such as faxing multiple clients at a time—that grow out of the sex trade.

25 Jo Doezema, describes the distinction between "voluntary" and "forced" prostitution that creates divisions between sex workers by reproducing the "whore /

madonna division within the category 'prostitute.' " She writes, "the madonna is the 'forced prostitute'—the child, the victim of trafficking; she, who by virtue of her victim status, is exonerated from sexual wrong-doing." While "the 'whore' is the voluntary prostitute: because of her transgression, she deserves whatever she gets" (1998: 46–47). In the international human rights arena, the distinction between "voluntary" and "forced" has derailed feminist agendas that seek to secure sex workers' rights—rights of all women in the sex trade regardless of how they entered it.

26 Bars in other parts of the Dominican Republic, however, sometimes pay middlemen who recruit women from throughout the country. Renaldo Pareja and Santo Rosario (1992) write about these recruiters in their overview of the sex trade in the Dominican Republic.

27 It also must be noted that because there were no pimps in Sosúa, I believe my safety as a researcher frequenting boardinghouses and bars was not in jeopardy. I do not know if I would have been as safe—or have had access to women selling sex—if there were a network of pimps keeping watch over the sex workers. For another example of a sex-tourism setting in which pimps do not play a major role, see a case in Australia (Banach and Metzenrath 2000).

28 Groups such as COYOTE (Call off Your Old Tired Ethics), based in the United States, demand women's right to determine how to use their bodies. They argue that "voluntary prostitution" (as opposed to forced prostitution) is a form of work over which women should have control. Other groups, such as WHISPER (Women Hurt in Systems of Prostitution Engaged in Revolt), maintain that all "prostitutes" are victims and therefore cannot "choose" to enter the sex trade. Similar debates exist in the Dominican Republic. Yet as I attended the Primer Congreso Dominicano Sobre la Situación de las Trabajadoras Sexuales o Mujeres Prostituidas (First Dominican Congress on the Situation of Sex Workers or Prostituted Women) in Santo Domingo in May 1995, I heard sex workers, scholars, activists, social workers, and lawyers insist on women's right to choose their work.

29 Feminist scholars' contribution to "transnational feminist theory" is particularly valuable since it emphasizes the particularized, historical contexts of women's experiences (Grewal and Kaplan 1994). This contextualizing has profound consequences for the question of agency / choice in sex work because consideration of sex worker's experiences in various contexts throughout the globe challenges the view that sex workers experience a monolithic set of oppressions in the sex trade.

30 For more on what Carla Freeman (2000: 37) calls scholarship on "gender, power, and agency in transnational capitalism," see Ong (1987), Safa (1995a), Yelvington (1995), Wolf (1992), and Kim 1997.

31 Since I argue that Dominican sex workers' opportunity for agency is highly nuanced, Sherry Ortner's discussion of "partial hegemonies" in her "subaltern version of practice theory" helps to conceptualize the thorny territory of

agency in the sex trade. Her analysis—which looks for the "slippages in repro-
ductions," the "disjunctions" in the "loop in which structures construct subjects and practices" and "subjects and practices reproduce structures"—allows
for seeing how Dominican women try to find ways in the sex trade to get
ahead (progresar) (Ortner 1996: 17–18).

32 Dominican resort workers (men and women) also tell stories of foreign tourists' false promises, which I explore in chapter 3.

33 Constance Clark describes a similar dependency on foreign Asian men's whims
as Chinese women wait for these men to pick one of them out from marriage
introduction agencies' video collections. She draws on Doreen Massey's idea of
"power geometry" that "some are more in charge of [mobility] than others"
with Clark's potential brides, much like Sosúa's sex workers, on the "receiving
end of mobility" (Clark 2001: 104; Massey 1993: 61).

34 Sex workers who have regularly corresponded with foreign men, and who
might have visited or lived with men in their home countries, learn to ratchet
down their expectations of foreign men in the future. Once romance does not
blossom on the women's part and their foreign partners do not treat them
dramatically better than Dominican partners, they often settle for what the
relationship can offer them: greater financial security.

35 This is not a setting in which women engage in transactional sex on the side of
other paid jobs, which Alysia Vilar describes as occurring in Cuba's sex tourist
trade (2003).

36 Anne Allison notes that this definition of sex is only one of many "possible
constructions" that is based on Sigmund Freud's ideas of what he considered
"'normal' adult sexuality: acts of genital intercourse with a gendered other
that ends in climax" (1994: 20 drawn from Freud 1962: 107–8).

37 See essays in Manderson and Jolly 1997, Kempadoo and Doezema 1998, Kempadoo 1999, Williams 1999, and Thorbek and Pattanaik 2002.

38 Elizabeth Bernstein tackles this question of "what is 'really' purchased in the
prostitution transaction" through interviews with male clients of sex workers
and the state agents "entrusted with regulating them" in cities in California
and Western Europe (2001: 392).

39 These Chinese women's transactional use of marriage, Constance Clark writes,
has earned them a reputation similar to that of Sosúan sex workers as "gold
diggers" searching for foreign "airplane tickets" (2001: 105).

40 Eva Ilouz explores the connections between romantic love and the marketplace (1997). Marriage has long served, in many cultures, as a site for the exchange of wealth. She comments that until the beginning of the twentieth century marriage was considered to be, by all classes except for those who could
not afford a ceremony, "one of the most, if not the most, important financial
operations of their lives" (1997: 9). Of course, reality television shows—such as
For Love or Money, in which participants have to perform love convincingly
enough to win money—have certainly served as crass pop cultural reminders

that all marriages potentially contain transactional elements. In contrast, Laura Ahearn charts how Nepalese women's increased literacy has allowed them to seek love marriages—facilitated through love-letter writing—rather than "capture" or arranged marriages (Ahearn 2001).

41 Eithne Luibhéid's research on the U.S. immigration control system examines how "historically laws and procedures granted 'preferred' admission to wives, while mandating the exclusion of lesbians, prostitutes, and other 'immoral' women" (2002: xi).

42 For research on third-world women's factory labor see Fuentes and Ehrenreich (1985), Ong (1987), Safa (1995a), Freeman (2000), Kim (1997), Lim (1990), Fernández-Kelly (1983), and Wolf (1992); for research on third-world women's domestic labor see Bunster and Chaney (1985), Constable (1997), Chaney and Castro (1989), Romero (1992), and Hondagneu-Sotelo (2001); and for research on third-world women's sexual labor see Phongpaichit (1982), Caldwell, Galster, and Steinzor (1997), Enloe (1989), Moon (1997), Sturdevant and Stoltzfus (1992), Kempadoo and Doezema (1998), Kempadoo (1999), Brussa (1989), Tabet (1989), Truong (1990), and Thorbek and Pattanaik (2002).

43 In his work with Dominican male sex workers, Mark Padilla observes that such major economic shifts have resulted in constructing the Dominican Republic as a "reservoir of a new kind of sexual labor" (2003: 3).

44 Sassen writes about a "narrative of eviction" that "excludes a whole range of workers, firms, and sectors that do not fit the prevalent images of globalization" (1998: 82).

45 Inderpal Grewal and Caren Kaplan note this omission: "Several decades of feminist research" on "topics such as [the] gendered division of labor, [and] sex tourism" have been ignored by "recent approaches to global capital" (1999: 352). Grewal and Kaplan are particularly concerned with the effects of scholarship which lumps all "subaltern" or "proletariat" together, thus eliding the "uneven divisions between men and women, as well as between first and third world constructions of class as inflected by race" (1999: 353).

46 Similarly, in his book *Global Sex*, Dennis Altman quotes Bruce Rich on how Bangkok has come to be known as a "global brothel" (Altman 2001: 10 on Rich 1994: 2). For a detailed political-economic analysis of the growth of Thailand's sex trade out of the "rest and recreation" industry for the U.S. military during the Vietnam War, see Truong (1990).

47 Mary Louise Pratt examines travel accounts from the colonial period, in which "native" women were bought by European men "to serve as sexual and domestic partners for the duration of their (the men's) stay" (1992: 95). One Dutch traveler wrote about this "concubinage" as "essential to Europeans survival, since the women knew how to prepare local food and medicine, and could tend Europeans when they were sick" (1992: 96).

48 Kamala Kempadoo notes that Frantz Fanon's notion of " 'Black Bodies, White Faces' seems to capture the post-colonial Caribbean ideology of female sexual

attractiveness," which "revolves around a synthesis of racialized stereotypes of a heightened sensuality, uninhibited sexual passion and physical desirability of the Black African female body and fine or 'delicate' facial features and silky hair of the White Euro-American woman" (1998: 131).

49 Fusco explains this stereotype evolved from the colonial roles of many mixed race women as both the " 'love children' and mistresses of white men." She cites an old Cuban adage of the Caribbean plantation that "white women were for marrying, black women were for work and *mulatas* were for sex" (1998: 155).

50 Claims to a "less traumatic and more socially desirable" Indian ancestry—from the Taino Indians who were exterminated by the Spanish—has helped past and present Dominican elites " 'whiten' their own perception of their color and race" (Sagás 2000: 35). Writing about identity discourse in the Dominican Republic, Kimberly Simmons describes the indio identity as a "defining characteristic of Domincanness" which differentiates between Haitians and Dominicans (Simmons 2001: 92).

51 For more on the massacre and racism against Haitians, see Lauren Derby's "Haitians, Magic, and Money: Raza and Society in the Haitian-Dominican Borderlands" (1994) as well as Edwidge's Danticat fictional account of the massacre, *The Farming of Bones* (1998). The number of Haitians massacred is disputed and ranges from 10,000 to 20,000. The historian Eric Roorda estimates, for example, that 12,000 Haitians were killed during a week of violence (1998: 127).

52 There are a number of studies on Haitian agricultural labor in the Dominican Republic. Martin Murphy (1991), Saskia K. S. Wilhelms (1994), and Franc Báez Evertsz (1986) have written on the working and living conditions of Dominican and Haitian labor on Dominican sugar plantations. Senaida Jansen and Cecilia Millán (1991) specifically have addressed the condition of Haitian women in Dominican *bateyes* (living quarters for agricultural workers). Also, see a photo essay that documents the inhuman living and working conditions of Haitian cane workers in the Dominican Republic (Kratochvil and Wilenz 2001).

53 Why do these tourists choose to vacation in the Dominican Republic over other Caribbean destinations, and why do Germans make up the majority of those visitors? For Europeans traveling on package tours, since the mid-1990s the Dominican Republic has been the cheapest beach vacation destination. "Price continues to be the driving force behind the country's meteoric rise from tourism obscurity five years ago to the Caribbean's most popular destination today," notes a European travel publication (Travel Trade Gazette Europa 1997). A German tour operator also attributed German travel to the Dominican Republic to the price: "Two-thirds of Germans going to the Caribbean go to one destination, and that is the Dominican Republic. This is not because they like it more than the others, it is because it is large and the real key is the price. You have fully-inclusives for U.S.$50 per night. You cannot get a similar holiday in Europe for that price" (Travel Trade Gazette Europa 1997). It is not a

surprise to travel industry experts who have described Germans in terms such as "world champion travelers" (Atkinson 1994) that German travelers have taken advantage of the inexpensive package tours to the Dominican Republic. Per capita, Germans spend more on foreign travel than citizens of any other country in the world (Travel Industry World Yearbook 1999: 6, 109).

54　It is unclear if these white foreign tourists would have spoken so freely to me about how they associated Afro-Dominican women's skin color with sexual proficiency and passion (see chapter 6), if my own skin color were not white.

55　See Gutmann (1996) and Safa (1995a).

56　Christian Krohn-Hansen describes the meaning of *tíguere* in the Dominican Republic: "the Dominican mythology of the *tíguere* has shaped, and continues to shape, a man who is both astute and socially intelligent; both courageous and smart; both cunning and convincing; and a gifted talker who gets out of most situations in a manner that is acceptable to others, while he himself does not at any time step back, stop chasing, or lose sight of his aim (be it women, money, a job, a promotion, etc.)" (1996: 108–9).

57　Sosúa's twist on what qualifies as "macho" or on who is a *tíguere*, dismantles hegemonic and unitary notions of "the Latin American male." Matthew Gutmann (1996) explores the varied and diverse interpretations and expectations of maleness and machismo in Mexico City. In contrast to Dominican men in Sosúa, who often embrace the term *tíguere* and revel in being perceived as macho, Gutmann found that Mexican men are resistant to being typecast as the "typical" Mexican macho.

58　In migration scholarship alone, references to things "transnational" are so varied that Mahler catalogs some of the terms that make up this "confusion": "transnational social field; transnational migrant circuit; binational society; transnational community; network; global ethnoscape; and socio-cultural system" (1998: 75). Far from being an "established field," research on transnational processes is a "highly contested approach that has yet to form a common agenda for research and analysis" (1998: 74).

59　For discussions on how the study of transnational migration evolved, see Mahler (1998), Glick Schiller (1999), Smith and Guarnizo (1998), and Glick Schiller, Basch, and Szanton-Blanc (1992, 1994).

60　Glick Schiller writes about transnational migration as "a pattern of migration in which persons, although they move across international borders and settle and establish social relations in a new state, maintain social connections within the polity from which they originated" (1999: 96). Glick Schiller also clearly distinguishes things global from transnational: whereas she writes about things global as "processes that are not located in a single state but happen throughout the entire globe" (such as the development of capitalism), she uses the term *transnational* "to discuss the political, economic, social, and cultural processes that extend beyond the borders of a particular state, include actors that are not states, but are shaped by the policies and institutional practices of states" (1999: 96).

61 Writing about these kinds of transnational ties that are "episodic and often imagined rather than realized," Mahler and Pessar choose the "more open descriptor" of "transnational spaces / contexts" since it is "broader and more inclusive than transnational social fields" (2001: 444).

62 Two important studies document Dominican migration to New York: Grasmuck and Pessar (1991) and Georges (1990). Peggy Levitt (2001) analyzes ties between Miraflores in the Dominican Republic, and Jamaica Plain (a neighborhood in Boston). These studies shed light on Dominican migration strategies and transnational ties which link Dominican sending communities to communities in the United States.

63 As of October 2000, more than 1 million Dominicans resided in the United States. Roughly one in nine Dominicans is now thought to live, legally or illegally, in the United States.

64 Many Sosúans refer to places off the island, whether in Europe or the United States, as *fuera*. Throughout the book I use the term as Sosúans do, to refer to any place not inside the Dominican Republic.

65 This preoccupation led Patricia Pessar to title her 1995 book on Dominican migration *A Visa for a Dream: Dominicans in the United States*, after Guerra's popular song.

66 However, a valid U.S. passport is now recommended for U.S. citizens for entry to and exit from the Dominican Republic. The U.S. Department of State issued a consular information sheet on 23 March 2000, advising U.S. citizens to carry a valid passport, or a certificate of naturalization / citizenship, or a U.S. birth certificate and photo identification.

67 The U.S. Coast Guard interdicted 4,047 Dominican migrants at sea in 1995; 5,430 in 1996; 1,143 in 1997; 831 in 1998; 531 in 1999; 781 in 2000; 279 in 2001; 801 in 2002; and 285 in the first two months of 2003 (U.S. Coast Guard 2003).

68 The concept of social field, Glick Schiller writes, "facilitates an analysis of the processes by which immigrants become incorporated into a new state and maintain ongoing social relationships with persons in the sending state" (1999: 98). José Itzigsohn, Carlos Dore Cabral, and Esther Hernández Medina describe the transnational social field as "constructed through the daily life and activity of immigrants affecting all aspects of their life, from their economic opportunities, to their political behavior, to their individual and group identities" (1999: 318). In response to the problem of whom to include within a transnational community and what types of practices should be considered transnational, they distinguish between "narrow" and "broad" transnational practices. They define transnationality in a "narrow" sense as referring "to those people involved in economic, political, social, or cultural practices that involve a regular movement within the geographic transnational field" (1999:

323). Whereas they define transnationality in a "broad" sense to refer "to a series of material and symbolic practices in which people engage that involve only sporadic physical movement between the two countries" (1999: 323), what I suggest as qualifying as part of a transnational social field in Sosúa might not involve any movement at all.

69 Since "much of what people actually do transnationally is foregrounded by imagining, planning, and strategizing," Mahler and Pessar emphasize, "these must be valued and factored into people's agency" (2001: 447). They point out that there are instances in which "people may not take any transnational actions that can be objectively measured (such as remitting funds, writing letters, or joining transnational organizations), yet live their lives in a transnational cognitive space" (2001: 447).

70 In the case of sex workers in Sosúa, I am referring to images they see on television of life in Europe (and in the United States). They also see firsthand how European and Canadians live in the expatriate residential sections of Sosúa.

71 For more on inequalities and globalization see Smith and Guarnizo (1998) and Sassen (1998); and for more on gender, inequalities, and globalization see Bergeron (2001) and Moghadam (1999).

72 *Gringo*, in Dominican parlance, generally refers to white individuals from North America or Europe.

73 Although I would like to acknowledge these women by name, as with all other sex workers mentioned in this study, I promised I would conceal their identities.

74 Since many sex workers could not read, I discussed these questions with them.

75 Interviews were conductd in either Spanish or English. Most of the Haitian sex workers I interviewed spoke some Spanish; if not, their friends with better Spanish-language skills would help the conversations along. Similarly, most European tourists and residents spoke some English. In some cases, the foreign residents spoke Spanish better than English, in which case the interviews took place in Spanish.

76 Enloe's (1993) research on the sex industry around military bases is one notable exception. She even provides a lengthy list of men whose "actions may contribute to the construction and maintenance of prostitution around any government's military base"; the list includes (among others) husbands and lovers; bar and brothel owners, local and foreign; national finance ministry officials; local male soldier customers; and foreign male soldier customers (153). Saundra Sturdevant and Brenda Stoltzfus (1992) also make explicit the individuals who make possible and benefit from local women selling sex to foreign men (and local men in some cases).

77 Rather than investigate an unflattering aspect of Japanese culture, Allison was urged to turn her interests toward more "traditional" areas of "Japaneseness," such as tea ceremonies (1994).

1   The term *contact zone* invokes the colonial encounter, which is how Mary Louise Pratt uses the term in her book on travel writing: "[Contact zone] refer[s] to the space of colonial encounters, the space in which peoples geographically and historically separated come into contact with each other and establish ongoing relations, usually involving conditions of coercion, radical inequality, and intractable conflict" (Pratt 1992: 6).

2   Individuals are considered residents of the Dominican Republic when they have remained in the country for more than 182 days, continuously or discontinuously, in the fiscal period of 1 January through 31 December of each year. The Tax Code (Law 11 of 16 May 1992) applies a fixed tax rate towards individuals for all financial income received from Dominican and foreign sources as of the third year of residency in the Dominican Republic (Russin and Bonetti 2000a).

3   Although prostitution is not illegal in the Dominican Republic, the police often operate as if it were. In Sosúa, the police demand bribes from women and men whom they arrest for allegedly prostituting themselves. Iris de la Soledad Valdéz writes about the ambiguous legal position of prostitution in the Dominican Republic (de la Soledad Valdéz 1996). The Domestic Violence Law, Ley 24-97, was enacted in 1997 and prohibits acting as an intermediary in a transaction of prostitution. The government has used this law to prosecute third parties who derive profit from prostitution (U.S. Department of State, Bureau of Democracy, Human Rights, and Labor 2000).

4   In her chapter on a United Fruit Company banana enclave in Columbia, LeGrand describes enclaves to be commonly understood as "economic zones created by foreign direct investment where capital, technology, management, and sometimes labor are introduced from the outside" (1998: 334).

5   *Hallo* is no longer in existence. *DomRep Magazin* is another German magazine focused on news in the Dominican Republic. It can be accessed online at http://www.domrep-magazin.de/. There also are two Dominican radio stations that broadcast in the German language.

6   Bateyes are the living quarters for agricultural workers, usually Haitian workers. The word originates from a Taino Indian word meaning "stone clearing."

7   In the fall of 1994, the state water company turned the water on twice a day (half an hour in the morning and half an hour at night) during which time Sosúans could fill buckets and drums with water. Yet by the spring of 1995, water shortages increased. The state water company turned water on only once or twice a week. Sosúans resorted to buying water from trucks carrying siphoned and often polluted river water.

8   There are a few colmados on the outskirts of El Batey; motorcycle taxi drivers stop at these to buy a soda or chunks of bread and cheese for lunch.

9   Revenue from tourism in the Dominican Republic was U.S.$2.14 billion in 1998, the highest of any Caribbean nation (Association of Caribbean States 2001a).

Tourism accounted for 13.52 percent of the Dominican Republic's gross domestic product in 1998 and has been above 13 percent every year since 1994 (Association of Caribbean States 2001b). Receipts from tourism totaled $2.86 million in 2000 and $2.68 million in 2001 (World Tourism Organization 2002).

10 Guests at these hotels pay a fixed price in their home countries and generally spend little money in the Dominican Republic. The packages include airfare, hotel, meals, and sometimes drinks and even cigarettes.

11 The exact number is not known. I have seen a range of estimates; Richard Symanski and Nancy Burly (1973), for example, write about 1,000 Jewish refugees, whereas a recent article by Debbie Blumberg (2003) cites 645.

12 These are the Jewish settlers' real names and are the only real names I identify in the book. The settlers agreed to be identified. Also, I decided to use their real names because they have been interviewed and identified by name many times before (by journalists, travel writers, and scholars of Jewish history) as well as in fellow settler Josef David Eichen's testimonial, *Sosúa: Una colonia hebrea en La República Dominicana* (1980).

13 I am grateful to Sylvie Papernik, Otto's daughter, who generously shared her father's memoir with me.

14 From 1980 to 1996, the average annual growth rate of tourist arrivals to the Dominican Republic was 10.62 percent. Among the world's top tourism destinations, the Dominican Republic was one of only eleven nations which boasted an average growth rate over 10 percent (World Tourism Organization 1998: 13). International tourist arrivals grew by 12.1 percent in 1999–2000; arrivals, however, decreased by 6.6 percent in 2000–2001. The Caribbean experienced a regional decline in tourist arrivals after September 11, 2001. The average regional decline was 6 percent in the months following the terrorist attacks, while arrivals to the Dominican Republic dropped by 5 percent (World Tourism Organization 2002).

15 The U.S. Department of State reported the 1998 labor force to be 2,889,000 (unemployment rate: 14.4 percent) and the 1999 labor force to be 2,965,000 (unemployment rate: 13.8 percent) (U.S. Department of State, Bureau of Economic and Business Affairs 2001). Economists estimate that 141,000 were employed in Dominican hotels, restaurants, and bars in 1999 (Economist 2000: 9). The estimated labor force in 2000 was 3,785,521, of which 1,224,114 were women, a participation rate of 37.6 percent (Báez 2000: 45, 49, 51).

16 The term *sanky-pankies* evolved from "los hanky-pankies." These men do not work for a set fee but for gifts, meals, and other expenses at the discretion of tourists. They hang out on the beaches by day and in the nightclubs at night, looking for foreign women. The original sankies' trademark, in the early 1980s, was dreadlocks, sometimes bleached by the sun. Dominican men who do not want to be labeled sankies thus avoid having dreadlocks or long hair. In the early 1980s, sankies were rumored to have sexual encounters with both men and women, but as the threat, and stigma, of AIDS increased, sankies' homosex-

ual liaisons have gone underground. A beachgoer or nightclubber today is more likely to see sankies hitting on women. For more on Dominican sankies, see de Moya et al. (1992).

17 For example, see Rebecca Scott (1985) on cities in colonial Cuba.

18 The following examine this theme of the "dangers" female sex workers represent: Donna Guy (1990) on late nineteenth- and early twentieth-century Buenos Aires; Carroll Smith-Rosenburg (1985) on U.S. cities in the late nineteenth century; Judith Walkowitz (1980) and (1992) on Victorian London; and Luise White (1990) on colonial Nairobi.

19 When I returned to Sosúa in 1999, everyone I asked about the fire at the Anchor told me unhesitatingly that they believed it was arson.

20 The Dominican police have been criticized by the U.S. Department of State for frequent human rights abuses, including extrajudicial killings, disappearances, and torture or inhumane treatment. The police also have been cited for their reluctance to handle rape cases and for frequent encouragement of victims to seek assistance from NGOS (U.S. Department of State, Bureau of Democracy, Human Rights, and Labor 2000).

21 In 1995, when the arrests I recount in this chapter took place, the average police officer was earning 900 pesos a month (U.S.$75.00), one of the lowest-paying jobs in the Dominican Republic.

22 The meeting was conducted entirely in German, but I sat with a German friend who translated the discussions for me into English.

23 The suspect was dubbed the "gentleman robber," since his modus operandi was to politely question his victims as to where everything was while they were blindfolded and tied up. He always apologized before he left. Many believed he had lived in the United States because his English was so polished. He hit at least half a dozen houses or apartments in and around Sosúa and Cabarete.

24 Despite these women's perceptions of the exclusivity of the meeting, one of the first items discussed was that the seal of the association could not have colors from the German flag, since the organization must be an international group.

25 Carlos was referring to an insufficient number of schools in the countryside. Many schools are understaffed and have few books or supplies.

26 Although Europeans are customers, I am unaware of any foreigners who own these kinds of bars with rooms in the back.

3 *Performing Love*

1 "Un Amor en el Caribe" by Lorena S. Victoria appeared on 21 November in one of the Dominican Republic's most well-respected news magazines, *Rumbo* (1994: 43).

2 Judith Butler's groundbreaking theorization on "performance" in relation to

gender has become a central concept in gender studies. For this project I am interested in her writing on "gender parody," which we see, for example, in drag that "implicitly reveals the imitative structure of gender itself—as well as its contingency" (1990: 137). If I were to write about a "love parody" in the Butlerian sense, however, I would be suggesting that there is no "original." Below I further explore this idea of distinguishing the "real thing" from false, inauthentic, or fabricated "love."

3   Catherine Lutz (1988: 145) summarizes James Averill's (1985) description of love in "American understandings" as "idealization of the other, suddenness of onset, physical arousal, and commitment to the other." In Sosúa, local understandings of what I am calling "real love" mirror Averill's description.

4   Linda-Anne Rebhun was also interested in how people "describe sentiment" but moved past "vocabulary to discourse: what people talk about in relation to sentiment, how they communicate, what they say, as well as what they leave unsaid and they act out in wordless practice" (1999: 11).

5   Catherine Lutz writes about the attachment of local meanings to emotion in her research with the Ifaluk: "Emotion can be a cultural and interpersonal process of naming, justifying, and persuading people in relationship to each other. Emotional meaning is then a social rather than an individual achievement—an emergent product of social life" (1988: 5).

6   The November 1994 double wedding also was widely publicized in the British press. In the wake of these stories, another British woman came forward with a cautionary tale. Four years earlier, Sharon Kelly had met and married Rafael Gutiérrez, a Dominican tour company driver, after an eight-week courtship. They married in the Dominican Republic and then successfully applied for a British visa for Rafael. Soon after their move to Sharon's home in Norwich, Rafael expressed a desire to obtain a visa to visit the United States. Denied once, he applied again and received a tourist visa. He left England with a one-way ticket to the Dominican Republic via New York but not before emptying Sharon's bank account, maxing out her credit card, and stealing her most valuable jewelry. Although they spoke by phone when he was in New York, as of November 1994 Sharon had not heard from Rafael since May 1992 (Hardy 1994).

7   Karen Kelsky explains that the term *yellow cab* was "allegedly coined by American men, [but] yellow cab was in fact invented and popularized by Japanese journalists to imply that Japanese women are, from a foreigner's perspective, 'yellow' and can be hailed as easily as a taxi" (1994: 465).

8   Angela Gilliam (2001) and Susanne Thorbek (2002a, 2002b) examine the relationship between the colonial eroticization of non-European women and the contemporary exoticization of third-world sex workers. In particular, both essays consider the role the brutal display in Paris's Musée de l'Homme of Saartje Baartman (a young woman taken from what is now South Africa to be exhibited like an animal in Europe) has played in shaping colonial and contem-

porary views of black women's sexuality. The display of her body "was placed at the unsavory intersection of slavery, an Enlightenment classificatory system, and quasi-pornographic notions of medicine" (Gilliam 2001: 179).

9 Men who are gossiped about as sankies do not use this term to describe themselves. Mark Padilla's findings in a research project with 200 male sex workers in Santo Domingo and Boca Chica suggest that only a small minority of those interviewed use this term to describe themselves. Rather, more commonly, the men pejoratively apply the term to others, and sometimes use it when ribbing one another. Padilla finds that the term carries less stigma than the terms *puta* or *prostituta* for female sex workers, because male sex work (with female clients) in comparison with female work seems less transgressive and more in line with norms of male gender and sexuality (Padilla 2003).

10 Activity directors organize social events for hotel guests, such as dancing lessons or sporting events.

11 Remittances to the Dominican Republic grew by 85 percent between 1996 and 2000. In 2000 remittances totaled approximately $1.7 billion, 80 percent of which came from Dominicans living in the United States (Latin Finance 2001).

12 When I started fieldwork in the Dominican Republic in 1993, the official bank rate was around 12 pesos to the U.S.$1. In the summer of 2003, the rate climbed to 33 pesos.

13 Between 1993 and 1994, the Dominican Republic was the country with the highest increase in immigration in the United States (6,171 people, or 13.7 percent). This increase is attributed to an influx of immediate relatives of U.S. citizens (an increase of 9,503 between the fiscal years 1993 and 1994) (U.S. Department of Justice, Immigration and Naturalization Service, 2001a).

14 Boca Chica is another tourist beach town with a lively sex trade. It is on the south coast of the Dominican Republic, outside of the capital, Santo Domingo.

15 Sex workers usually do not receive faxes written in German or in languages other than English or Spanish. In the case of their clients / boyfriends who do not speak any English or Spanish, the men appear to have received help from friends in translating their faxes so that the Dominican women can read them.

16 Other Dominican customers at this branch of Codetel are internal migrants who are in Sosúa to work in the tourist trade. They generally use the service to phone their families back home.

17 Sex workers do not have access to phones at the boardinghouses; nor do they have phones, other than cell phones, in their apartments or houses.

18 Although there are new cybercafés in El Batey, e-mail is not—as of yet—a form of communication between sex workers and their clients. Since literacy is low among sex workers, and their familiarity with computers is nonexistent, it is not likely that this will become a widely used form of communication.

19 For more on letter writing between clients and sex workers, see *Hello My Big, Big Honey*, a collection of love letters that foreign men have sent Thai "bar girls" in Bangkok (Walker and Ehrlich 1992).

20 With only a third-grade education, Nanci could not read or write. In order to correspond with her suitors, she sought the help of more literate sex workers.

21 The leading source countries for spouses of U.S. citizens in fiscal year 1994, for example, were Mexico (19,828) and the Dominican Republic (14,894). The number of spouses of U.S. citizens admitted from the Dominican Republic increased by 52 percent between fiscal years 1993 and 1994 (U.S. Department of Justice, Immigration and Naturalization Service, 2001b).

4 Sosua's Sex Workers

1 Multiple interests in the household and resulting complex power dynamics have been handled well in women-and-migration research. Studies such as Sherri Grasmuck and Patricia Pessar's (1991) on Dominican migration to New York and Pierrette Hondagneu-Sotelo's (1994) on Mexican migration have shown that decisions about which member(s) of a household migrates where, when, and how are a function of power dynamics in the household. This is especially true when one examines who has access to the resources necessary for migration. Dispelling the notion of the household as a homogenous, income-pooling "black box," this body of research reveals the household as a site of unequal and hierarchical relations. For more on power dynamics in the household, see Blumberg (1991), Dwyer and Bruce (1988), Whitehead (1984), and Young, Wolkowitz, and McCullagh (1984).

2 José Itzigsohn (2000) also includes migrant remittances on this list of growth sectors.

3 Clara Báez reports that the economic participation rate for women grew from 29.7 percent in 1985 to 32.6 percent in 1990, 35.3 percent in 1995, and 37.6 percent in 2000. The average growth rate for Dominican women in the work force from 1995 to 2000 was 3.4 percent, compared to 2.2 percent for men (Baez 2000: 51).

4 In 2000 it was estimated that a family of five requires 5,400 pesos a month for basic necessities (World Bank 2001)

5 Women working in free-trade zones are subject to constant discrimination, including low wages and sexual harassment by supervisors (Organization of American States 1999). Human Rights Watch reported in 1996 that pregnancy tests are widespread in the factories, in spite of national laws prohibiting them (Htun 1996). Oxfam also cites abuses such as forced overtime, repression of unions, sterilization certificates, and insufficient bathroom breaks or work recesses as rampant throughout the free-trade zones (Hernández Medina 2002).

6 Reductions in U.S. sugar quotas from the Dominican Republic, which had previously accounted for half of the quota from the Caribbean Basin, forced many men out of work. Sugar export revenues declined from U.S.$555 million in 1980, to U.S.$191 million in 1989 (Safa 1995: 21). In 1999, sugar refining

accounted for a mere 0.5 percent of the country's gross domestic product (Economist 2000).

7   Who spends money is just as important in understanding household dynamics as who earns it and what they earn. Members of households not only act with different interests and levels of authority, but their income allocation decisions greatly affect household members' well-being, especially children's. Patricia Engle (1995) found that women's ability to attend to children's immediate needs hinges on their independent control of household income. When they have that control, children's nutrition levels are higher. Mercedes González de la Rocha found that among the working class in Mexico, for example, women allocate their wages to the household, while men generally only give half their wages, keeping the rest for their own expenses (1994).

8   Their work decisions, in turn, will affect their daughters' education and work trajectories as is underscored by Lourdes Benería and Martha Roldán's (1987) study of women piecemeal workers' households in Mexico City. Benería and Roldán describe that girls are passed over when deciding which household members will receive an elementary education as well as that girls help with household tasks that are understood to be women's work, such as acting as "substitute mother[s] for younger brothers and sisters." Their research calls attention to the significant link between gender hierarchies in the household, girls' educational levels, and their future work trajectories (1987: 84).

9   It is unlikely, however, that Ani would have been able to send her daughter to college without help from her daughter's grandparents.

10 She elaborates that households without mothers at the center to hold them together "cease to exist," while "a household without men, either male head or sons, can go on" (González de la Rocha 1994: 161).

11 I was extremely worried about Maribel once I pieced together her age. Although throughout my fieldwork I made a point of appearing to not judge the women's decisions on any level, I urged Maribel to stay out of the bars. I had not given this advice to any sex worker before, nor have I since.

12 Scholars have written a great deal on women in extended families who raise one another's children to overcome problems of absentee fathers. Edith Clarke's *My Mother Who Fathered Me* (1957) remains one of the most well-known works on women in the Caribbean. In this classic study on Jamaican families, household composition, and conjugal unions, Clarke examined both single-parent households as well as what she called grandmother and great-grandmother households.

13 Data on female-headed households in the Dominican Republic reveal an increase in recent decades, with 19.6 percent of households headed by women in 1971, 24.1 percent in 1984 (Gómez 1989), and 29.5 percent in 1991 (Ramírez 1993). The United Nations reports that 25 percent of Dominican households are headed by women (United Nations Statistics Division 2000).

14 Feminist scholars have written extensively on this designation of women's

wages as supplementary to men's wages. Eleanor Fapohunda (1988), for example, writes about nonpooling households with gender-specific expenditure patterns, noting that the Yoruba distinguish between men's income as purchasing "essential" items while women's income covers "supplementary" goods.

15 Owners who do not live at the bar and oversee its daily operations hire administrators to live at and manage the business.

16 Interviewing Dominican sex workers who work in the houses that line the canals in the heart of Amsterdam's red-light district, I found that those sex workers, in contrast, have mirrored walls or ceilings, pink or red bedspreads or curtains, and sex toys that double as decorations.

17 Although I only met one female bar owner, I did find several female administrators.

18 The stereotypes the dependents hold of the independents, and vice versa, are not wholly inaccurate. Although some women pick pockets outside of the tourist bars, by no means is this a widespread practice. Women who work with tourists similarly condemn those who steal, since they bring a bad reputation to all sex workers and provide the police with another reason to closely monitor sex workers' actions.

19 No women worked as sex workers at their bar.

20 Because these women do not work for pimps, I believe my safety as a researcher frequenting boardinghouses and bars was not an issue. I do not know if I would have felt as safe and comfortable if there were a network of men keeping watch over the sex workers. At the very least, I would not have had as much access to the women. Also, within a system of pimps, I could have compromised the sex workers' safety by talking with them.

21 The Anchor was closed during the day, as are most other nightclubs like it.

5 Advancement Strategies

1 There were adult men who dressed as women and worked the bars. I rarely saw them, however, since they tried to keep a low profile—as much as they could and still look for clients—from the police.

2 Rita is the only sex worker I met in Sosúa who was still married (in a consensual union).

3 The police do not enter the bars or nightclubs to make arrests but rather arrest women as they arrive from Los Charamicos by motoconcho taxis, or as they mill around outside the bars.

4 For sex workers, starting a small business such as a colmado, provides security in times of crises. Many of the goods on a colmado's shelf—rum, for example— are not perishable and thus are an investment. Also, since colmados can be run out of the home, there are few costs other than start-up capital necessary to purchase the stock.

5   As Diane Elson points out, "The absence of a husband leaves most women worse off. The core of gender subordination lies in the fact that most women are unable to mobilize adequate resources (both material and in terms of social identity) except through dependence on a man" (Elson 1992: 41).

6   Rhoda Halperin's (1990) research on kin-based social networks in Appalachia uncovered a similar economic strategy, the "Kentucky way."

7   Since tourists staying in all-inclusive hotels with strict entry requirements wear bracelets that serve as entry "passes," sex workers know that men wearing these hotel bracelets cannot bring them back to their hotels.

8   After observing migrant Turkish women's mental health in Denmark, G. M. Mirdal (1984) concluded that migration is a considerably "stressing" life event and that close family ties can protect migrants from mental illness and other forms of trauma.

9   In all my interviews I have never met a sex worker who claimed to have had more than two or three clients in an evening. Most women have one client a night—or none at all.

10 In this scenario I am describing opportunities held out mainly to the independents, not to the dependents.

11 New consumption possibilities are a part of many rural to urban migrants' experiences, regardless of their type of work. Mary Beth Mills, for example, writes of Thai women factory workers who compensated for low wages and repetitive tasks by purchasing consumer items and participating in weekend outings (Mills 1997).

12 Dolores is the sex worker I wrote about in chapter 4 who worked at a Dominican bar, the Seabreeze. She had a roster of regular clients and had worked overseas in Curaçao and Panama. Dolores did not realize that CEPROSH could not require an HIV-infected sex worker to stop working.

13 Pierrette Hondagneu-Sotelo and Ernestine Avila define transnational motherhood as "the circuits of affection, caring and financial support that transcend national borders" (1997). Like transnational mothers, sex workers in Sosúa are engaged in improvising new meanings and arrangements of motherhood. They must rely on expanded "caring circuits" that replace the "epoxy glue" view of motherhood as mothers and children under one roof (Blum and Deussen 1996, cited in Hondagneu-Sotelo and Avila 1997).

14 Just as Sosúa's sex workers view women who spend money on themselves or on boyfriends as "bad mothers," Pierrette Hondagneu-Sotelo and Ernestine Avila's (1997) informants, who had children who lived with them in California, criticized transnational mothers as "bad women."

15 This scholarship documents women throughout the world "trying to better their conditions as crucial aspects of globalization," which contradicts "the assumption that globalization is a process imposed solely from above by powerful states or multinational corporations" (Basu et al. 2001: 944).

6 Transnational Disappointments

1 Jeffrey Peck (1995) explores how right-wing violence targeted at nonwhites and non-Germans has made Germany a dangerous place for immigrants.

2 For research on women and migration that tackles the issue of reconfiguration or reaffirmation of gender roles through the migration process, see Hondagneu-Sotelo (1994), Mahler (1997 and 1998), and Pessar (1996). And for research on women's increased authority in the household through wage work—and the experience of migration—see Hirsch (1999), Kibria (1993), Pessar (1984), Repack (1995), Safa (1995a), and Zavella (1991).

3 A rich stew of meats, fish, and vegetables.

4 And these transnational social networks linking Sosúa and Germany are increasingly efficient, as Luisa's reversal of fortune that I wrote about in chapter 5 indicates. Luisa stopped receiving money wires from her German boyfriend only after a former coworker of hers from Sosúa's sex trade blew the whistle on her.

5 When Maria's German boyfriend came to visit her on several occasions, Juan moved out temporarily.

6 In her research with "mail-order brides," Nicole Constable found that most women did not want to leave their home countries for marriage. Moving was part of the marriage business transaction, not something they sought in and of itself (Constable 2003).

7 See the narratives in *Showing Our Colors: Afro-German Women Speak Out* (Opitz, Oguntoye, and Schultz 1992) for a poignant glimpse of life in Germany for German citizens who are not white.

8 I monitored these two sites to get a sense of how sex tourists might find out about sex-tourist destinations on the Internet. The addresses for these sites are http://www.worldsexguide.org and http://www.tsmtravel.com. They claim to post writings from alleged sex tourists. I should note that I do not know with certainty the citizenship of the men who submit postings to these Internet sites. However, since I am trying to unravel how German men in Germany find out about Sosúa and Dominican women, I found these Internet sites through a German search engine. While the World Sex Guide is a free web site through which "volunteer researchers" post information about sex-tourist destinations, TSM charges a monthly membership fee. This on-line travel service uses "satisfied customer" testimonials as a way to entice new members, which is where I saw these postings about Dominican women.

9 Nicole Constable has found that Japanese and Singaporean men also looked for "traditional" women through marriage agencies. As a result, the women "engage in practices that are 'self-orientalizing' " as they act out what they think the men desire in a "traditional" woman—in some cases even explicitly stating "I am a very traditional woman"—in the videotapes the men can pay to watch (Constable 2003: 119).

10 None of the bars or clubs in Sosúa had strip shows. Here I am referring to women dancing solo, fully clothed, on the dance floor to merengue or club music.

11 Unlike the passivity of pornographic films, in sex shows women are "able to bounce back images, and invert, caricature, tease, manipulate and exploit those who use their bodies" (Manderson 1992: 465).

12 This is a play on words, since in this case *geiler* (better) also means "hornier."

13 Julia O'Connell Davidson believes this kind of arrangement appeals to "situational tourists," tourists who do not travel with the sole purpose of buying sex, but, like some of the sex tourists in Sosúa, engage in the sex trade once they are there. Since these men can tell themselves they are "involved in a genuine and reciprocal sexual-emotional relationship," the "incredibly low price" for sexual services "helps men like this to delude themselves" (1996: 43).

14 The dashes (——) indicate where the message board's moderator had deleted parts of the text.

15 I have replaced individuals' names and the places at which they work with XX.

16 Dominican newspapers have been full of stories over the past decade about Dominican women's participation in the sex trade in Europe. An estimated 50,000 Dominican women have either migrated or were trafficked in the sex trade in Europe in the 1980s and early 1990s (Parejo and Rosario 1992; Gallardo 2002). One researcher estimated that during this time thirty to forty trafficking rings specialized in the international trafficking of Dominican women (Van Den Berg 1991). However, a number of European countries, such as Spain, have made it more difficult to obtain "entertainment" visas, which were used to traffic women in the 1980s.

17 I consider her story about her time as a dancer to be reliable: she was quite candid about traveling through Europe, several years later, as a sex worker in part of an organized sex tour, and therefore had little incentive to be untruthful about the folk dancing tour.

Conclusion Changes for Sex Workers

1 I helped Elena pay for these computer classes. She was taking the classes to gain the skills needed to work in office jobs.

GLOSSARY

allá: over there; used by Dominicans in Sosúa to refer to places off the island. Used in the same way as *fuera*.

amiga / o: friend. Dominican sex workers sometimes refer to Dominican clients or Dominican boyfriends as amigos.

aquí: here; used by Dominicans in Sosúa to mean on the island.

arroz con pollo: rice with chicken.

bateyes: living quarters for agricultural workers.

caliente: hot; can mean "sexy."

calle: street. If a woman is said to be in the calle, she is selling sex; if a man is running around in the calle, he is cheating on his wife or girlfriend.

campesina / o: peasant, farmer.

campo: countryside.

Centro de Promoción y Solidaridad Humana (CEPROSH): a Dominican non-governmental organization that conducts HIV / AIDS educational programs. CEPROSH was formerly called Comité de Vigilancia y Control del Sida (COVICOSIDA).

charlas: talks, workshops.

chulo: pimp.

clientes fijos: regular clients.

Codetel: phone company in the Dominican Republic.

colmado: small Dominican grocer, often out of one's home, that sells basic food-stuffs such as rice, beans, and cooking oil.

contaminación: contamination.

corrupción: corruption.

de aquí: from here.

dependent: a sex worker who works with Dominican clients in Dominican-owned bars where the women also live.

(el) diablo: (the) devil.

dinero rápido: fast money.

dominicanas: female Dominicans.

Dominicanidad: Dominicanness.

El Batey: the section of Sosúa where most tourist-related businesses are located (hotels, shops, and restaurants) and where most foreign residents live.

esposa/o: spouse.

flaca: skinny.

fuera: outside; used by Dominicans in Sosúa to refer to places off the island. Used in the same way as *allá*.

gringa/o: a North American or European.

hombre de la calle: man of the street; used to refer to men who are unfaithful to their girlfriends or wives.

hombre de la casa: man of the house; used to refer to men who are faithful to their girlfriends or wives.

hombre serio: serious man; used to refer to men who are sincere and trustworthy and also try to provide financially for their families.

independent: a sex worker who works "freelance" with foreign tourists. They meet in tourist bars, nightclubs, or on the beach. Independents live on their own, either renting an apartment or house or paying for a room in a boardinghouse.

india/o clara/o, india/o oscura: within a Dominican racial taxonomy, racial categories which lay claim to an Indian past.

ladrones (sing. ladrón): thieves.

loca/o: crazy.

Los Charamicos: the section of Sosúa where most Dominican-owned businesses are located and where most Dominicans live.

machista: adjective form of *machismo;* masculine.

mensajeras de salud: health messengers; CEPROSH's peer educators.

mi amor: an endearing term meaning "my love."

morena: within a Dominican racial taxonomy, a racial category that lays claim to ancestry that is somewhere between white (*blanco*) and black (*negro*). The category avoids explicit claims to African ancestry.

motoconcho: motorcycle taxi driver

motor: motorcycle

negra: black; within a Dominican racial taxonomy, a racial category that typically is reserved to refer to Haitians.

pelo bueno: "good" hair; refers to hair that is not curly or kinky. A woman who has pelo bueno is often talked about as blanca, "white." A woman who has pelo malo is typically talked about as being morena, or some racial category other than blanca.

peso: Dominican currency. Throughout the book, unless otherwise indicated, I use the rate of 12 pesos for every U.S.$1.

(los) pobres: the poor.

por amor: for love.

por residencia: for residence.

progresar: to get ahead economically.

promoción: job in Sosúa's tourist trade that involves passing out flyers on street corners to advertise restaurants, stores, and nightclubs.

prostituta: prostitute.

Puerto Plata: largest city on the north coast of the Dominican Republic.

puta: whore.

residencia: residence; often refers to visas to visit, work, or live in countries off the island.

(los) ricos: the rich;. often used by Dominicans in Sosúa to refer to tourists.

(la) ropa sexi: sexy clothes.

(la) salida: fee of 30–50 pesos (U.S.$2.50–$4.15) that Dominican clients pay to bar owners for the use of a room at the bar. The client pays a sex worker for her services.

sancocho: Dominican stew, usually made with vegetables, meat, and fish.

sanky-panky: evolved from the term *hanky-panky;* refers to Dominican men who seduce foreign tourists (female or male) to acquire gifts—including money—as well as meals and other expenses at the discretion of the tourists. They do not work for a set fee.

señoras: older women.

señoritas: young (unmarried) women.

SIDA: AIDS.

sobreviviendo: surviving.

tíguere: literally "tiger"; in Sosúa, it refers to a man who is overconfident, philandering, and only looks out for himself. Sosúans also use the term to refer to men who are involved with drug dealing and other illegal activities.

transculturación: transculturation, changes in culture.

visa para un sueño: visa for a dream.

Vocero: a now-defunct Dominican newspaper published in Sosúa.

yola: small boat; used by some to try to leave the country without visas, for example to go to Puerto Rico.

zonas francas: export-processing zones.

BIBLIOGRAPHY

Abu-Lughod, Lila. 1987. *Veiled Sentiments: Honor and Poetry in a Bedouin Society*. Berkeley: University of California Press.

——. 1990. "The Romance of Resistance: Tracing Transformations of Power through Bedouin Women." *American Ethnologist* 17 (1): 41–55.

——. 1993. *Writing Women's Worlds: Bedouin Stories*. Berkeley: University of California Press.

Abu-Lughod, Lila, and Catherine A. Lutz. 1990. "Introduction: Emotion, Discourse and the Politics of Everyday Life." In *Language and the Politics of Emotion*. Lila Abu-Lughod and Catherine A. Lutz, eds. Pp. 1–23. Cambridge: Cambridge University Press.

Ahearn, Laura M. 2001. *Invitations to Love: Literacy, Love Letters, and Social Change in Nepal*. Ann Arbor: University of Michigan Press.

Alexander, Priscilla. 1997. "Feminism, Sex Workers, and Human Rights." In *Whores and Other Feminists*. Jill Nagle, ed. Pp. 83–97. London: Routledge.

Allison, Anne. 1994. *Nightwork: Sexuality, Pleasure, and Corporate Masculinity in a Tokyo Hostess Club*. Chicago: University of Chicago Press.

Alloula, Malek. 1986. *The Colonial Harem*. Myrna Godzich and Wlad Godzich, trans. Vol. 21. Minneapolis: University of Minnesota Press.

Altman, Dennis. 1999. "The Globalisation of Sex." *The Age*. 15 July.

——. 2001. *Global Sex*. Chicago: University of Chicago Press.

Alvarez-López, Luis, et al. 1997. *Dominican Studies: Resources and Research Questions*. New York: CUNY Dominican Studies Institute.

Appadurai, Arjun. 1990. "Disjuncture and Difference in the Global Cultural Economy." *Public Culture* 2 (2): 1–24.

——. 1991. "Global Ethnoscapes: Notes and Queries for a Transnational Anthropology." In *Recapturing Anthropology: Working in the Present*. Richard Fox, ed. Pp. 191–210. Santa Fe, N.M.: School of American Research Press.

——. 1996. *Modernity at Large: Cultural Dimensions of Globalization*. Vol. 1. Minneapolis: University of Minnesota Press.

——. 2000. "Grassroots Globalization and the Research Imagination." *Public Culture* 12 (1): 1–19.

Armbrust, Walter. 2000. "Introduction: Anxieties of Scale." In *Mass Mediations: New*

Approaches to Popular Culture in the Middle East and Beyond. Walter Armbrust, ed. Pp. 1–31. Berkeley: University of California Press.

Association of Caribbean States. 2001a. *Revenues from Tourism for ACS Countries in US $ (millions) 1990–98*. Vol. 2001. Association of Caribbean States. http://www.acs-aec.org.

———. 2001b. *Revenues from Tourism for ACS Countries in % of GDP*. Vol. 2001. Association of Caribbean States. http://www.acs-aec.org.

Atkinson, Rick. 1994. "The Well-Wandered German." *Washington Post*. 28 July, p. C1.

Austerlitz, Paul. 1997. *Merengue: Dominican Music and Dominican Identity*. Philadelphia: Temple University Press.

Averill, James, R. 1985. "The Social Construction of Emotion: With Special Reference to Love." In *The Social Construction of the Person*. Kenneth J. Gergen and Keith E. Davis, eds. Pp. 89–109. New York: Springer-Verlag.

Báez, Clara. 2000. *Estadísticas para la planificación social con perspectiva de género*. Secretaría de Estado de la Mujer, Programa de las Naciones Unidas para el Desarrollo, Fondo de Población de las Naciones Unidas. Santo Domingo: Editora Búho.

Báez, Clara, and Ginny Taulé. 1993. "Posición socio-cultural y económica de la mujer en La República Dominicana." *Género y Sociedad* 1 (2).

Báez-Evertsz, Franc. 1986. *Braceros Haitianos en La República Dominicana*. Santo Domingo: Instituto Dominicano de Investigaciones Sociales.

Balaguer, Joaquín. 1984. *La Isla al revés: Haití y el destino dominicano*. Santo Domingo: Librería Dominicana.

Banach, Linda, and Sue Metzenrath. 2000. *Principles for Model Law Reform*. Sydney, Australia: Scarlet Alliance and the Federation of AIDS Organizations.

Barry, Tom, Beth Wood, and Deb Preusch. 1984. *The Other Side of Paradise: Foreign Control in the Caribbean*. Albuquerque: Resource Center.

Basu, Amrita, et al. 2001. Editorial. *Signs* 26 (4): 943–48.

Baumann, Zygmunt. 1996. "From Pilgrim to Tourist—or a Short History of Identity." In *Questions of Cultural Identity*. Stuart Hall and Paul du Gay, eds. Pp. 18–36. Thousand Oaks, Calif.: Sage.

Bell, Laurie, ed. 1987. *Good Girls, Bad Girls: Feminists and Sex Trade Workers Face to Face*. Toronto: Seal Press.

Bell, Shannon. 1994. *Reading, Writing, and Rewriting the Prostitute Body*. Bloomington: Indiana University Press.

Benería, Lourdes, and Martha Roldán. 1987. *The Crossroads of Class and Gender: Industrial Homework, Subcontracting and Household Dynamics in Mexico City*. Chicago: University of Chicago Press.

Berg, Van Den, Martina. 1991. "Tráfico de mujeres y prostitución de mujeres de La República Dominicana en Holanda." Manuscript.

Bergeron, Suzanne. 2001. "Political Economy Discourses of Globalization and Feminist Politics." *Signs* 46 (4): 983–1006.

Bernstein, Elizabeth. 2001. "The Meaning of the Purchase: Desire, Demand and the Commerce of Sex." *Ethnography* 2 (3): 389–420.

——. 2002. "Border Wars: Migration and the Regulation of Sex Work in the New Europe." Paper presented at the American Anthropological Association annual meeting. November, New Orleans.

Bhabba, Homi K. 1990. "DissemiNation: Time, Narrative, and the Margins of the Modern Nation." In *Nation and Narration*. H. K. Bhabba, ed. Pp. 291–322. New York: Routledge.

Bishop, Ryan, and Lillian S. Robinson. 1998. *Night Market: Sexual Cultures and the Thai Economic Miracle*. New York: Routledge.

Blumberg, Debbie. 2003. "In Search of Sosúa's Synagogue." *Reform Judaism*. 31 (4): 66–68.

Blumberg, Rae Lesser. 1991. "Income under Female versus Male Control: Hypotheses from a Theory of Gender Stratification and Data from the Third World." In *Gender, Family and Economy: The Triple Overlap*. Rae Lesser Blumberg, ed. Pp. 97–127. London: Sage Publications.

——. 1995. "Introduction: Engendering Wealth and Well-Being in an Era of Economic Transformation." In EnGENDERing *Wealth and Well-Being: Empowerment for Global Change*. Rae Lesser Blumberg, Cathy A. Rakowski, Irene Tinker, and Michael Monteon, eds. Pp. 1–14. Boulder, Colo.: Westview Press.

Bolles, Lynn A. 1992. "Sand, Sea, and the Forbidden." *Transforming Anthropology* 3 (1): 30–34.

Boorstin, Daniel J. 1961. *The Image: A Guide to Pseudo-events in America*. New York: Harper and Row.

Bourgois, Philippe, and Eloise Dunlap. 1993. "Exorcising Sex-for-Crack: An Ethnographic Perspective from Harlem." In *Crack Pipe as Pimp: An Ethnographic Investigation of Sex-for-Crack Exchanges*. Mitchell S. Radner, ed. Pp. 97–132. Lexington, Mass.: Lexington Books.

Bowman, Glenn. 1986. "Fucking Tourists: Sexual Relations and Tourism in Jerusalem's Old City." *Critique of Anthropology* 9 (2): 77–93.

Brea, Ramonina, and Isis Duarte. 1999. *Entre la calle y la casa: Las mujeres dominicanas y la cultura política a finales del siglo XX*. Santo Domingo: Profamilia y Editora Búho.

Brennan, Denise. 1998. "Everything Is for Sale Here: Sex Tourism in Sosúa, the Dominican Republic." Ph.D. diss., Yale University.

——. 2001. "Tourism in Transnational Places: Dominican Sex Workers and German Sex Tourists Imagine One Another." *Identities: Global Studies in Culture and Power* 7 (4): 621–63.

——. 2002. "Selling Sex for Visas: Sex Tourism as Stepping Stone to International Migration for Dominican Women." In *Global Woman*. Barbara Ehrenreich and Arlie Russell Hochschild, eds. Pp. 154–68. New York: Metropolitan Books.

Broring, Georg. 1992. " 'AIDS and Mobility': The Impact of International Mobility on the Spread of HIV and the Need and Possibility for AIDS/HIV Prevention Programmes. With a Specific Focus on Central/Eastern Europe." Amsterdam: National Committee on AIDS Control.

Bruner, Edward M. 1996. "Tourism in the Balinese Borderzone." In *Displacement, Diaspora and Geographies of Identity*. Smadar Lavie and Ted Swedenburg, eds. Pp. 157–79. Durham, N.C.: Duke University Press.

———. 1999. Return to Sumatra: 1957, 1997. *American Ethnologist* 26 (2): 461–77.

Brussa, Licia. 1989. "Migrant Prostitutes in the Netherlands." In *Vindication of the Rights of Whores*. Gail Pheterson, ed. Pp. 227–240. Seattle: Seal Press.

Bunster, Ximena, and Elsa M. Chaney. 1985. *Sellers and Servants: Working Women in Lima, Peru*. New York: Praeger.

Burkhalter, Byron. 1999. "Reading Race Online: Discovering Racial Identity in Usenet Discussions." In *Communities in Cyberspace*. Marc A. Smith and Peter Kollock, eds. Pp. 60–75. London: Routledge.

Bush, Barbara. 1990. *Slave Women in Caribbean Society 1650–1838*. London: James Currey.

Butler, Judith. 1990. *Gender Trouble: Feminism and the Subversion of Identity*. New York: Routledge.

———. 1993. *Bodies That Matter: On the Discursive Limits of "Sex."* New York: Routledge.

Cabezas, Amalia L. 1999. "Women's Work Is Never Done: Sex Tourism in Sosúa, the Dominican Republic." In *Sun, Sex, and Gold: Tourism and Sex Work in the Caribbean*. Kamala Kempadoo, ed. Pp. 93–123. Lanham, Md.: Rowman and Littlefield Publishers.

Caldwell, Gillian, Steven Galster, and Nadia Steinzor. 1997. *Crime and Servitude: An Exposé of the Traffic in Women for Prostitution from the Newly Independent States*. Washington, D.C.: Global Survival Network.

Cassirer, Bruce. 1992. *Travel and the Single Male*. Channel Island, Calif.: TSM Publishing.

Castaneda, Quetzil E. 1996. *In the Museum of Maya Culture: Touring Chichén Itzá*. Minneapolis: University of Minnesota Press.

Chaney, Elsa M., and Mary Garcia Castro, eds. 1989. *Muchachas No More: Household Workers in Latin America and the Caribbean*. Philadelphia: Temple University Press.

Chant, Sylvia. 1997a. "Gender and Tourism Employment in Mexico and the Philippines." In *Gender, Work and Tourism*. M. Thea. Sinclair, ed. Pp. 120–79. London: Routledge.

———. 1997b. *Women-Headed Households: Diversity and Dynamics in the Developing World*. London: Macmillan Press.

Chant, Sylvia, and Cathy McIlwaine. 1995. *Women of a Lesser Cost: Female Labour, Foreign Exchange and Philippine Development*. London: Pluto Press.

Chapkis, Wendy. 1997. *Live Sex Acts: Women Performing Erotic Labor*. New York: Routledge.

———. 2000. "Power and Control in the Commercial Sex Trade." In *Sex for Sale:*

Prostitution, Pornography, and the Sex Industry. Ronald Weitzer, ed. Pp. 181–201. New York: Routledge.

Clark, Constance D. 2001. "Foreign Marriage, 'Tradition,' and the Politics of Border Crossings." In *China Urban: Ethnographies of Contemporary Culture*. Nancy N. Chen, Constance D. Clark, Suzanne Z. Gottschang, and Lyn Jeffry, eds. Pp. 104–22. Durham, N.C.: Duke University Press.

Clark, Gary. 1998. *Your Bride Is in the Mail! How To Find the Woman You Really Want by Corresponding with Ladies in Foreign Countries*. Las Vegas: Words That Work Publications.

Clarke, Edith. 1957. *My Mother Who Fathered Me*. London: George Allen and Unwin.

Clifford, James. 1997. *Routes: Travel and Translation in the Late Twentieth Century*. Cambridge, Mass.: Harvard University Press.

Cohen, Erik. 1971. "Arab Boys and Tourist Girls in a Mixed Jewish Arab Community." *International Journal of Comparative Sociology* 12 (4): 217–33.

———. 1982. "Thai Girls and Farang Men: The Edge of Ambiguity." *Annals of Tourism Research* 9 (3): 403–28.

Cohen, Judith, Priscilla Alexander, and Constance Wofsy. 1988. "Prostitutes and AIDS: Public Policy Issues." *AIDS and Public Policy Journal* 3 (2): 16–22.

COIN. 1996. *Juntarnos: Memorias 1er congreso dominicano de trabajadoras sexuales*. Santo Domingo: COIN.

———. 1998. *Trabajo, salud y SIDA: Compilación de investigaciones*. Santo Domingo: COIN.

———. 2000. *Mujeres unidas: Nuestros primeros pasos (1995–2000)*. Santo Domingo: MODEMU (Movimiento de Mujeres Unidas, Inc.) and COIN.

Cole, Jeffrey. 1997. *The New Racism in Europe: A Sicilian Ethnography*. Cambridge: Cambridge University Press.

Constable, Nicole. 1997. *Maid to Order in Hong Kong: Stories of Filipina Workers*. Ithaca, N.Y.: Cornell University Press.

———. 2003. *Romance on a Global Stage: Pen Pals, Virtual Ethnography, and "Mail-Order" Marriages*. Berkeley: University of California Press.

Conway, S., P. Gillies, and R. Slack. 1990. *The Health of Travellers: A Report on a Study of People in Nottingham, Concentrating upon Sexual Behavior Whilst Traveling Abroad and Risk-Taking in the Context of STD- and HIV-Transmission*. Nottingham, England: University of Nottingham and Nottingham Health Authority.

Corten, André, and Isis Duarte. 1995. "Five Hundred Thousand Haitians in the Dominican Republic." *Latin American Perspectives* 22 (3): 94–110.

COVICOSIDA (Comité de Vigilancia y Control del SIDA). 1993. *Proyecto Hoteleros: Resultados de la intervención educativa para prevención VIH/SIDA/ETS en empleados de hotelería*. Puerto Plata, Dominican Republic: COVICOSIDA.

Crang, Philip. 1997. "Performing the Tourist Product." In *Touring Cultures: Transformations of Travel and Theory*. Chris Rojek and John Urry, eds. Pp. 137–54. London: Routledge.

Crassweller, Robert D. 1966. *Trujillo: The Life and Times of a Caribbean Dictator*. New York: Macmillan.

Crompton, Rosemary, and Kay Sanderson. 1990. *Gendered Jobs and Social Change*. London: Unwin Hyman.

Dalby, Liza. 1983. *Geisha*. Berkeley: University of California Press.

Dank, Barry M. 1999. "Sex Work, Sex Workers, and Beyond." In *Sex Work and Sex Workers*. Vol. 2 of *Sexuality and Culture*. Barry M. Dank and Roberto Refinetti, eds. Pp. 1–6. New Brunswick, N.J.: Transaction Publishers.

Danticat, Edwidge. 1998. *The Farming of Bones: A Novel*. New York: Soho Press.

Davies, Jessica. 1994. "Secret Weddings that Stunned Two Families." In *Daily Mail*. Vol. 2001. London.

Davis, John. 1977. *People of the Mediterranean*. London: Routledge.

Deere, Carmen Diana, et al., eds. 1990. *In the Shadows of the Sun: Caribbean Development Alternatives and U.S. Policy*. Boulder, Colo.: Westview Press.

de Filippis, Daisy Cocco, ed. 1992. *Combatidas, combativas y combatientes: Antología de cuentos escritos por mujeres dominicanas*. Santo Domingo: Librería Trinitaria e Instituto del Libro.

Delacoste, Frederique, and Priscilla Alexander, eds. 1987. *Sex Work: Writings By Women in the Sex Industry*. Pittsburgh: Cleis Press.

de la Soledad Valdéz, Iris A. 1996. "Leyes y Prostitución en República Dominicana." In *Juntarnos: Memorias 1er congreso dominicano de trabajadoras sexuales*. Pp 96–101. COIN. Santo Domingo: Imprenta La Union.

del Castillo, José, and Martin F. Murphy. 1986. "Migration, National Identity and Cultural Policy in the Dominican Republic." *Journal of Ethnic Studies* 15 (3): 49–70.

de Moya, Antonio, et al. 1992. "Sosúa's Sanky-Pankies and Female Sex Workers: An Exploratory Study." Manuscript.

Derby, Lauren. 1994. "Haitians, Magic, and Money: Raza and Society in the Haitian-Dominican Borderlands." *Comparative Studies in Society and History* 36 (2): 488–526.

——. 1998. "Gringo Chickens with Worms: Food and Nationalism in the Dominican Republic." In *Close Encounters of Empire: Writing the Cultural History of U.S.-Latin American Relations*. Gilbert M. Joseph, Catherine C. LeGrand, and Ricardo D. Salvatore, eds. Pp. 451–93. Durham, N.C.: Duke University Press.

——. 2000. "The Dictator's Seduction: Gender and State Spectacle during the Trujillo Regime." In *Latin American Popular Culture: An Introduction*. William H. Beezley and Linda A. Curcio-Nagy, eds. Pp. 213–39. Wilmington, Del: Scholarly Resources, Inc.

de Zalduondo, Barbara O. 1991. "Prostitution Viewed Cross-Culturally: Toward Recontextualizing Sex Work in AIDS Intervention Research." *Journal of Sex Research* 28 (2): 223–48.

Díaz, Junot. 1996. *Drown*. New York: Riverhead Books.

Doezema, Jo. 1998. "Forced to Choose: Beyond the Voluntary v. Forced Prostitution Dichotomy." In *Global Sex Workers: Rights, Resistance and Redefinition*. Kamala Kempadoo and Jo Doezema, eds. Pp. 34–50. New York: Routledge.

Duany, Jorgé. 1994. *Quisqueya on the Hudson: The Transnational Identity of Dominicans in Washington Heights*. New York: Dominican Studies Institute, City University of New York.

———. 1998. "Reconstructing Racial Identity: Ethnicity, Color, and Class among Dominicans in the United States and Puerto Rico." *Latin American Perspectives* 25 (3): 147–72.

Duarte, Isis. 1986. *Trabajadores urbanos: Ensayos sobre fuerza laboral en República Dominicana*. Santo Domingo: Editora Universitaria.

———. 1989. "Household Workers in the Dominican Republic: A Question for the Feminist Movement." In *Muchachas No More: Household Workers in Latin America and the Caribbean*. Elsa M. Chaney and Mary Garcia Castro, eds. Pp. 197–219. Philadelphia: Temple University Press.

Dwyer, Daisy, and Judith Bruce, eds. 1988. *A Home Divided: Women and Income in the Third World*. Stanford, Calif.: Stanford University Press.

Economist. 2000. Country Profile: "Dominican Republic." In *Economist Intelligence Unit*. Pp. 9–19. London: Economist Intelligence Unit.

———. 2003. "Swindled." In The Americas section. June 14. London.

Ehrenreich, Barbara, and Arlie Russell Hochschild. 2002. Introduction. In *Global Woman: Nannies, Maids, and Sex Workers in the New Economy*. Barbara Ehrenreich and Arlie Russell Hochschild, eds. Pp. 1–3. New York: Metropolitan Books.

Eichen, Josef David. 1980. *Sosúa: Una colonia hebrea en La República Dominicana. Santiago: República Dominicana*. Santiago: UCMM (Universidad Católica Madre y Maestra).

El Saadawi, Nawal. 1975. *Women at Point Zero*. Atlantic Highlands, N.J.: Zed Books.

Elson, Diane. 1992. "From Survival Strategies to Transformation Strategies: Women's Needs and Structural Adjustment." In *Unequal Burden: Economic Crises, Persistent Poverty, and Women's Work*. Lourdes Benería and Shelley Feldman, eds. Pp. 26–48. Boulder, Colo.: Westview Press.

Engle, Patricia L. 1995. "Father's Money, Mother's Money, and Parental Commitment: Guatemala and Nicaragua." In ENGENDERing *Wealth and Well-Being: Empowerment for Global Change*. Rae Lesser Blumberg, Cathy A. Rakowski, Irene Tinker, and Michael Monteon, eds. Pp. 155–79. Boulder, Colo.: Westview Press.

Enloe, Cynthia. 1989. *Bananas, Beaches and Bases: Making Feminist Sense of International Politics*. Berkeley: University of California Press.

———. 1992. "It Takes Two." In *Let the Good Times Roll: Prostitution and the U.S. Military in Asia*. Saundra Pollock Sturdevant and Brenda Stoltzfus, eds. Pp. 22–29. New York: New Press.

———. 1993. *The Morning After: Sexual Politics at the End of the Cold War*. Berkeley: University of California Press.

Espinal, Rosario. 1995. "Economic Restructuring, Social Protest, and Democratization in the Dominican Republic." *Latin American Perspectives* 22 (3): 63–79.

Europa Publications. 2000. *Regional Surveys of the World: South America, Central America and the Caribbean*. London: Europa Publications.

Fanon, Frantz. 1967. *Black Skin, White Masks*. New York: Grove Press.

Fapohunda, Eleanor R. 1988. "The Nonpooling Household: A Challenge to Theory." In *A Home Divided: Women and Income in the Third World*. Daisy Dwyer and Judith Bruce, eds. Pp. 143–54. Stanford, Calif.: Stanford University Press.

Farmer, Paul. 1992. *AIDS and Accusation: Haiti and the Geography of Blame*. Berkeley: University of California Press.

——. 1999. *Infections and Inequalities: The Modern Plagues*. Berkeley: University of California Press.

Featherstone, Mike, ed. 1999. *Love and Eroticism*. London: Sage Publications.

Ferguson, Marjorie. 1992. "The Mythology about Globalization." *European Journal of Communication* 7: 69–93.

Fernández-Kelly, María Patricia. 1983. *For We Are Sold, I and My People: Women and Industry in Mexico's Frontier*. Albany: State University of New York Press.

Fong, Timothy P. 1994. *The First Suburban Chinatown: The Remaking of Monterey Park, California*. Philadelphia: Temple University Press.

Ford, N., and M. Inman. 1992. "Safer Sex in Tourist Resorts." *World Health Forum* 13 (1): 77–80.

Fosado, Gisela. 2003. A Woman's Journey into the World of Male Sex Work. In *Contemporary Cuba*. Denise Blum and Peter McLaran, eds. Lanham, Md.: Rowan and Littlefield Publishers.

Franco, Franklin J. 1989. *Los negros, los mulatos y la nación dominicana*. Santo Domingo: Editora Nacional.

Frank, Katherine. 2002. *G-Strings and Sympathy: Strip Club Regulars and Male Desire*. Durham, N.C.: Duke University Press.

Freeman, Carla. 2000. *High Tech and High Heels in the Global Economy: Women, Work and Pink-Collar Identities in the Caribbean*. Durham, N.C.: Duke University Press.

Freud, Sigmund. [1925] 1962. *Three Essays on the Theory of Sexuality*. James Strachey, trans. New York: Avon Books.

Friedman, Jonathan. 1994. *Cultural Identity and Global Process*. London: Sage Publications.

Friedrichsmeyer, Sara, Sara Lennox, and Susanne Zantop, eds. 1998. *The Imperialist Imagination: German Colonialism and Its Legacy*. Ann Arbor: University of Michigan Press.

Fuentes, Annette, and Barbara Ehrenreich. 1985. *Women in the Global Factory*. Boston: South End Press.

Fusco, Coco. 1998. Hustling for Dollars: "*Jineterismo* in Cuba." In *Global Sex Workers: Rights, Resistance and Redefinition*. Kamala Kempadoo and Jo Doezema, eds. Pp. 151–66. New York: Routledge.

Gallardo Rivas, Gina. 2002. "Tráfico de mujeres y explotación sexual en la Republica Dominicana." In *El Género en la agenda pública dominicana: Estudios de casos y análisis comparativo*. Denise Paiewonsky, ed. Pp. 181–97. Santo Domingo: Tecnologico de Santo Domingo.

——. 1995. *Buscando la vida: Dominicanas en el servicio doméstico en Madrid*. Santo

Domingo: Coedición IEPALA-CIPAF (Centro de Investigación para la Acción Femenina).

García, Rafael. 1991. "Tourism and AIDS: A Dominican Republic Study." *AIDS and Society* 2 (3): insert, 1–3.

Georges, Eugenia. 1990. *The Making of a Transnational Community: Migration, Development and Cultural Change in the Dominican Republic*. New York: Columbia University Press.

Gewertz, Deborah B., and Frederick K. Errington. 1991. *Twisted Histories, Altered Contexts: Representing the Chambri in a World System*. New York: Cambridge University Press.

Giddens, Anthony. 1990. *The Consequences of Modernity*. Stanford, Calif.: Stanford University Press.

———. 1993. "Dare to Care, Conserve and Repair." *New Statesman and Society* 6, 29 October 1993, p. 18–20.

Gilliam, Angela M. 2001. "A Black Feminist Perspective on the Sexual Commodification of Women in the New Global Culture." In *Black Feminist Anthropology: Theory, Politics, Praxis, and Poetics*. Irma McClaurin, ed. Pp. 150–86. New Brunswick, N.J.: Rutgers University Press.

Gilmore, David D. 1990. *Manhood in the Making: Cultural Concepts of Masculinity*. New Haven, Conn.: Yale University Press.

Glick Schiller, Nina. 1999. "Transmigrants and Nation-States: Something Old and Something New in the U.S. Immigrant Experience." In *The Handbook of International Migration: The American Experience*. Charles Hirschman, Philip Kasinitz, and Josh DeWind, eds. Pp. 94–119. New York: Russell Sage Foundation.

Glick Schiller, Nina, Linda Basch, and Cristina Szanton-Blanc. 1992. "Towards a Transnationalization of Migration: Race, Class, Ethnicity, and Nationalism Reconsidered." In *Towards a Transnational Perspective on Migration: Race, Class, Ethnicity, and Nationalism Reconsidered*. Nina Glick Schiller, Linda Basch, and Cristina Szanton-Blanc, eds. Pp. 1–24. New York: New York Academy of Sciences.

———. 1994. *Nations Unbound: Transnational Projects, Postcolonial Predicaments and Deterritorialized Nation-States*. Langhorne, Pa.: Gordon and Breach Science Publishers.

———. 1995. "From Immigrant to Transmigrant: Theorizing Transnational Migration." *Anthropological Quarterly* 68 (1): 48–63.

Goldring, Luin. 1998. "The Power of Status in Transnational Social Fields." In *Transnationalism From Below*. Michael P. Smith and Luis E. Guarnizo, eds. Pp. 165–95. Vol. 6. Comparative Urban and Community Research series. New Brunswick, N.J.: Transaction Publishers.

Goldstein, Donna. 1999. "'Interracial' Sex and Racial Democracy in Brazil: Twin Concepts?" *American Anthropologist* 101 (3): 563–78.

Gómez, Carmen Julia. 1989. *La problemática de las jefas de hogar: Evidencia de la insubordinación social de las mujeres*. Santo Domingo: Ediciones Populares Feministas.

Gonzalez, David. 2003a. "Pan American Games: Games Lift Spirits in Santo Domingo." *New York Times*, 8 August, p. D1.

——. 2003b. "Back Talk: Protesting through the Streets." *New York Times*, 10 August, sec. 8, p. 11.

González de la Rocha, Mercedes. 1994. *The Resources of Poverty: Women and Survival in a Mexican City*. Oxford: Blackwell Publishers.

Graburn, Nelson H. 1983. "The Anthropology of Tourism." *Annals of Tourism Research* 10: 9–33.

Grasmuck, Sherri, and Patricia R. Pessar. 1991. *Between Two Islands: Dominican International Migration*. Berkeley: University of California Press.

Greenberg, H. R. 1991. "Rescrewed: Pretty Woman's Co-opted Feminism." *Journal of Popular Film and Television* 19 (1): 9–13.

Grewal, Inderpal, and Caren Kaplan. 1994. "Introduction: Transnational Feminist Practices and Questions of Postmodernity." In *Scattered Hegemonies: Postmodernity and Transnational Feminist Practices*. Inderpal Grewal and Caren Kaplan, eds. Pp. 1–31. Minneapolis: University of Minnesota Press.

——. 1999. "Transnational Feminist Cultural Studies: Beyond the Marxism / Poststructuralism / Feminism Divides." In *Between Woman and Nation: Nationalisms, Transnational Feminisms, and the State*. Caren Kaplan, Norma Alarcón, and Minoo Moallem, eds. Pp. 349–63. Durham, N.C.: Duke University Press.

Guarnizo, Luis Eduardo. 1994. "Los Dominicanyorks: The Making of a Binational Society." *ANNALS* 553: 70–83.

Guarnizo, Luis Eduardo, and Michael Peter Smith. 1998. "The Locations of Transnationalism." In *Transnationalism from Below*. Michael P. Smith and Luis E. Guarnizo, eds. Pp. 3–34. Vol. 6. Comparative Urban and Community Research series. New Brunswick, N.J.: Transaction Publishers.

Gutmann, Mathew C. 1996. *The Meanings of Macho: Being a Man in Mexico City*. Berkeley: University of California Press.

Guy, Donna J. 1990. *Sex and Danger in Buenos Aires: Prostitution, Family, and Nation in Argentina*. Lincoln: University of Nebraska Press.

Haberman, Clyde. 1997. "In Citizenship, in Sickness, and in Health." *New York Times*, 21 February, p. A32

Haggerty, Richard, ed. 1991. *Dominican Republic and Haiti Country Studies*. Washington, D.C.: Library of Congress, Federal Research Division.

Hall, Joan Kelly. 1993. "Oye oye lo que ustedes no saben: Creativity, Social Power, and Politics in the Oral Practice of Chismeando." *Journal of Linguistic Anthropology* 3 (1): 75–98.

Hall, Michael R. 2000. *Sugar and Power in the Dominican Republic: Eisenhower, Kennedy and the Trujillos*. Westport, Conn.: Greenwood Press.

Hall, Stuart. 1997. "The Local in the Global: Globalization and Ethnicity." In *Culture, Globalization and the World-System: Contemporary Conditions for the Representation of Identity*. Anthony D. King, ed. Pp. 19–39. Minneapolis: University of Minneapolis.

Halperin, Rhoda. 1990. *The Livelihood of Kin: Making Ends Meet "The Kentucky Way."* Austin: University of Texas Press.

Hamilton, Annette. 1997. "Primal Dream: Masculinism, Sin and Salvation in Thailand's Sex Trade." In *Sites of Desire, Economies of Pleasure: Sexualities in Asia and the Pacific*. Lenore Manderson and Margaret Jolly, eds. Pp. 145–65. Chicago: University of Chicago Press.

Hardy, Frances. 1994. "How I Bitterly Regret My Paradise Marriage." *London Daily Mail*, 18 November, pp. 20–21.

Harvey, David. 1996. *Justice, Nature and the Geography of Difference*. Cambridge, Mass.: Blackwell.

———. 2000. *Spaces of Hope*. Berkeley: University of California Press.

Hawkes, S. 1992. "Travel and HIV / AIDS." *AIDS Care* 4 (4): 446–49.

Heikhaus, Jorg. 1995a. "Im Bermuda-Dreieck Bleibt Keiner Allein" [No One Remains Single in the Bermuda Triangle]. Part of a series, Sex, Suff and Sonnenbrand [Sex, Boozing it Up, and Sunburn]. *Express* (Cologne, Germany), 22 May.

———. 1995b. "Heisse Nachte in Sosúa: Die Sundigste Meile der Karibe" [Hot Nights in Sosúa: The Most Sinful Mile in the Caribbean]. Part of a series, Sex, Suff und Sonnenbrand [Sex, Boozing it Up, and Sunburn]. *Express* (Cologne, Germany), 23 May.

Hernández, Ramona, and Francisco Rivera-Batiz. 1997. *Dominican New Yorkers: A Socioeconomic Profile, 1997*. New York: Dominican Research Monographs, CUNY Dominican Studies Institute.

Hernández, Ramona, Francisco Rivera-Batiz, and Roberto Agodini. 1995. *Dominican New Yorkers: A Socioeconomic Profile, 1990*. New York: Dominican Research Monographs, CUNY Dominican Studies Institute.

Hernández Medina, Esther. 2002. *A Brief Profile of Free Trade Zones in the Dominican Republic, 2002*. Santo Domingo: CIPAF (Centro de Investigación para la Acción Femenina).

Herold, Edward, et al. 1992. "Canadian Tourists and Sex Workers in the Dominican Republic." Paper presented at the conference Culture, Sexual Behavior, and AIDS. July 24–26, Amsterdam.

Herzfeld, Michael. 1985. *The Poetics of Manhood: Contest and Identity in a Cretan Mountain Village*. Princeton: Princeton University Press.

Hirsch, Jennifer S. 1999. "En el norte la mujer manda: Gender, Generation, and Geography in a Mexican Transnational Community." *American Behavioral Scientist* 42 (9): 1332–49.

———. 2003. *A Courtship after Marriage: Sexuality and Love in Mexican Transnational Families*. Berkeley: University of California Press.

Hochschild, Arlie Russell. 1983. *The Managed Heart*. Berkeley: University of California Press.

Hommes, Mary, and Hans van der Vleugel. 1993. *Materials for HIV / AIDS Education Aimed at Travellers, Ethnic Minorities and Migrant Communities*. Amsterdam: National Committee on AIDS Control, European Project on AIDS and Mobility.

Hondagneu-Sotelo, Pierrette. 1994. *Gendered Transitions: Mexican Experiences of Immigration*. Berkeley: University of California Press.

———. 2001. *Doméstica: Immigrant Workers Cleaning and Caring in the Shadows of Affluence*. Berkeley: University of California Press.

Hondagneu-Sotelo, Pierrette, and Ernestine Avila. 1997. "'I'm Here, But I'm There': The Meanings of Latina Transnational Motherhood." *Gender and Society* 11 (5): 548–71.

Howard, David. 2001. *Coloring the Nation: Race and Ethnicity in the Dominican Republic*. Oxford: Signal Books.

Htun, Mala. 1996. *Women's Rights and Opportunities in Latin America: Problems and Prospects*. P. 17. Generated by the ICRW's Women's Leadership Conference of the Americas.

Hunter, Mark. 2002. "The Materiality of Everyday Sex: Thinking beyond 'Prostitution.'" *African Studies* 61 (1): 99–120.

Illouz, Eva. 1997. *Consuming the Romantic Utopia: Love and the Cultural Contradictions of Capitalism*. Berkeley: University of California Press.

International Labour Organization, Bureau of Statistics. 1998–2000. LABORSTA (Labour Statistics Database). Vol. 2001. http://laborsta.ilo.org.

International Monetary Fund. 2001. *International Financial Statistics*. Washington, D.C.: International Monetary Fund.

International Organization for Migration. 1996. *Trafficking in Women from the Dominican Republic for Sexual Exploitation*. http://www.iom.int.

Intros.net. 2001. *Dominican Girls: Pen Pals*. http://www.4personals.org/philippines.htm.

Itzigsohn, Jose. 2000. *Developing Poverty: The State, Labor Market Deregulation, and the Informal Economy in Costa Rica and the Dominican Republic*. University Park: Pennsylvania State University Press.

Itzigsohn, Jose, Carlos Dore Cabral, and Esther Hernández Medina. 1999. "Mapping Dominican Transnationalism: Narrow and Broad Transnational Practices." *Ethnic and Racial Studies* 22 (2): 316–39.

Jankowiak, William. 1995. Introduction. In *Romantic Passion: A Universal Experience?* William Jankowiak, ed. Pp. 1–19. New York: Columbia University Press.

Jansen, Senaida, and Cecilia Millán. 1991. *Género, trabajo y etnia en los bateyes dominicanos*. Santo Domingo: Instituto Tecnológico de Santo Domingo (INTEC).

Jenness, Valerie. 1993. *Making It Work: The Prostitutes' Rights Movement in Perspective*. New York: Walter de Gruyter.

Jolly, Margaret. 1997. "From Point Venus to Bali Ha'i: Eroticism and Exoticism in Representations of the Pacific." In *Sites of Desire, Economies of Pleasure*. Lenore Manderson and Margaret Jolly, eds. Pp. 99–122. Chicago: University of Chicago Press.

Jordon, Howard. 1998. "Dominicans in New York: Getting a Slice of the Apple." Pp. 37–42. *NACLA Report on the Americas*. New York: NACLA (North American Conference on Latin America).

Kaplan, Caren, and Inderpal Grewal. 1999. "Transnational Feminist Cultural Studies: Beyond the Marxism/Poststructuralism/Feminism Divides." In *Between*

Woman and Nation. Caren Kaplan, Norma Alarcón, and Minoo Moallem, eds. Pp. 349–63. Durham, N.C.: Duke University Press.

Kearney, Michael. 1995. "The Local and the Global: The Anthropology of Globalization and Transnationalism." *Annual Review of Anthropology* 24: 547–65.

Kelsky, Karen. 1994. "Intimate Ideologies: Transnational Theory and Japan's 'Yellow Cabs.' " *Public Culture* 6: 465–78.

———. 2001. *Women on the Verge: Japanese Women, Western Dreams.* Durham, N.C.: Duke University Press.

Kempadoo, Kamala. 1998. "Introduction: Globalizing Sex Workers' Rights." In *Global Sex Workers: Rights, Resistance and Redefinition.* Kamala Kempadoo and Jo Doezema, eds. Pp. 1–28. New York: Routledge.

———. 1999. "Continuities and Change: Five Centuries of Prostitution in the Caribbean." In *Sun, Sex, and Gold: Tourism and Sex Work in the Caribbean.* Kamala Kempadoo, ed. Pp. 3–33. Lanham, Md.: Rowman and Littlefield Publishers.

———, ed. 1999. *Sun, Sex, and Gold: Tourism and Sex Work in the Caribbean.* Lanham, Md.: Rowman and Littlefield Publishers.

Kempadoo, Kamala, and Jo Doezema, eds. 1998. *Global Sex Workers: Rights, Resistance and Redefinition.* New York: Routledge.

Kennedy, Randy. 1997. "Deadline Fear Exposes Many Immigrants to Fraud." *New York Times,* 23 March, pp. 39, 43.

Kermath, Brian, and Robert N. Thomas. 1992. "Spatial Dynamics of Resorts: Sosúa, Dominican Republic." *Annals of Tourism Research* 19: 173–90.

Kerrigan, Deanna. 2000. "Individual, Relational and Environmental-Structural Determinants of Consistent Condom Use among Female Sex Workers and Their Regular Paying Partners in the Dominican Republic." Ph.D. diss. Baltimore: Johns Hopkins University School of Public Health.

Kerrigan, Deanna, Jonathan M. Ellen, Luis Moreno, Santo Rosario, Joanne Katz, David D. Celentano, and Michael Sweat. 2003. "Environmental-Structural Factors Significantly Associated with Consistent Condom Use among Female Sex Workers in the Dominican Republic." *AIDS* 17: 415–23.

Kerrigan, Deanna, Luis Moreno, Santo Rosario, and Michael Sweat. 2001. "Adapting the Thai 100% Condom Programme: Developing a Culturally Appropriate Model for the Dominican Republic." *Culture, Health, and Sexuality* 3 (2): 221–40.

Kibria, Nazli. 1993. *Family Tightrope: The Changing Lives of Vietnamese Americans.* Princeton, N.J.: Princeton University Press.

Kim, Seung-Kyung. 1997. *Class Struggle or Family Struggle: The Lives of Women Factory Workers in South Korea.* Cambridge: Cambridge University Press.

Kincaid, Jamaica. 1988. *A Small Place.* New York: Penguin Books.

King, Brian, Abraham Pizam, and Ady Milman. 1992. "Social Impacts of Tourism: Host Perceptions." *Annals of Tourism Research* 19: 650–65.

Kinnaird, Vivian, and Derek Hall, eds. 1994. *Tourism: A Gender Analysis.* New York: John Wiley and Sons.

Koenig, Ellen, et al. 1987. "Prevalence of Antibodies to Human Immunodeficiency

Virus in Dominicans and Haitians in the Dominican Republic." *Journal of the American Medical Association* 257 (5): 631–34.

Kratochvil, Antonin, and Amy Wilenz. 2001. "For the Haitians Who Toil on the Sugar Plantations of the Dominican Republic, There are No Sweet Rewards." In *Mother Jones* (September–October): 53–59.

Krohn-Hansen, Christian. 1996. "Masculinity and the Political among Dominicans: 'The Dominican Tiger.' " In *Machos, Mistresses, Madonnas: Contesting the Power of Latin American Gender Imagery.* Marit Melhuus and Kristi Anne Stolen, eds. Pp. 108–33. London: Verso.

Kulick, Don. 1998. *Travesti: Sex, Gender and Culture among Brazilian Transgendered Prostitutes.* Chicago: University of Chicago Press.

Larsen, Wanwadee. 1989. *Confessions of a Mail Order Bride.* New York: Harper Paperbacks.

Latin Finance 2001. "Reliance on Remittances." *Dominican Republic: A Diversifying Economy.* Supplement to *Latin Finance.* November, p. 32.

Lavie, Smadar, and Ted Swedenburg. 1996. "Introduction: Displacement, Diaspora, and Geographies of Identity." In *Displacement, Diaspora, and Geographies of Identity.* Smadar Lavie and Ted Swedenburg, eds. Pp. 1–25. Durham, N.C.: Duke University Press.

——, eds. 1996. *Displacement, Diaspora and Geographies of Identity.* Durham, N.C.: Duke University Press.

LeDuff, Charlie. 1997. "Little Room for Romance in Rush to Wed a Citizen." *New York Times,* 9 March.

LeGrand, Catherine C. 1995. "Deconstructing 'Enclaves,' 'Company Towns,' and 'Modernizing' Cities: Plantations, Mining Camps, and Urban Spaces in the Late Nineteenth and Twentieth Centuries." In *Rethinking the Post-Colonial Encounter: Transnational Perspectives on the Foreign Presence in Latin America.* Gilbert M. Joseph, Catherine C. LeGrand, and Ricardo D. Salvatore, eds. New Haven, Conn.: Yale University Press.

——. 1998. "Living in Macondo: Economy and Culture in a United Fruit Company Banana Enclave in Colombia." In *Close Encounters of Empire: Writing the Cultural History of U.S.-Latin American Relations.* Gilbert M. Joseph, Catherine C. LeGrand, and Ricardo D. Salvatore, eds. Pp. 333–68. Durham, N.C.: Duke University Press.

Leidholdt, Dorchen. 1993. "Prostitution: A Violation of Women's Rights." *Cardozo Women's Law Journal* 1 (1): 133–47.

Levitt, Peggy. 2001. *The Transnational Villagers.* Berkeley: University of California Press.

Lim, Linda. 1983. "Capitalism, Imperialism, and Patriarchy: The Dilemma of Third World Women Workers in Multinational Factories." In *Women, Men, and the International Division of Labor.* June Nash and Maria Patricia Fernández-Kelly, eds. Pp. 70–91. Albany: SUNY Press.

——. 1990. "Women's Work in Export Factories: The Politics of a Cause." In

Persistent Inequalities: Women and World Development. Irene Tinker, ed. Pp. 101–21. New York: Oxford University Press.

Littlewood, Ian. 2001. *Sultry Climates: Travel and Sex.* Cambridge, Mass.: Da Capo Press.

Lowe, Lisa. 1997. "Work, Immigration, Gender: New Subjects of Cultural Politics." In *The Politics of Culture in the Shadow of Capital.* Lisa Lowe and David Lloyd, eds. Pp. 354–74. Durham, N.C.: Duke University Press.

Lozano, Wilfredo. 1997. "Dominican Republic: Informal Economy, the State, and the Urban Poor." In *The Urban Caribbean: Transition to the New Global Economy.* Alejandro Portes, Carlos Dore-Cabral, and Patricia Landolt, eds. Pp. 153–89. Baltimore, Md.: Johns Hopkins University Press.

Luibhéid, Eithne. 2002. *Entry Denied: Controlling Sexuality at the Border.* Minneapolis: University of Minnesota Press.

Lutz, Catherine A. 1988. *Unnatural Emotions: Everyday Sentiments on a Micronesian Atoll and Their Challenge to Western Theory.* Chicago: University of Chicago Press.

Lutz, Catherine A., and Lila Abu-Lughod, eds. 1990. *Language and the Politics of Emotion.* Cambridge: Cambridge University Press.

MacCannell, Dean. 1976. *The Tourist: A New Theory of the Leisure Class.* New York: Schocken Books.

Mahler, Sarah J. 1997. "Bringing Gender to a Transnational Focus: Theoretical and Empirical Ideas." Paper. University of Vermont.

——. 1998. "Theoretical and Empirical Contributions toward a Research Agenda for Transnationalism." In *Transnationalism from Below.* Michael P. Smith and Luis E. Guarnizo, eds. Pp. 64–100. Vol. 6. Comparative Urban and Community Research series. New Brunswick, N.J.: Transaction Publishers.

——. 1999. "Engendering Transnational Migration: A Case Study of Salvadorans." *American Behavioral Scientist* 42 (4): 690–719.

Mahler, Sarah J., and Patricia R. Pessar. 2001. "Gendered Geographies of Power: Analyzing Gender across Transnational Spaces." *Identities* 7 (4): 441–59.

Manderson, Lenore. 1992. "Public Sex Performances in Patpong and Explorations of the Edges of Imagination." *Journal of Sex Research* 29 (4): 451–75.

Manderson, Lenore, and Margaret Jolly. 1997. "Sites of Desire / Economies of Pleasure in Asia and the Pacific." In *Sites of Desire, Economies of Pleasure.* Lenore Manderson and Margaret Jolly, eds. Pp. 1–26. Chicago: University of Chicago Press.

Martis, Jacqueline. 1999. "Tourism and the Sex Trade in St. Maarten and Curaçao." In *Sun, Sex, and Gold: Tourism and Sex Work in the Caribbean.* Kamala Kempadoo, ed. Pp. 201–15. Lanham, Md.: Rowman and Littlefield Publishers.

Massey, Doreen. 1993. "Power Geometry and a Progressive Sense of Place." In *Mapping the Future: Local Culture, Global Change.* John Bird, Barry Curtis, Tim Putnam, G. Robertson, and Lisa Tickner, eds. Pp. 59–69. New York: Routledge.

——. 1994. *Space, Place and Gender.* Minneapolis: University of Minnesota Press.

McClintock, Anne. 1993a. "Sex Workers and Sex Work: An Introduction." *Social Text* 11 (4): 1–10.

McClintock, Anne, ed. 1993b. "Special Section Explores the Sex Trade." *Social Text* 11 (4).

———. 1995. *Imperial Leather: Race, Gender, and Sexuality in the Colonial Conquest.* New York: Routledge.

Melhuus, Marit, and Kristi Anne Stolen, eds. 1996. *Machos, Mistresses, Madonnas: Contesting the Power of Latin American Gender Imagery.* New York: Verso.

Mignolo, Walter D. 2000. *Local Histories / Global Designs: Coloniality, Subaltern Knowledge, and Border Thinking.* Princeton, N.J.: Princeton University Press.

Mills, Mary Beth. 1999. *Thai Women in the Global Labor Force.* New Brunswick, N.J.: Rutgers University.

Mintz, Sidney W. 1960. *Worker in the Cane: A Puerto Rican Life History.* New York: W.W. Norton and Company.

———. 1974. *Caribbean Transformations.* New York: Columbia University Press.

———. 1989. "The Sensation of Moving, While Standing Still." *American Ethnologist* 16 (4): 786–96.

Mintz, Sidney W., and Sally Price, eds. 1985. *Caribbean Contours.* Baltimore, Md.: Johns Hopkins University Press.

Mirdal, G. M. 1984. "Stress and Distress in Migration: Problems and Resources of Turkish Women in Denmark." *International Migration Review* 18 (4): 984–1003.

Moghadam, Valentine M. 1999. "Gender and Globalization: Female Labor and Women's Mobilization." *Journal of World-Systems Research* 5 (2): 367–88.

Momsen, Janet Henshall. 1994. "Tourism, Gender and Development in the Caribbean." In *Tourism: A Gender Analysis.* Vivian Kinnaird and Derek Hall, eds. Pp. 106–20. New York: John Wiley and Sons.

———, ed. 1993. *Women and Change in the Caribbean.* Bloomington: Indiana University Press.

Mongia, Radhika Viyas. 1999. "Race, Nationality, Mobility: A History of the Passport." *Public Culture* 11 (3): 527–56.

Moon, Katherine. 1997. *Sex Among Allies: Military Prostitution in U.S.-Korea Relations.* New York: Columbia University Press.

Moreno, Luis, and Deanna Kerrigan. 2000. "HIV Prevention Strategies among Female Sex Workers in the Dominican Republic." *Research for Sex Work* (June): 8–10.

Morissey, Marietta. 1989. *Slave Women in the New World: Gender Stratification in the Caribbean.* Lawrence: University of Kansas Press.

Moya Pons, Frank. 1998. *The Dominican Republic: A National History.* Princeton, N.J.: Markus Wiener Publishers.

Murphy, Martin F. 1991. *Dominican Sugar Plantations: Production and Foreign Labor Integration.* New York: Praeger.

Nagle, Jill, ed. 1997. *Whores and Other Feminists.* London: Routledge.

Nelson, Nici. 1978. " 'Women Must Help Each Other': The Operation of Personal Networks Among Buzaa Beer Brewers in Mathare Valley, Kenya." In *Women United, Women Divided: Cross-Cultural Perspectives on Female Solidarity.* Janet Burja and Patricia Caplan, eds. New York: Tavistock Publications.

——. 1987. " 'Selling her kiosk': Kikuyu Notions of Sexuality and Sex for Sale in Mathare Valley, Kenya." In *The Cultural Construction of Sexuality*. Patricia Caplan, ed. Pp. 217–39. New York: Tavistock Publications.

O'Connell Davidson, Julia. 1996. "Sex Tourism in Cuba." *Race and Class* 38 (1): 39–48.

O'Connell Davidson, Julia, and Jacqueline Sanchez Taylor. 1999. "Fantasy Islands: Exploring the Demand for Sex Tourism." In *Sun, Sex, and Gold: Tourism and Sex Work in the Caribbean*. Kamala Kempadoo, ed. Pp. 37–54. Lanham, Md.: Rowman and Littlefield Publishers.

Omi, Michael, and Howard Winant. 1994. *Racial Formation in the United States: from the 1960s to the 1990s*. 2d ed. New York: Routledge.

O'Neill Richard, Amy. 2000. "International Trafficking in Women to the United States: A Contemporary Manifestation of Slavery and Organized Crime." Washington, D.C.: Center for the Study of Intelligence.

Ong, Aihwa. 1985. "Industrialization and Prostitution in Southeast Asia." *Southeast Asia Chronicle* 96: 2–6.

——. 1987. *Spirits of Resistance and Capitalist Discipline: Factory Women in Malaysia*. Albany: State University of New York Press.

——. 1999. *Flexible Citizenship: The Cultural Logics of Transnationality*. Durham, N.C.: Duke University Press.

Opitz, May, Katharina Oguntoye, and Dagmar Shultz, eds. 1992. *Showing Our Colors: Afro-German Women Speak Out*. Amherst: University of Massachusetts Press.

Organization of American States. 1999. *Country Report—Dominican Republic, 1999*. Washington, D.C.: Inter-American Commission on Human Rights.

——. 2001. *Support for OAS Tourism Activities*. Vol. 2001. Washington, D.C.: Organization of American States.

——. 2002. *Dominican Republic: Tourist Arrivals by Country of Residence, 1992–1996*. Vol. 2002. Washington, D.C.: Organization of American States.

Ortner, Sherry. 1984. "Theory in Anthropology Since the Sixties." *Comparative Studies in Society and History* 26 (1): 126–66.

——. 1996. *Making Gender: The Politics and Erotics of Culture*. Boston: Beacon Press.

Pacini Hernandez, Deborah. 1995. *Bachata: A Social History of a Dominican Popular Music*. Philadelphia: Temple University Press.

Padilla, Mark B. 2003. " 'Me la Busco': Male Sex Work, Political Economy, and Sexual Identity in the Dominican Republic." Ph.D. diss. (draft). Emory University.

Papernick, Otto. 1983. ". . . And That's My Story." Manuscript. Sosúa, Dominican Republic.

Pareja, Renaldo, and Santo Rosario. 1992. *Sexo, trabajo, SIDA y sociedad: El mundo del trabajo sexual, su dinámica, sus reglas y sus autores*. Santo Domingo: COIN.

Parker, Richard G., and John H. Gagnon, eds. 1995. *Conceiving Sexuality: Approaches to Sex Research in a Post Modern World*. London: Routledge.

Pasini, W. 1988. *Promotion and Protection of Health in Tourists*. WHO meeting, Rimini, Italy, 1988. Societa Italiana de Medicini del Turismo.

Pateman, Carole. 1998. *The Sexual Contract*. Cambridge: Polity Press.

Patton, Cindy. 2000. Migratory Vices. In *Queer Diasporas*. Cindy Patton and Benigno Sánchez-Eppler, eds. Pp. 15–37. Durham, N.C.: Duke University Press.

Peck, Jeffrey M. 1995. "Refugees as Foreigners: The Problem of Becoming German and Finding Home." In *Mistrusting Refugees*. E. Valentine Daniel and John Chr. Knudsen, eds. Pp. 102–25. Berkeley: University of California Press.

Pessar, Patricia R. 1984. "The Linkage between the Household and Workplace of Dominican Women in the U.S." *International Migration Review* 18 (4): 1188–211.

———. 1995a. *A Visa for a Dream: Dominicans in the United States*. Needham Heights, Mass.: Allyn and Bacon.

———. 1995b. "On the Homefront and in the Workplace: Integrating Immigrant Women into Feminist Discourse." *Anthropological Quarterly* 68 (1): 37–47.

———. 1999. "The Role of Gender, Households and Social Networks in the Migration Process: A Review and Appraisal." In *The Handbook of International Migration: The American Experience*. Charles Hirschman, Philip Kasinitz, and Josh DeWind, eds. Pp. 53–70. New York: Russell Sage Foundation.

———, ed. 1996. *Caribbean Circuits: Emigration, Remittances, and Return*. New York: Center for Migration Studies.

Pheterson, Gail. 1989. "Not Repeating History." In *A Vindication of the Rights of Whores*. Gail Pheterson, ed. Pp. 3–30. Seattle: Seal Press.

———. 1990. "The Category 'Prostitute' in Scientific Inquiry." *Journal of Sex Research* 27 (3): 397–407.

———. 1996. *The Prostitution Prism*. Amsterdam: Amsterdam University Press.

———, ed. 1989. *A Vindication of the Rights of Whores*. Seattle: Seal Press.

Phongpaichit, Pasuk. 1982. *From Peasant Girls to Bangkok Masseuses*. Geneva: International Labor Office.

Pichardo, Franklin F. 1997. *Sobre racismo y antihaitianismo (y otros ensayos)*. Santo Domingo: Impr. Librería Vidal.

Piscitelli, Adriana. 2001. Of " 'Gringos' and 'Natives': Gender and Sexuality Discussed in the Context of International Sex Tourism in Fortaleza, Brazil." Paper presented at the meeting of the Latin American Studies Association, Washington, D.C. Pp. 1–23.

Pratt, Mary Louise. 1992. *Imperial Eyes : Travel Writing and Transculturation*. London: Routledge.

Pred, Allan. 2000. *Even in Sweden: Racisms, Racialized Spaces, and the Popular Geographical Imagination*. Berkeley: University of California Press.

Pruitt, Deborah, and Suzanne LaFont. 1995. "For Love and Money: Romance Tourism in Jamaica." *Annals of Tourism Research* 21 (2): 422–40.

Ramírez, Nelson. 1993. *La fuerza de trabajo en La República Dominicana*. Santo Domingo: Instituto de Estudio de Población y Desarrollo.

Randall, Laura. 1995. "Golden Cage." In *American Eagle's Latitudes South*. Pp. 18–22.

Rebhun, Linda-Anne. 1999. *The Heart Is Unknown Country: Love in the Changing Economy of Northeast Brazil*. Stanford, Calif.: Stanford University Press.

Repack, Terry A. 1995. *Waiting on Washington: Central American Workers in the Nation's Capital*. Philadelphia: Temple University Press.

Reyes, Quintina, and Magaly Pineda. 1985. *Paternidad responsable: Un estudio sobre la ley 2402*. Santo Domingo: CIPAF-PROFAMILIA (Centro de Investigación para la Acción Femenina).

Roberts, Nickie. 1992. *Whores in History: Prostitution in Western Society*. London: Harper Collins Publishers.

Rodríguez, Natalia. 1992. *Sexismo y discriminación en la educación técnica en La República Dominicana*. Santo Domingo: Centro de Investigación para la Acción Femenina.

Rofel, Lisa. 1999. *Other Modernities: Gendered Yearnings in China after Socialism*. Berkeley: University of California Press.

Rojek, Chris. 1993. *Ways of Escape: Modern Transformations in Leisure and Travel*. Lanham, Md.: Rowman and Littlefield Publishers.

Rojek, Chris, and John Urry. 1997. "Transformations of Travel and Theory." In *Touring Cultures: Transformations of Travel and Theory*. Chris Rojek and John Urry, eds. Pp. 1–19. London: Routledge.

Romero, Mary. 1992. *Maid in the U.S.A.* New York: Routledge.

Roorda, Eric Paul. 1998. *The Dictator Next Door: The Good Neighbor Policy and the Trujillo Regime in the Dominican Republic, 1930–1945*. Durham, N.C.: Duke University Press.

Roseberry, William. 1998. "Social Fields and Cultural Encounters." In *Close Encounters of Empire: Writing the Cultural History of U.S.-Latin American Relations*. Gilbert M. Joseph, Catherine C. LeGrand, and Ricardo D. Salvatore, eds. Pp. 515–24. Durham, N.C.: Duke University Press.

Rouse, Roger. 1991. "Mexican Migration and the Social Space of Postmodernism." *Diaspora* 1 (1): 8–23.

———. 1992. "Making Sense of Settlement: Class Transformation, Cultural Struggle, and Transnationalism among Mexican Migrants in the United States." In *Towards a Transnational Perspective on Migration*. Nina Glick Schiller, Linda Basch, and Cristina Szanton-Blanc, eds. Pp. 25–52. New York: New York Academy of Sciences.

Russin, Vecchi, and Heredia Bonetti. 2000a. *Tax Code Q & A*. Vol. 2002. http://www.rvhb.com/faq_11.htm.

———. 2000b. *General Rules Governing Foreign Investment in the DR*. Vol. 2002. http://www.rvhb.com/faq_5.htm.

Safa, Helen I. 1995a. *The Myth of the Male Breadwinner: Women and Industrialization in the Caribbean*. Boulder, Colo.: Westview Press.

———. 1995b. "Gender Implications of Export-Led Industrialization in the Caribbean Basin." In *ENGENDERing Wealth and Well-Being*. Rae Lesser Blumberg, Cathy A. Rakowski, Irene Tinker, and Michael Monteon, eds. Pp. 89–112. Boulder, Colo.: Westview Press.

———. 1999a. "Free Markets and the Marriage Market: Structural Adjustment, Gender Relations and Working Conditions among Dominican Women Workers." *Environment and Planning* 31: 291–304.

——. 1999b. "Women Coping with Crisis: Social Consequences of Export-Led Industrialization in the Dominican Republic." *The North-South Agenda* 36: 1–22.

Sagás, Ernesto. 2000. *Race and Politics in the Dominican Republic.* Gainesville, Fla.: University Press of Florida.

Sánchez-Eppler, Benigno, and Cindy Patton. 2000. "Introduction: With a Passport Out of Eden." In *Queer Diasporas.* Cindy Patton and Benigno Sánchez-Eppler, eds. Pp. 1–14. Durham, N.C.: Duke University Press.

Sanjek, Roger. 1994. "Introduction: The Enduring Inequalities of Race." In *Race.* Steven Gregory and Roger Sanjek, eds. Pp. 1–17. New Brunswick, N.J.: Rutgers University Press.

Sassen, Saskia. 1988. *The Mobility of Labor and Capital: A Study in International Investment and Labor Flow.* Cambridge: Cambridge University Press.

——. 1998. *Globalization and Its Discontents.* New York: New Press.

Schloss, Glenn. 1999. "Customs Officers Learning Thai after Prostitute Row." *South China Morning Post* (Hong Kong), 15 July, p. 3.

Schwartz, Rosalie. 1997. *Pleasure Island: Tourism and Temptation in Cuba.* Lincoln: University of Nebraska Press.

Scott, James C. 1985. *Weapons of the Weak.* New Haven, Conn.: Yale University Press.

Scott, Julie. 1995. "Sexual and National Boundaries in Tourism." *Annals of Tourism Research* 22 (2): 385–403.

Scott, Rebecca J. 1985. *Slave Emancipation in Cuba: The Transition to Free Labor, 1860–1899.* Princeton, N.J.: Princeton University Press.

Seabrook, Jeremy. 1996. *Travels in the Skin Trade: Tourism and the Sex Industry.* London: Pluto.

Simmons, Kimberly Elson. 2001. "A Passion for Sameness: Encountering a Black Feminist Self in Fieldwork in the Dominican Republic." In *Black Feminist Anthropology: Theory, Politics, Praxis, and Poetics.* Irma McClaurin, ed. Pp. 77–101. New Brunswick, N.J.: Rutgers University Press.

Sinclair, M. Thea. 1997. "Issues and Theories of Gender and Work in Tourism." In *Gender, Work and Tourism.* M. Thea Sinclair, ed. Pp. 1–15. London: Routledge.

——, ed. 1997. *Gender, Work and Tourism.* London: Routledge.

Skrobanek, Siriporn, Nataya Boonpakdee, and Chutima Jantateero. 1997. *The Traffic in Women: Human Realities of the International Sex Trade.* London: Zed Books.

Sleightholme, Carolyn, and Indrani Sinha. 1996. *Guilty without Trial: Women in the Sex Trade in Calcutta.* New Brunswick, N.J.: Rutgers University Press.

Smith, Michael Peter, and Luis Eduardo Guarnizo. 1988. "The Locations of Transnationalism." In *Transnationalism from Below.* Michael P. Smith and Luis E. Guarnizo, eds. Pp. 3–34. New Brunswick, N.J.: Transaction Publishers.

——, eds. 1998. *Transnationalism from Below.* Vol. 6. Comparative Urban and Community Research series. New Brunswick, N.J.: Transaction Publishers.

Smith, Valene L., ed. 1989. *Hosts and Guests: The Anthropology of Tourism*. Philadelphia: University of Pennsylvania Press.

Smith-Rosenburg, Carroll. 1985. *Disorderly Conduct: Visions of Gender in Victorian America*. New York: Alfred A Knopf.

Soja, Edward W. 1996. *Thirdspace: Journeys to Los Angeles and Other Real-and-Imagined Places*. Oxford: Basil Blackwell.

Sørensen, Ninna Nyberg. 1998. "Narrating Identity across Dominican Worlds." In *Transnationalism from Below*. Michael P. Smith and Luis E. Guarnizo, eds. Pp. 241–69. Vol. 6. Comparative Urban and Community Research series. New Brunswick, N.J.: Transaction Publishers.

Sotero Peralta y Asociados, and Horwath Consulting. 1994. *La Industria Hotelera Dominicana / The Dominican Hotel Industry*. Santo Domingo: Horwath International.

Spacks, Patricia Meyer. 1985. *Gossip*. New York: Alfred A. Knopf.

Span, Paula. 2003. "What's Love Got to Do With It?" *Washington Post*, 3 March, p. B7.

Standing, Guy. 1989. "Global Feminization through Flexible Labor." *World Development* 17 (7): 1077–96.

Stoler, Ann Laura. 1995. *Race and the Education of Desire: Foucault's History of Sexuality and the Colonial Order of Things*. Durham, N.C.: Duke University Press.

——. 1997a. "Sexual Affronts and Racial Frontiers: European Identities and the Cultural Politics of Exclusion in Colonial Southeast Asia." In *Tensions of Empire: Colonial Cultures in a Bourgeois World*. Frederick Cooper and Ann Laura Stoler, eds. Pp. 198–237. Berkeley: University of California Press.

——. 1997b. "Educating Desire in Colonial Southeast Asia: Foucault, Freud and Imperial Sexualities." In *Sites of Desire, Economies of Pleasure*. Lenore Manderson and Margaret Jolly, eds. Pp. 27–47. Chicago: University of Chicago Press.

Sturdevant, Saundra Pollock, and Brenda Stoltzfus, eds. 1992. *Let the Good Times Roll*. New York: New Press.

Swain, Margaret Byrne. 1995. "Gender in Tourism." *Annals of Tourism Research* 22 (2): 247–66.

Symanski, Richard, and Nancy Burley. 1973. "The Jewish Colony of Sosúa." *Annals of the Association of American Geographers* 63 (3): 366–78.

Tabet, Paola. 1989. "I'm the Meat, I'm the Knife: Sexual Service, Migration, and Repression in Some African Societies." *Feminist Issues* 11 (1): 3–21.

Tamayo, Juan O. 1997. "Dominican Prostitution: Cheap, Prevalent and Accepted." *Miami Herald*, 24 June.

Tejeda Ortiz, Dagoberto. 1998. "África en Santo Domingo: De los orígenes a la identidad." In *Cultura popular e identidad nacional*. Dagoberta Tejeda Ortiz, ed. Vol. 3. Santo Domingo: Consejo Presidencial de Cultura y Instituto Dominicano de Folklore.

Thorbek, Susanne. 2002a. "The European Inheritance: Male Perspectives." In *Trans-*

national Prostitution: Changing Global Patterns. Susanne Thorbek and Bandana Pattanaik, eds. Pp. 24–41. New York: Zed Books.

———. 2002b. Introduction. In *Transnational Prostitution: Changing Global Patterns.* Susanne Thorbek and Bandana Pattanaik, eds. Pp. 1–9. New York: Zed Books.

Thorbek, Susanne, and Bandana Pattanaik, eds. 2002. *Transnational Prostitution: Changing Global Patterns.* New York: Zed Books.

Torgovnick, Marianna. 1990. *Gone Primitive: Savage Intellects, Modern Lives.* Chicago: University of Chicago Press.

Torres-Saillant, Silvio. 1995. "The Dominican Republic." In *No Longer Invisible: Afro-Latin Americans Today.* Pp. 109–38. London: M. R. Group.

———. 1998. "The Tribulations of Blackness: Stages in Dominican Racial Identity." *Latin American Perspectives* 25 (3): 126–46.

———. 1999. *Introduction to Dominican Blackness.* New York: CUNY Dominican Studies Institute.

Torres-Saillant, Silvio, and Ramona Hernández. 1998. *The Dominican Americans.* Westport, Conn.: Greenwood Press.

Travel Trade Gazette Europa. 1997. "No Sign of Island Leader Slowing." In *Travel Trade Gazette Europa.* P. 20. CMP Information, Ltd.

Trawick, Margaret. 1990. *Notes on Love in a Tamil Family.* Berkeley: University of California Press.

Trouillot, Michel-Rolph. 1994. "Culture, Color, and Politics in Haiti." In *Race.* Steven Gregory and Roger Sanjek, eds. Pp. 146–74. New Brunswick, N.J.: Rutgers University Press.

Truong, Thanh-dam. 1990. *Sex, Money, and Morality: Prostitution and Tourism in South-East Asia.* London: Zed Books.

United Nations, Economic Commission on Latin America and the Caribbean. 2001. *Foreign Investment in Latin America and the Caribbean.* Vol. 2001. Santiago: United Nations, Economic Commission on Latin America and the Caribbean.

United Nations Statistics Division. 2000. *The World's Women 2000: Trends and Statistics.* Table 2.B, Indicators on Households and Childbearing. Vol. 2002. New York: United Nations.

———. 2002. *Indicators on Unemployment.* Vol. 2002. New York: United Nations Statistics Division.

Urry, John. 1990. *The Tourist Gaze: Leisure and Travel in Contemporary Society.* London: Sage Publications.

U.S. Coast Guard. 2003. *Alien Migrant Interdiction: Migrant Interdiction Statistics, 1982–Present.* http://www.uscg.mil/hq/g-o/g-opl/mle/amiostats1.htm.

U.S. Department of Justice, Immigration and Naturalization Service. 1997. *1996 Statistical Yearbook of the Immigration and Naturalization Service.* Washington, D.C.: U.S. Government Printing Office.

———. 2001a. *Characteristics of Legal Immigrants.* Vol. 2002. Washington, D.C.: U.S. Government Printing Office.

——. 2001b. *Immigration in Fiscal Year 1994*. Vol. 2002. Washington, D.C.: U.S. Government Printing Office.

U.S. Department of State. 2001. *FY 2001 Country Commercial Guide: Dominican Republic*. Vol. 2001. Washington, D.C.: U.S. Department of State.

U.S. Department of State, Bureau of Democracy, Human Rights, and Labor. 2000. *Dominican Republic: Country Reports on Human Rights Practices*. Vol. 2002. Washington, D.C.: U.S. Department of State.

U.S. Department of State, Bureau of Economic and Business Affairs. 2001. *2000 Country Reports on Economic Policy and Trade Practices: Dominican Republic*. Vol. 2002. Washington, D.C.: U.S. Department of State, Bureau of Economic and Business Affairs.

U.S. Department of State, Bureau of Western Hemisphere Affairs. 2000. *Background Notes: Dominican Republic*. Washington, D.C.: U.S. Department of State, Bureau of Public Affairs.

Van Duifhuizen, Rinske, and George Broring. 1993. *A Manual for the Implementation of HIV/AIDS Prevention Activities Aimed at Travellers and Migrants*. Amsterdam: National Committee on AIDS Control, European Project AIDS and Mobility.

Vargas-Lundius, Rosemary. 1991. *Peasants in Distress: Poverty and Unemployment in the Dominican Republic*. Boulder, Colo.: Westview Press.

Victoria, Lorena S. 1994. "Un Amor en el Caribe." *Rumbo* (21 November): 42–46.

Vilar, Alysia. 2003. Havana Honey. 21–23 May. http://www.salon.com.

Visweswaran, Kamala. 1994. *Fictions of Feminist Ethnography*. Minneapolis: University of Minnesota Press.

Vollman, William. 1993. Sex Slave. *Spin* 9 (9).

Walker, Dave, and Richard Ehrlich. 1992. *Hello My Big Big Honey: Love Letters to Bangkok Bar Girls and Their Revealing Interviews*. Bangkok: Dragon Dance Publications.

Walkowitz, Judith R. 1980. *Prostitution and Victorian Society: Women, Class, and the State*. New York: Cambridge University Press.

——. 1992. *City of Dreadful Delight: Narratives of Sexual Danger in Late-Victorian London*. Chicago: University of Chicago Press.

Weitzer, Ronald. 2000. "Why We Need More Research on Sex Work." In *Sex for Sale: Prostitution, Pornography, and the Sex Industry*. Ronald Weitzer, ed. Pp. 1–13. New York: Routledge.

White, Luise. 1990. *The Comforts of Home: Prostitution in Colonial Nairobi*. Chicago: University of Chicago Press.

Whitehead, Ann. 1984. "I'm Hungry, Mum: The Politics of Domestic Budgeting." In *Of Marriage and the Market*. Kate Young, Carol Wolkowitz, and Roslyn McCullagh, eds. Pp. 93–116. London: Routledge and Kegan Paul.

Wilhelms, Saskia K. S. 1994. *Haitian and Dominican Sugarcane Workers in Dominican Bateyes: Patterns and Effects of Prejudice, Stereotypes and Discrimination*. Hamburg: LIT.

Williams, Eric. 1984. *From Columbus to Castro: The History of the Caribbean*. New York: Vintage Books.

Williams, Phil, ed. 1999. *Illegal Immigration and Commercial Sex: The New Slave Trade*. London: Frank Cass.

Wolf, Diane Lauren. 1992. *Factory Daughters: Gender, Household Dynamics, and Rural Industrialization in Java*. Berkeley: University of California Press.

Wolf, Margery. 1992. *A Thrice-Told Tale: Feminism, Postmodernism, and Ethnographic Responsibility*. Stanford, Calif.: Stanford University Press.

World Bank. 2001. *Dominican Republic Poverty Assessment: Poverty in a High-Growth Economy (1986–2000)*. Poverty Reduction and Economic Management Unit, Latin America and the Caribbean. Volume 1: Main Report. 17 December.

World Bank, Caribbean Country Management Unit, Latin America and the Caribbean Region. 1999. *Memorandum of the President of the International Bank for Reconstruction and Development to the Executive Directors on a Country Assistance Strategy of the World Bank Group for the Dominican Republic*. P. 15. Washington, D.C.: World Bank.

World Tourism Organization. 1998. *Yearbook of Tourism Statistics*. Vol. 1. Madrid: World Tourism Organization.

World Tourism Organization. 2002. *Tourism Highlights 2002*. http:// www.world-tourism.org/market_research/facts&figures/menu.htm.

World Tourism Organization, Statistics and Market Research Department. 2000. *Tourism Highlights 2000*. Madrid: World Tourism Organization.

Yediot Aharonot. 1999. *Russian Envoy on Immigrants, Peace Process, Iranian Arms*. Tel Aviv.

Yelvington, Kevin A. 1995. *Producing Power: Ethnicity, Gender, and Class in a Workplace*. Philadelphia, Pa.: Temple University Press.

Young, Kate, Carol Wolkowitz, and Roslyn McCullagh, eds. 1984. *Of Marriage and the Market: Women's Subordination Internationally and Its Lessons*. London: Routledge and Kegan Paul.

Zantop, Susanne. 1997. *Colonial Fantasies: Conquest, Family, and Nation in Precolonial Germany, 1770–1870*. Durham, N.C.: Duke University Press.

Zavella, Patricia. 1991. "Mujeres in Factories: Race and Class Perspective on Women, Work, and Family." In *Gender at the Crossroads of Knowledge*. Micaela di Leonardo, ed. Pp. 312–36. Berkeley: University of California Press.

INDEX

Fosado, Gisela, 224 n.11
Frank, Katherine, 29, 200, 218
Freeman, Carla, 226 n.30
Fusco, Coco, 34–35, 229 n.49

Georges, Eugenia, 101
Germans: community in Sosúa, 53, 54–
56, 76, 209, 224 n.14, 235 n.22; Dominican men and, 190; economic influence of, 42, 54–56, 80; expatriate
community in Sosúa, 54–56, 76, 209,
235 n.22; images of sex workers, 204;
imperialist imagination of, 54–55;
mobility of, 37, 42; negative image of,
53, 82–84; sex workers' relationships
with, 2–9, 26–27, 108–9, 152, 188, 208,
209; travel to Dominican Republic,
37, 229 n.53
Germany: media advertisements for sex
tourism, 197–98; migration to, 2–9,
26–27, 107, 187–93; racism in, 188,
192, 193, 242 n.1; social isolation in,
191–93
Gewertz, Deborah, 84
Giddens, Anthony, 39, 223 n.5
Gilliam, Angela, 224 n.9, 236 n.8
Glick Schiller, Nina: on globalization,
223 n.6; on transnational migration,
39, 230 n.60; transnational social
field, 41, 231 n.68
Globalization: citizenship, 20, 42, 43,
77–78; defining, 223 n.4; gender divisions of labor, 31–32, 228 n.42, 228
n.45; marriage and, 30–31, 227 n.40;
media images of European middle-
class comfort, 45, 46, 232 n.70; sexscapes and, 15–17, 31–35, 95, 199, 228
n.46; stereotypes disseminated by,
194, 198–99, 242 n.8; transnational
migration and, 39–41, 230 n.58, 230
n.60; travel and, 28–29, 32, 37, 62, 199,
200, 229 n.53, 243 n.13; United Fruit
Company, 18, 225 n.16, 233 n.4;

women's agency, 182, 241 n.15;
women's work, 31–32, 228 n.42. *See
also* Migration; Sex tourism; Transnationalism
González de la Rocha, Mercedes, 124,
171, 239 n.7
Gossip: on AIDS transmission, 141–42,
175, 179–80, 241 n.12; on child support, 177–78; on enjoyment of sex
work, 177–78; on failed relationships,
213–14; on Haitian sex workers, 180;
on life in Europe, 192–94; love in, 97–
98; on reputations of sex workers,
175–79; sex workers as pickpockets,
142, 240 n.18; social networks and, 22,
172–74, 188–89, 196–97, 242 n.4; on
women's support of men, 178
Grasmuck, Sherri, 101, 238 n.1
Greenberg, H. R., 225 n.20
Grewal, Inderpal, 228 n.45
Guarnizo, Luis Eduardo, 21, 42, 43, 205
Guerra, Juan Luis, 40
Gutmann, Matthew, 230 n.57
Guy, Donna, 235 n.18

Haitians: massacre of, 35, 58, 229 n.51; as
negra (black), 35, 36; as sex workers,
2, 36, 180; as sugarcane workers, 36,
229 n.52; Rafael Trujillo and, 35, 229
n.51
Hall, Stuart, 223 n.4
Halperin, Rhoda, 241 n.6
Hamilton, Annette, 32, 33, 37, 204
Hernández Medina, Esther, 231 n.68
Hess, Luis, 59
Hochschild, Arlie, 98
Hondagneu-Sotelo, Pierrette, 128, 238
n.1, 241 nn.13–14, 242 n.2
Households: food preparation in, 7, 221
n.7; income allocation decisions in,
122, 238 n.1, 239 n.7; men as heads of,
106, 124, 239 n.10; sisters in, 2, 4, 128–
29; women as heads of, 127, 129, 193,

Households (*continued*)
205, 239 nn.12–13; women's income
in, 122–23, 131, 239 n.7, 239 n.14
Housing: in bars, 132, 133–35; boarding
houses, 147–49 (*148*), 172; home ownership, 99, 164–65; private dwellings,
149–50; rent payments, 170; supported
by foreign men, 4–5, 168, 209, 211
Howard, David, 35
Hunter, Mark, 168

Ilouz, Eva, 227 n.40
Imagination: economic realities and,
46–47, 71–72, 74–75; German imperialism, 54–55; nationalities identified
with sex work, 205; sexscapes, 15–17,
31–35, 95, 199; of Sosúa as paradise,
72, 73–75
Income strategies: colmados, 4, 68, 221
n.8, 240 n.4; consumption opportunities, 177–78, 211; for economic
advancement strategies (*progresar*),
22–24, 225 n.21; of former workers,
26, 210–11; marriage as, 166–67, 208;
men's support as, 4–6, 26, 112–13,
129–30, 168–71, 190, 209, 211; migration to Europe, 20; remittances from
diasporic family members, 101, 103,
237 n.11; savings plans as, 162–64; unpredictability and, 3–4, 7–8, 171
Internet, 42, 194, 197–99, 201–3, 218, 242
n.8
Itzigsohn, José, 231 n.68, 238 n.2

Jansen, Senaida, 229 n.52
Japan, 27, 99, 236 n.7, 242 n.9
Jewish community of Sosúa, 13, 56, 58–
60, 73, 234 nn.11–12
Jolly, Margaret, 224 n.9

Kaplan, Caren, 228 n.45
Kearney, Michael, 51, 224 n.7
Kelsky, Karen, 99, 236 n.7

Kempadoo, Kamala, 25–26, 34, 97, 228
n.48
Koch, Felix, 59, 60
Krohn-Hansen, Christian, 38, 230 n.56

LaFont, Suzanne, 98, 104
Lavie, Smadar, 225 n.17
LeGrand, Catherine, 53, 225 n.16, 233 n.4
Los Charamicos: Dominican bars in,
132–39, 140–44, 197; Dominican presence in, 221 n.3; living conditions in,
60–61, 65, 79; sex workers in, 67; water supply of, 56, 233 n.7
Love: changing definitions of, 95, 236
n.3; emotions and, 95–96, 236 nn.3–5;
gossip about, 97–98; marriage and,
30, 91, 97–98, 209, 236 n.6; as migration strategy, 3, 21, 97–99, 101, 103–4,
201–2, 208; performance of, 21, 91,
97–98, 201–2, 227 n.40, 235 n.1
Lowe, Lisa, 223 n.4
Luibhéid, Eithne, 228 n.41
Lutz, Catherine, 236 n.3, 236 n.5

Mahler, Sarah: migration and gender
roles, 242 n.2; on transnationalism,
15, 224 n.7, 224 n.12, 230 n.58, 231 n.61,
232 n.69
Manderson, Lenore, 197, 243 n.11
Marriage: as business transaction, 30–
31, 227 n.40; consensual unions, 5,
140, 167, 221 n.7, 222 n.9; for docu-
mentation purposes, 113–14; Dominican men and, 91–95, 106, 202–3, 236
n.6; for economic advancement, 213;
employment abroad and, 113–14;
failures of, 189, 213; as financial security, 166–67, 241 n.5; for green
cards (por residencia), 3, 21–22, 99,
113–14, 208; idealization of, 9, 165; introduction agencies, 30, 31, 205, 227
n.39; lifestyle changes after, 193; for
love, 30, 91, 95–98, 209, 236 n.6; mi-

13, 193, 204, 238 n.20; dancing, 197, 217–18, 243 n.10; in Europe, 91, 97–98, 188–89, 193, 236 n.6, 242 n.4, 243 n.16; fashion of, 2, 143–44, 151, 187–88, 216–17; fax communication with clients, 4, 21, 22, 107, 110–11, 170, 225 n.24, 237 n.15; Haitians as, 2, 36, 180; independent, 144–52; Internet images of, 194, 197–99, 201–2, 218, 242 n.8; male, 202–3, 228 n.43, 240 n.1; motherhood and, 123–29, 174, 177–79, 181, 213, 222 n.9, 241 n.13; multiple relationships of, 31, 108–9, 212; parents' support of, 125; pimps and, 22–23, 182, 222 n.2, 226 n.27, 240 n.20; police and, 1, 52, 65, 120, 158–59, 164, 233 n.3, 240 n.1, 240 n.4; pregnancy and, 6, 123, 222 n.10; prostitution and, 23, 175, 205, 222 n.2, 225 n.25, 227 n.38, 233 n.3, 237 n.9; recruitment of, 22, 226 n.26; relationships for green cards (por residencia), 3, 21–22, 99, 107, 113–14, 208; rescue fantasy of, 20–21, 225 n.18, 225 n.20; risks of, 64, 154–61, 165, 176, 190–91, 235 n.18; *sanky-panky* and, 64, 91–95, 100, 103–4, 217, 234 n.16, 237 n.9; self-descriptions of, 174–76, 196–97, 222 n.2; social class (*campesinas*), 144–45, 180; success stories, 139–41; supplementary employment, 26–27, 127, 168, 208–9, 227 n.35; work routine of, 150–51; young girls as, 126–27, 239 n.11. *See also* Bars; Children; Germans; Households; Housing; Income strategies; Love; Marriage; Men (Dominican, foreign); Migration; Race and racism
Sex workers' rights advocacy, 222 n.2
Simmons, Kimberly, 229 n.50
Smith, Michael Peter, 21, 42, 43, 205
Smith-Rosenberg, Carroll, 235 n.18
Social class: in colonialism, 34–35, 83, 228 nn.47–48; media images of European middle-class comfort, 45, 46, 232 n.70; sex workers (*campesinas*) and, 144–45, 180; of tourists, 20, 29, 33–34, 37, 44, 77–79

Social networks, 22, 172–74, 188–89, 196–97, 242 n.4
Sørensen, Ninna Nyberg, 40
Sosúa: airplane travel to, 62; children in, 67, 85–86; corruption in, 64–65, 69–70, 75–76; Dominican identity of, 18, 53–54, 82–84, 85; El Batey, 2, 3, 56–58, 65–67, 80, 85–87, 221 n.3; German community in, 54–56, 76, 209, 235 n.22; Jewish community in, 13, 56, 58–60, 73, 234 nn.11–12; Los Charamicos, 56, 60–61, 65, 67, 79, 221 n.3, 233 n.7; as paradise, 19, 72, 73–75; as sexscape, 15–16; tourism in, 29–30, 52, 74–75, 215–16; as transnational space, 14, 17; United Fruit Company, 18, 58–59, 225 n.16, 233 n.4; urban blight in, 72–73. *See also* Germans; Migration; Sex workers
Spacks, Patricia Meyer, 179
Standing, Guy, 181–82
Stereotypes: Domincanness as sexual availability, 200; of European women, 33, 195–96; Internet and, 194, 197–99, 201–3, 218, 242 n.8; Russian women as prostitutes, 205; sexual appeal of Dominican women, 196–98; skin color, 35, 199, 200; of Thai women, 33–34, 204
Stoler, Ann Laura, 34, 199
Stoltzfus, Brenda, 224 n.10, 232 n.76
Sturdevant, Saundra, 224 n.10, 232 n.76
Swedenburg, Ted, 225 n.17
Symanski, Richard, 234 n.11

Thailand: condom use program in, 222 n.10; as sexscape, 32, 228 n.46; sex tourism in, 28, 33–34, 37, 97, 198, 205; social class of male tourists, 37

Denise Brennan is an Assistant Professor of
Anthropology in the Department of Sociology and
Anthropology at Georgetown University.

Library of Congress Cataloging-in-Publication Data
Brennan, Denise.
What's love got to do with it? : transnational desires and
sex tourism in the Dominican Republic / Denise Brennan.
p. cm. — (Latin America otherwise)
Includes bibliographical references and index.
ISBN 0-8223-3259-0 (cloth : alk. paper)
ISBN 0-8223-3297-3 (pbk. : alk. paper)
1. Sex tourism—Republic—Sosúa. 2. Prostitution—
Dominican Republic. I. Title. II. Series.
HQ162.5.S68B74 2004   306.74′097293′58—dc22
2003025002